Dominant Culture
and the Education of Women

Dominant Culture and the Education of Women

Edited by

Julia C. Paulk

Cambridge Scholars Publishing

Dominant Culture and the Education of Women, Edited by Julia C. Paulk

This book first published 2008 by

Cambridge Scholars Publishing

15 Angerton Gardens, Newcastle, NE5 2JA, UK

British Library Cataloguing in Publication Data
A catalogue record for this book is available from the British Library

Copyright © 2008 by Julia C. Paulk and contributors

All rights for this book reserved. No part of this book may be reproduced, stored in a retrieval system, or transmitted, in any form or by any means, electronic, mechanical, photocopying, recording or otherwise, without the prior permission of the copyright owner.

ISBN (10): 1-84718-573-8, ISBN (13): 9781847185730

TABLE OF CONTENTS

Acknowledgements viii

Part I:
Medieval and Early Modern Eras: Early Forays into Education for Women

Women Who Know Latin: An Introduction to *Dominant Culture and the Education of Women*
Julia C. Paulk 1

Latin Literacy in Medieval Women's Writing
Jane E. Jeffrey 10

A Cultural "Novelty": Christine de Pizan, a Self-Educated Single Mom in Medieval France
Dorothée Mertz-Weigel 23

"But till some household cares me tie, / My books and Pen I will apply": Early Modern Women's Writings and the Debate on Female Education
Ulrike Tancke 36

Chemistry by a Lady for Ladies: Education in the Alchemical Arts
Sandy Feinstein 53

Part II:
The Nineteenth Century: Women in Europe and the Ottoman Empire

The Liberatory Positioning of British Female Rhetoric: Bathsua Makin's *An Essay to Revive the Antient Education of Gentlewomen*, Mary Wollstonecraft's *The Education of Daughters*, and Lucy Wilson's *The Education of Women*
Julia Kiernan 68

Female Education in Nineteenth-Century Germany: Caroline de la Motte
Fouqué and the Rejection of Bourgeois Models of Domesticity
Karin Baumgartner 82

The Education of a Young Creole: The Countess of Merlin's Memoirs
Claire Emilie Martin 98

The First Generation of German Female Students: Autobiographical
Perspectives on the Contested Space of Gender and Knowledge
Magdalena Tarnawska 110

In Their Own Ways: Emilia Pardo Bazán and María Martínez Sierra's
Struggle for Women's Education in Turn-of-the-Century Spain
Mar Soria López 128

"Knowledgeable Ottoman Girls": Ottoman Women's Education
in the Nineteenth Century
Hülya Yıldız 143

Part III:
The Nineteenth Century: Women in the Americas

Contradictory Designs: Mary Lyon's Mount Holyoke Female Seminary
Beatrice Jacobson 156

Teaching, Preaching, and Practice: Nísia Floresta's Shifting Vision
of Women's Education in Nineteenth-Century Brazil
Charlotte Liddell 169

Beyond the American Home: The Contributions of Catharine Beecher
and Clorinda Matto de Turner to Women's Education
Julia C. Paulk 184

The Struggle for the Independence and Education of the African
American Woman in the Works of Frances Ellen Watkins Harper
Terry Novak 197

Work among the People: How Susan La Flesche Picotte and Zitkala
Sa used Boarding School Education for the Benefit of their Tribes
Sarah Jayne Hitt 209

Part IV:
The Twentieth Century and Beyond: Facing Dominant Cultures

Education for Marriage or Education for Life? The Challenge of Post-War Spanish Women Novelists to the Francoist Approach to the Education of Women
Patricia O'Byrne 221

Cultural Preservation through Education and Literacy: Isabel Juárez Espinosa
Abbey Poffenberger 236

Contributors 256

Index 260

ACKNOWLEDGEMENTS

Dominant Culture and the Education of Women began as a conference panel for the 2006 Midwest Modern Language Association Annual Convention in Chicago, Illinois, and, with the encouragement of Cambridge Scholars Publishing, has grown into this essay collection. A Gettel Faculty Research Grant awarded by the Department of Foreign Languages and Literatures at Marquette University for the summer of 2006 supported my initial research for this study. I would particularly like to thank the contributors to this volume for their hard work and dedication to the topic of women's education. Several contributors, including Claire Emilie Martin, Karin Baumgartner, and Patricia O'Byrne, provided thoughtful commentary on the early draft of the introduction; I would like to recognize their insightful comments here. I would also like to thank my husband, Sumit Dhar, and my family, who make all of my accomplishments possible.

CHAPTER ONE

WOMEN WHO KNOW LATIN:
AN INTRODUCTION TO *DOMINANT CULTURE
AND THE EDUCATION OF WOMEN*

JULIA C. PAULK

To study the education of women is to enter into an exploration of women's relationship to society as a whole and of how female identity is shaped by a variety of factors, including class, race, religion, nationality, and historical era. Therefore, this essay collection, *Dominant Culture and the Education of Women*, is intended to be inclusive and to augment our knowledge of the great variety in women's experiences regarding education in the Western world.[1] In contrast to existing anthologies on this topic, which tend to focus on a more limited time period or single national tradition, this collection traces developments in the education of women from the fourth to the twenty-first century in Europe and the Americas. A comprehensive presentation of such a lengthy interval would be difficult to achieve; this collection offers something more akin to snapshots of different women at key moments in time. Ironically, despite the effort to address the diversity of female experiences, certain concerns regarding female education present themselves as recurring themes in these essays. Women who have sought to gain entry into educational institutions have had to negotiate similar obstacles when facing opposition from what might be called the dominant culture. Although notable differences arise and indeed need to be recognized, women are in many ways united in this struggle. Thus, in this introduction and essay collection, both shared concerns and important divergences will be examined in order to identify recurring problems and to promote greater understanding of the particular educational needs of women from marginalized cultures and communities.

Access to and control of language form one of the common threads tying together the studies included in *Dominant Culture and the Education of Women*. For centuries in Europe, Latin was the language of the educated and therefore was the language of power. A woman's efforts to learn Latin have become highly symbolic, and one cannot help but recall the Spanish expression in use as recently as the last century, "Mujer que sabe latín no tiene marido ni tiene buen fin".[2] That is to say, an educated woman is not fit to find personal happiness through her designated role in the domestic sphere; without a man to support her, this woman will meet a bad end. This saying reflects the notion that a woman who has gained knowledge of the discourse of power is a threat to the dominant culture. Although formal education in the Western world has been conducted in the vernacular for quite some time, the issue of access to the dominant language through educational institutions still arises for women from marginalized cultures in the Western world. For example, fluency and literacy in the standardized, prioritized languages of English and Spanish are indicators of a woman's level of education in many parts of the Americas today.

Perhaps the most frequently mentioned concern regarding the education of women in the studies included here is the question of the relationship between morality and education. From the writings of Jerome to the present day, virtue is intimately tied to female education and helps demonstrate the delicate balancing act women have had to perform over the centuries. Women have undertaken careful negotiations with the dominant culture in order to gain increasingly greater access to instruments and institutions of knowledge by attempting to allay fears that they, and therefore society, will be hopelessly corrupted or thrown into chaos in the process. As a result, those supporting female education have frequently argued that education preserves rather than undermines female virtue. Control over the bodies of both the female educator and the female student enters into the discussion of female education in a way that it does not appear to do in the education of male students. For centuries, women were taught in separate institutions and studied different subjects from men, beginning with convents and private tutors in the medieval era to women's schools and colleges in the modern age, in order to safeguard respectability.

Closely related to notions of female virtue are beliefs in a woman's principal and essential role as a wife and mother. Like those who argued that an education would help preserve and promote female virtue, supporters of female education have proposed that a highly literate woman makes a better companion for her husband and a better educator of her child. Following the move for women of all classes to nurse and raise their own children, women have been extolled as the most natural and best choice to educate their own children. Once again, the careful negotiations undertaken with and against the dominant culture come to the fore. In order to justify seeking an education, women have had to take recourse to notions of a woman's "proper" place in order to push the boundaries of that same sphere. Highlighting the benefits of female education for husbands and children is a tactic used repeatedly by the women studied in this collection. With the rise of nationalism in the nineteenth century, a woman's role in the home took on a new importance as those supporting female education were able to argue that women are nation-builders who raise future citizens. The debate over women's roles continues today as the taboo against women working outside the home after marriage or after childbirth has persisted in some areas into the twenty-first century.

Despite the prevalence of the idea that a woman's proper place is in the home, women from the Middle Ages to the present have discovered that marriage does not always guarantee financial security. Many of the women studied in *Dominant Culture and the Education of Women* were either widowed or married to men unable to support their families. In the fourteenth century, Christine de Pizan found herself with children to support after the death of her husband and undertook a career as a writer in order to do so. This pattern is repeated over the centuries. Writing and teaching, two careers requiring an education, have consistently been described as "appropriate," "decent," and "natural" for women, particularly those from the middle and upper classes. This argument aligns itself with the hegemonic idea that women should prioritize family and behave according to a certain decorum. However, as the years go by, greater numbers of women sought education and the "proper" careers that literacy makes available as an alternative to marriage in the first place. Female educators such as Mary Lyon and Catharine Beecher from the United States stand out as examples of professional women who never married and thereby provided alternative models for women seeking financial independence. Other women have pushed the boundaries even further by studying and writing about male-dominated subjects such as chemistry and anatomy. The question of whether or not a woman should work or marry or both is, of course, one of privilege and should be recognized as an area in which women of different classes and cultures have had varying experiences.

The association between men and what is generally termed the public sphere and that between women and the private or domestic space appears often in *Dominant Culture and the Education of Women* and thus would seem to be a continuing feature of Western culture. Education has traditionally been perceived as an activity that will prepare men for their more highly valued roles in the public sphere. To protect girls and women from the dangers lurking beyond the home, some early texts about the education of women, such as the work of Jerome, advocated the cloistering of women in a private space to protect their virtue. Later works, such as Fray Luis de León's *La perfecta casada (The Perfect Wife)*, which promoted silence and domestic isolation for women, were still being taught in the twentieth century. However, a number of women crossed the boundaries separating the male and female, public and private realms by pursuing careers as court writers, *salonnières*, professionals, and, most often, as writers and teachers.

Dominant Culture and the Education of Women begins with two essays addressing the education of women in medieval Europe. "Latin Literacy in Medieval Women's Writing" by Jane E. Jeffrey and "A Cultural 'Novelty': Christine de Pizan, a Self-Educated Single Mom in Medieval France" by Dorothée Mertz-Weigel demonstrate the singularity of women seeking an education during that era and outline the barriers which they faced. In medieval Europe, access to literacy, particularly in Latin, was limited to the upper class and was understood as belonging to the male domain. In their quest for knowledge, women such as Radegund and Hildegard of Bingen had to seek the isolation of the convent in order to learn and, as in the case of Heloise, submit bodily to the authority of male educators. As Mertz-Weigel demonstrates, Christine de Pizan broke new ground for women through her career as a writer with royal patronage and as a feminist scholar who sought to elevate the status of women and increase their access to literacy skills. Pizan was particularly unusual in that her writings tended to have a more secular orientation and gained entry into the all-male literary canon of the age.

Many of the difficulties facing women seeking an education continued in the early modern era in Europe despite the spread of humanism and more egalitarian ideals regarding knowledge and education. Ulrike Tancke's "'But till some household cares me tie, / My books and Pen I will apply': Early Modern Women's Writings and the Debate on Female Education" examines the tensions inherent in women's writings about education in sixteenth and seventeenth century England. Rather than suggest that these women are unsuccessful in their efforts to move beyond the parameters established for them by the dominant society, Tancke concludes that women's ambiguity towards education, or their simultaneous self-assertion and adherence to convention, should be understood as a strategy of self-definition. Sandy Feinstein's "Chemistry by a Lady for Ladies: Education in the Alchemical Arts" analyzes a text specifically written to educate women in the early modern era in France. Marie Meurdrac's chemistry primer pushes the boundaries of both genre and gender through its concurrent reliance on the discourses of alchemy and of the developing, modern science of chemistry in a text intended for those who were at that time excluded from institutions of higher learning.

The nineteenth century marks a period of great change in Europe and the Americas in that women begin to make their way into the public sphere and educational institutions in increasingly larger numbers. Texts addressing the education of women reflect many of the major trends of the era, such as independence in the Americas, industrialization, the rise of nationalism, and the consolidation of universities in their contemporary form, to name just a few. Julia Kiernan's essay, "The Liberatory Positioning of British Female Rhetoric: Bathsua Makin's *An Essay to Revive the Antient Education of Gentlewomen*, Mary Wollstonecraft's *The Education of Daughters*, and Lucy Wilson's *The Education of Women*" reflects these changes as she traces the move over several centuries in England to finally include working class women in educational institutions in the nineteenth century. Not only do supporters of female education continue to rely on more traditional arguments regarding the formation of successful wives and mothers, but proponents such as Lucy Wilson also address upward class mobility in their support of female education.

In the nineteenth century, women at all levels of the class spectrum pushed the boundaries of their assigned roles by redefining what constitutes the public sphere and female education's role in it. Karin Baumgartner's "Female Education in Nineteenth-Century Germany: Caroline de la Motte Fouqué and the Rejection of Bourgeois Models of Domesticity" examines Fouqué's relocation of the family and social network into the public domain as she argued for women's centrality and duty to the state. At the center of her family and in her *salon*, an educated, upper class woman not only raises dutiful citizens but also shapes public policy. Claire Emilie Martin also studies the formation of a *salonnière* in her essay, "The Education of a Young Creole: The Countess of Merlin's Memoirs." María de las Mercedes de Santa Cruz y Montalvo, Condesa Merlin, was born in Cuba to a wealthy family but required a European education to make the transition from life in the colony to that in the metropole. Her memoirs, written for publication, illustrate her understanding of and misgivings regarding Jean Jacques Rousseau's theories on the education of women and the effects of his theories on her self-development.

As the century progressed, middle and working-class women broke new ground as they entered universities and pursued wider fields of study and professional work. "The First Generation of German Female Students: Autobiographical Perspectives on the Contested Space of Gender and Knowledge", by Magdalena Tarnawska, analyzes the memoirs of the first

German women admitted to previously all-male universities. Their writings reflect their clear understanding of themselves as test cases for later women and the survival strategies they were forced to develop as "interlopers" into the male domain. Mar Soria López's "In Their Own Ways: Emilia Pardo Bazán and María Martínez Sierra's Struggle for Women's Education in Turn-of-the-Century Spain" demonstrates the ways in which two influential female writers relied on both pressing national concerns, particularly the loss of empire and therefore national identity and prestige, and traditional notions of womanhood to promote female education. Hülya Yıldız traces the developments in education for Ottoman women in her essay, "'Knowledgeable Ottoman Girls': Ottoman Women's Education in the Nineteenth Century" through an analysis of historical developments in the Ottoman Empire, women's periodicals and Fatma Aliye Hanım's novel, *Re'fet*. As in Western Europe, the nineteenth century marked a time when the Ottoman Empire first established public schools that allowed lower class women access to literacy and the careers such skills made available.

In the same era in the Americas, women were not only entering schools and universities in increasing numbers, they were also establishing their own. After carefully studying other institutions for women in the United States, Mary Lyon developed a model for a female institution for higher learning that found enduring success, as Beatrice Jacobson describes in "Contradictory Designs: Mary Lyon's Mount Holyoke Female Seminary". Lyon's Mount Holyoke reflects the paradox present in many projects related to female education in that it promoted both an ambitious academic curricula and proficiency in domestic chores. In Brazil, Nísia Floresta's school and texts about female education similarly reflect the pressures facing female educators and female students, which Charlotte Liddell demonstrates in "Teaching, Preaching, and Practice: Nísia Floresta's Shifting Vision of Women's Education in Nineteenth-Century Brazil". To be considered acceptable to the dominant culture, a girls' school needed to prepare young women in domestic skills; to meet the high academic standards a female teacher has for her students, it must also incorporate demanding subjects. The goals and pressures shared by female educators in the Americas is also highlighted in "Beyond the American Home: The Contributions of Catharine Beecher and Clorinda Matto de Turner to Women's Education" by Julia C. Paulk. As these two writers and educators demonstrate, conceptions of women's roles and education became increasingly radicalized over the course of the century even while relying on more traditional notions of True Womanhood for acceptance within the larger culture.

Class privilege was not the only unfair advantage being contested in the Americas in the nineteenth century. Restrictions imposed upon women that were based on a racial hierarchy were also being challenged in the realm of education. A woman who was very conscious of the role that education might play in promoting social change was Frances Harper. Terry Novak's "The Struggle for the Independence and Education of the African American Woman in the Works of Frances Ellen Watkins Harper" analyzes Harper's theories of the education of African American women, particularly as it appears in her works of fiction, and their unique needs both during and after slavery. "Work among the People: How Susan La Flesche Picotte and Zitkala Sa Used Boarding School Education for the Benefit of their Tribes", by Sarah Jayne Hitt, analyzes the potential of education within the dominant culture to destroy or seriously undermine practices, languages, and beliefs of marginalized communities in her study of the boarding school educations of two Native American women. Like Frances Harper, Susan La Flesche Picotte and Zitkala Sa used the skills they gained through mainstream education to become advocates for their people.

Despite the great inroads made by women of varying class, race, and national origins over the centuries, the essays dedicated to women of the twentieth and twenty-first centuries indicate that entirely equal access to education and the corresponding power structures has not yet been achieved. Patricia O'Byrne's "Education for Marriage or Education for Life? The Challenge of Post-War Spanish Women Novelists to the Francoist Approach to the Education of Women" examines the education of women under a conservative, totalitarian regime. Despite severe censorship and efforts to bar women from serious academic achievement or entry into the working world, women such as Carmen Martín Gaite, Carmen Kurtz, and Susana March nonetheless found a way to critique limitations placed on women through their literary texts. Totalitarianism ended in Spain with Franco's death in 1975 but certainly has not vanished from today's world. In contemporary Mexico, increasing access to computer technology and reinvigorated commitment to solidarity has provided new instruments for the preservation and promotion of indigenous cultures, as Abbey Poffenberger outlines in "Cultural Preservation through Education and Literacy: Isabel Juárez Espinosa". Writing in both her native Tzeltal and in Spanish, Juárez Espinosa prioritizes both cultural preservation and elevation of the status of women in her prose and theater works. Embracing the oral and theatrical traditions of Mayan peoples, Júarez Espinosa relies on activist theater to reach and educate as wide an audience as possible, reminding us that the written word is not necessarily more powerful than the spoken one.

The United States Census Bureau recently reported that there are now more women earning bachelor's degrees from universities in the United States than men but also that, above the age of twenty-five, men holding such degrees still outnumber women with similar qualifications.[3] Similarly, studies outlining wage gaps between men and women indicate that men continue to have greater earning power than women in similar jobs and that race is a factor in earnings. Surprisingly, the earnings gap between men and women is the greatest for those who have achieved the highest levels of education. Although educated women tend to earn more and have greater autonomy than women who did not finish high school or earn bachelor's degrees, theorists propose that the domestic and family expectations placed upon women still prevent them realizing their full potential with regard to salary.[4] In other words, women's increasing access to education is providing them with concrete benefits, but inequities between men and women have not yet been eliminated. Perhaps the struggles and successes illustrated in *Dominant Culture and the Education of Women* will inspire those who are interested in achieving full equality for women from all walks of life to continue to push the boundaries imposed by the hegemonic culture's beliefs and practices.

Notes

[1] The essays included in this collection address Europe, the Ottoman Empire, and several countries from the Americas. Henceforth, "the Western world" and "Europe" should be understood as including what is now Turkey. I do this for the sake of brevity and do not intend it as a political statement.

[2] "A woman who knows Latin has no husband and no future" (original translation). The title of the introduction is adapted from this saying. A similar expression in English is the following: "Men don't make passes at women who wear glasses".

[3] Hermes, "Young Women Outpace Young Men in Degree Attainment, Census Shows." This information was reported in early 2008.

[4] Powers, "Doing the Daily Grind: The Effects of Domestic Labor on Professional, Managerial, and Technical Workers' Earnings," 4. Powers's article raises a number of interesting issues related to the gender wage gap. She concludes that domestic work significantly reduces earnings potential for working women who are employed in professional, managerial, and technical positions.

Works Cited

Primary Sources

Fatma Aliye. *Re'fet*. İstanbul: Kırk Ambar Matbaası, 1314.
León, Luis de. *La perfecta casada*. Barcelona: Casa Miquel-Rius, 1930.

Secondary Sources

Hermes, J. J. "Young Women Outpace Young Men in Degree Attainment, Census Shows." *The Chronicle of Higher Education* (January 11, 2008). http://www.chronicle.com (accessed January 11, 2008).
Powers, Rebecca S. "Doing the Daily Grind: The Effects of Domestic Labor on Professional, Managerial, and Technical Workers' Earnings." *Gender Issues* 21.1 (2003): 3-23.

CHAPTER TWO

LATIN LITERACY IN MEDIEVAL WOMEN'S WRITING

JANE E. JEFFREY

The Middle Ages is an expansive historical period, usually defined as the period between the fall of the Roman Empire in the fifth century and the invention of the printing press in 1455. Historical context is important when defining "literacy" because standards of literacy shift as cultural priorities change.[1] For the history of women and literacy, the medieval period more accurately begins with the political rise of Catholicism, which placed a high value on Latin literacy, and ends with the political challenge of the Protestant Reformation, which encouraged study in the vernacular. Literacy in the early Middle Ages, when there was no formally organized school system, meant education in Christian texts: the Vulgate, the Latin translation of the Bible by Jerome; scriptural commentary and other writings by the Church Fathers; and lives of the Saints.

The etymology of *literacy* derives from *litterator*, a masculine noun meaning philologist or grammarian, and medieval literacy means knowing Latin grammar, its vocabulary, case endings, conjugations, and, at the advanced level, rhetorical and literary forms. The use of Latin by women allowed them to participate in the dominant Christian culture that required strict adherence to form, tradition, and authority.

In 384 A.D., Jerome wrote one of the earliest works on women's education, the "Letter to Eustochium," in which he emphasized the virtues of an ascetic life of silence, obedience, and, especially, virginity. Recounting the victories and rewards of virgins throughout the letter, Jerome asserted that Christ's first sacrifice was spending nine months in Mary's womb, where "For our salvation the Son of God is made the Son of Man. Nine months He awaits His birth in the womb, undergoes the most revolting conditions, and comes forth covered with blood...."[2] In other words, Jerome asked Eustochium, why would a woman marry when even a virgin birth produced abject bodily shame? The ascetic life was the only way to ensure that one's body never acted on hunger, thirst, companionship, or love, a severe restriction of human experience by stopping the flow of physical desire. Jerome's instructions to read scripture and repeat prayers incessantly were intended to compel women to use their education to control, and thus save, their bodies. Moreover, Jerome believed in virginity of the whole body, exhorting women not to live among men. Following Jerome's principles, Eustochium left Rome to reside in Bethlehem, where she pursued a life of asceticism and chastity and founded the first convent for religious women.

Jerome's curriculum prohibited teaching classical Roman literature. In the "Letter to Eustochium," Jerome described a dream wherein God punished Jerome for reading Cicero and Plautus. Jerome

> ...was caught up in the spirit and dragged before the judgment seat of the Judge; and here the light was so bright, and those who stood around were so radiant, that I cast myself upon the ground and did not dare to look up. Asked who and what I was I replied: 'I am a Christian.' But He who presided said: 'Thou liest, thou art a follower of Cicero and not of Christ. For 'where thy treasure is, there will thy heart be also.' Instantly I became dumb, and amid the strokes of the lash--for He had ordered me to be scourged--I was tortured more severely still by the fire of conscience....He might still, they urged, inflict torture on me, should I ever again read the works of the Gentiles.[3]

Jerome's abhorrence of classical writing was in part a result of early Christian condemnation of pagan writers. Yet more important than tradition for Jerome was his personal experience of not being in command of his desire to read non-Christian literature.

Jerome wrote a more detailed account of his pedagogical practice for girls in the "Letter to Laeta," written to a woman who had asked Jerome for advice about educating her young daughter. Jerome told Laeta to teach her daughter the alphabet first by sight and sound. Laeta should place before her daughter

> ...a set of letters made of boxwood or of ivory and call each by its proper name. Let her play with these, so that even her play may teach her something. And not only make her grasp the right order of the letters and see that she forms their names into a rhyme, but constantly disarrange their order and put the last letters in the middle and the middle ones at the beginning that she may know them all by sight as well as by sound.[4]

By tracing the letters over and over again, the girl would physically internalize the alphabet into memory:

...so [as] soon as she begins to use the stylus upon the wax, and her hand is still faltering, either guide her soft fingers by laying your hand upon hers, or else have simple copies cut upon a tablet; so that her efforts confined within these limits may keep to the lines traced out for her and not stray outside of these....

Stressing the importance of staying within the lines alleviated Jerome's fear that a girl would read outside the Christian curriculum and fall defenseless into the works of classical writers whose language explored the physicality of existence. In his explanation of the Song of Solomon to Eustochium, Jerome argued that the Ethiopian bride was meant to show how a girl's body was more receptive to physical sensation than was her mind, which must be filled in with lessons to discipline her body. Jerome's letter persuaded Laeta to send her daughter to Eustochium's convent, setting the precedent for convent schools as the best place to teach girls.

Convents were organized according to a Rule. A century after Jerome, the Rule of St. Caesarius was the first rule written for a convent.[5] It required that every member of the convent learn how to read and write. Margaret L. King has argued that "the root of the modern female intellectual experience" might be found in convent communities, where girls and women heard Latin read, sung, prayed, and taught every hour of the day.[6] The first convent to adopt the Rule of St. Caesarius was Radegund's sixth-century Convent of the Holy Cross. While in the convent, Radegund wrote an epic on the war between her country, Thurgundia, and the invading Franks, who killed most members of her family. After eleven-year-old Radegund was kidnapped by the King of the Franks, who intended to marry her, she lived with other royal Frankish women, learned Latin, and began following the practices of Christian asceticism set forth by Jerome. The Frankish aristocracy admired pagan Roman culture and wanted their women to learn Latin as a way of maintaining Roman tradition, while the women learned Latin as a means of strengthening their knowledge of Christian culture. Later as queen, Radegund used her knowledge and influence to persuade her husband to build a convent for her. Adopting the Rule of St. Caesarius, Radegund was able to safeguard the convent from invaders, possible dissidents within the convent, and outside influence from the Church because the Rule emphasized not only literacy, but also enclosure, which was important for Christian women because unconverted Germanic fathers and husbands could otherwise remove their daughters and wives at will. Radegund's final written work was the "Letter of Foundation," which Gregory of Tours included in his *History of the Franks*.[7] Fearing that one of the nuns would use family influence to dissolve the convent (which eventually happened), Radegund stressed how important it was that, after her death, the convent follow the Rule of St. Caesarius so that women could pursue a more studious and contemplative life than that offered by marriage. One of the girls educated at the Convent was Baudonivia, who wrote about Radegund's teaching, history's earliest account of a woman teaching women:

> When the psalms sung in her presence ended, her reading never ceased, neither day, or night, or for refreshing her body with a small amount of food. When the lesson was read, she would say, showing pious concern for the health of our souls, 'If you do not understand what you read, why not search carefully in the mirror of your souls.' And if, out of reverence, the younger members presumed to question her, she, with pious concern and maternal affection, would not cease from teaching what the lesson held for the health of our souls.[8]

Radegund's century marked the last time that Latin would be thought of as both a literary and a vernacular language. By the seventh century, according to Françoise Waquet,

> ...Latin that shaped the liturgy was in a run-of-the-mill, popular register, remote from the classical tongue; but it was also, from its beginnings, a literary language, different from the one generally spoken. The difference was self-accentuating: the language of the sacred text became a language of culture and acquired a patina of archaism that ended by placing it outside time and withdrawing it from common speech.[9]

Losing its vernacular presence, Latin became the language of the literate elite.

By the tenth century, classical Latin, including the works of the Latin writers whom Jerome abhorred, had become part of the convent curriculum. The most notable example of the influence of classical literature on a medieval woman was Hrotsvit of Gandersheim, whose six plays written in Latin were, she said, inspired by her reading of the comedies by the Roman playwright Terence. She also wrote a Latin account of the history of the Ottonian Empire, the history of Gandersheim, and eight saints' lives. There is debate over whether her plays were performed or, like her other writings, read aloud for the edification of the nuns. In either context, scholars agree that Hrotsvit used her writing to teach parts of the quadrivium (mathematics, geometry, astronomy, music); to reinforce the nuns' vows of marriage to Christ; and to provide a history for royal religious women that corresponded to the lives of women living at the Ottonian court. Ulrike Wiethaus argues that Hrotsvit's writings commemorate

> ...the patriarchal Christian idea of womanhood, defined as female strength in the service of male sexual ownership, female eloquence in the service of Christian ideology, female loyalty unto death to male authority figures who insist on their power over them.[10]

Although Hrotsvit used Latin to support the policies of the court and the legacy of the Church Fathers, her position as an aristocratic writer reinforced the idea that educated women were equal and sometimes superior to men, especially to men who did not understand Latin.

During the twelfth century, the evidence of women's participation as writers, readers, and patrons of the Latin tradition is very strong. Joan M. Ferrante writes that the

> ...enthusiasm for education in the twelfth century is real, not just because it has practical applications in religious life and society, but because it is perceived as a good in itself. Knowledge can provide wonderful powers, sometimes magical....In this period at least, we are meant to root for the brilliant heroine.[11]

Having studied Priscian's sixth-century Latin grammar, Marie de France wrote that she considered translating Latin stories into Anglo-Norman before choosing to translate oral tales into the written vernacular, marking an important change in the medieval definition of language literacy. Marie de France's decision to write in a vernacular allowed her to write outside the constraints of institutional authority, at least religious authority. Yet the choice between writing in Latin or a vernacular language carried certain implications for women because a woman who could understand Latin would be taken more seriously and her writing more likely preserved than would writing in the vernacular, a language which risked not being written down because of its association with domestic matters.[12]

The twelfth century also saw several changes in higher education: the curriculum was augmented with translations of Greek and Arabic literature, there was competition with vernacular literature, and a new technique of teaching was introduced, Abelard's dialectic method of scholarly inquiry, which advocated rigorous investigation in the place of unquestioning adherence to tradition and authority. Abelard's use of dialectic is fully detailed in his autobiography *Historia calamitatum* as a competitive and antagonistic form of argumentation that produces winners and humiliates losers. Abelard writes that when his

> ...own teaching gained so much prestige and authority from [dialetic] the strongest supporters of my master who had hitherto been the most violent among my attackers now flocked to join my school....Within a few days of my taking over the teaching of dialectic, William [Abelard's teacher] was

eaten up with jealousy and consumed with anger to an extent it is difficult to convey, and being unable to control the violence of his resentment for long, he made another artful attempt to banish me.[13]

In contrast to Baudonivia's heartfelt tribute to Radegund's teaching is Abelard's epistolary vilification of one of Paris's most famous teachers, Anselm of Laon. Over the years, according to Abelard's description, Anselm's mind had become dry rot and his lessons empty:

> Anyone who knocked at his door to seek an answer to some question went away more uncertain than he came. Anselm could win the admiration of an audience, but he was useless when put to the question. He had a remarkable command of words but their meaning was worthless and devoid of all sense. The fire he kindled filled his house with smoke but did not light it up; he was a tree in full leaf which could be seen from afar, but on closer and more careful inspection proved to be barren. I had come to this tree to gather fruit, but I found it was the fig tree which the Lord cursed, or the ancient oak of which Lucan compares Pompey:
> There stands the shadow of a noble name
> Like a tall oak in a field of corn.[14]

The quotations cited from Jerome and Abelard are saturated with an aggressive and violent language of learning that often characterizes a masculine professoriate, a dominant culture, in contrast to a supportive, tolerant way of teaching and learning described by Baudonivia, a way of teaching thought appropriate for children, girls, and women, but not for future ecclesiastical, court, and civic leaders.

Marie's contemporaries Heloise and Hildegard of Bingen were members of religious orders and wrote exclusively in Latin. The education of Heloise presents one of the best documented accounts of a student-teacher relationship; in fact, Heloise's reputation for being educated is what attracted Abelard, who wrote, "In looks she did not rank lowest, while in the extent of her learning she stood supreme. A gift for letters is so rare in women that it added greatly to her charm and had won her renown throughout the realm."[15] As a girl in the convent school at Argenteuil, Heloise studied scriptures and commentary written by Jerome as well as classical authors who entered the curriculum in the tenth century. To educate Heloise, Abelard modified the aggressive disciplinary methods of the university to using the premise of education to seduce Heloise. The rhetorical and physical violence expressed in Jerome's writings on acquiring an education is heard six-hundred years later in Peter Abelard's teaching of Heloise:

> [Fulbert, Heloise's uncle] gave me complete charge over the girl, so that I could devote all the leisure time left me by my school to teaching her by day and night, and if I found her idle I was to punish her severely....In handing her over to me to punish as well as to teach, what else was he doing but giving me complete freedom to realize my desires, and providing an opportunity, even if I did not make use of it, for me to bend her to my will by threats and blows if persuasion failed?[16]

Abelard's physical punishments soon advanced to leaving "no stage of love-making untried." Women who learned to write in Latin engaged a language established through history and by convention as a canonical, authoritative language, yet, as in Heloise's case, the pedagogical practices of her day required the educated woman to submit to authority. If the authority was a male tutor and he demanded sexual exchange, then Heloise's physical submission to Abelard would seem to her fundamental for gaining status in the academic culture to which she aspired.

Although Abelard's teaching required Heloise to equate erotic submission with learning, as unfortunately has been a reality in higher education for many women, it was not until Heloise became pregnant and bore a son, after Abelard was castrated, and after Heloise was named abbess of the Paraclete that she used her knowledge of Latin to confront Abelard's power over her. She wrote him two letters that not only justified her love for Abelard, but also insisted that he fulfill his responsibilities to her as her husband. In response, Abelard ignored Heloise's many well-supported appeals and proofs and demanded that Heloise cease her mindless longing and concentrate her energy on praying for his welfare.

In a third letter, Heloise promised to say no more about love. Within a few lines, she turned from lover to student and asked Abelard to instruct her about needed changes in the convent's Rule so that it could be adapted to women's lives. She wanted him to recognize her now as a teacher in charge of the education of nuns, novices, and children. Heloise composed the *Problemata*, forty-two questions on scripture addressed to Abelard.[17] In these questions, Heloise shifted Abelard's attention from their sexual past to an intellectual and professional relationship. Heloise asked Abelard to help her write a Rule for women, one which acknowledged gender difference and held women to a high level of intellectual sophistication. Using the philosophy of dialectic, Heloise questioned what she has been taught concerning the differences between men and women, body and mind, and sin and judgment. Heloise's questions also raised textual and interpretative complexities in the Old and New Testaments, which, Heloise wrote, slowed down the nuns' reading of the Scriptures.[18] The final result was a Rule that respected women's bodies and their minds, not using one to punish the other, as had been the basis of Jerome's pedagogy. According to M. T. Clanchy, Heloise

> ...was probably the last medieval lay woman to be so highly trained in classical 'letters'; a century later even many nuns had stopped learning Latin....until the end of the nineteenth century, women remained excluded from the academic world, with which Heloise had been familiar and in which she had gained such distinction.[19]

Heloise served as abbess at the Paraclete for twenty years. Under her rule, five dependent priories were established, and the monastery earned a reputation as one of the most important educational centers for women in twelfth-century France.

In Germany, Hildegard of Bingen was born in 1098, the tenth child of a nobleman and his wife. When Hildegard was eight years old, her parents gave her to the Church as a tithe. She went to live with the anchoress Jutta in a cell attached to a Benedictine monastery. From Hildegard's many writings and from a biography written shortly after her death, we know the contents of her education. Hildegard's writings include quotations from the Bible, the writings of the Church Fathers, and a number of classical Roman sources, primarily Cicero. In the preface her longest work, *Scivias*, Hildegard wrote that at age forty-two,

> Heaven was opened and a fiery light of exceeding brilliance came and permeated my whole brain, and inflamed my whole heart and my whole breast....And immediately I knew the meaning of the exposition of the Scriptures, namely the Psalter, the Gospel and the other catholic volumes of both the Old and New Testaments....[20]

Although her understanding seems to come instantaneously, for the previous forty years Hildegard had been listening to, reading, and reciting biblical passages and interpretations. Hildegardwrotethat she kept her knowledge secret "because of doubt and a low opinion [of myself]." With the monk Volmar's help and encouragement, she began to write. At the time of her death at age eighty one, she had written three books of visionary writing, a book on diseases and cures, chants, a play, over four-hundred letters, and a work on natural history that contains sixty-three chapters on trees, seventy-two chapters on birds, and 230 chapters on plants.

Hildegard always said that her knowledge of Latin endings and cases was weak and that she depended on Volmar for help. Clanchy provides insight into the problems facing a writer of a non-native language: even though Hildegard might understand Latin when it was spoken or read, writing in Latin raises different epistemological problems:

> For a medieval writer the difficulties of getting the text on to parchment were relatively simple compared with the initial problem of converting one's thoughts into Latin. This required years of training. Because it was nobody's mother tongue and its rules of style and construction had been established more than a thousand years earlier, Latin tended to take over anyone who began to write it. To the rhetoric of the classical authors (Virgil, Cicero, Ovid, and so on) had been added the even more powerful models of the Latin Bible and the Latin liturgy, with which every monk and nun was in daily contact through chanting and hearing readings. [21]

In 1970, Peter Dronke described Hildegard's Latin songs as "a highly individual language, at times awkward and at times unclear; the adjectives can be repetitious and limited in range, the interjections excessive. It is the language not of a polished twelfth-century humanist but of someone whose unique powers of poetic vision confronted her more than once with the limits of poetic expression."[22] Twenty years later, Barbara Newman explained Hildegard's spiritual language not as meeting a linguistic limit, but as "unrhymed, unmetrical songs, wholly unpredictable as to line division, length, and stanzaic pattern, follow[ing] the rhythms of thought alone. Their content belongs to the twelfth century, but their form anticipates the twentieth." [23]

One of the most recent observations about Hildegard's use of Latin comes from the translators of her letters in 1994. They write that

> One of the greatest challenges in reading (and translating) Hildegard indeed comes not from her own difficulty with the scholarly language, but, as it were, from her very ease with it, her fecund and canny use of its creative possibilities....A marked feature of Hildegard's style is a general looseness of sentence structure, with phrase attracting phrase, and clause, clause, all strung rather adventitiously together on the thread of the thought. This fact, in and of itself, poses no real problem for the reader, and, in fact, has its own kind of simple charm. Still, at times, this accumulation of qualifying or merely additive elements without clear or unambiguous markers....[or] logical relationships among the ideas results in a passage of almost impenetrable opacity. [24]

Although "simple charm" resonates uneasily with Abelard's description of Heloise's education as "add[ing] greatly to her charm," Hildegard, unlike Heloise, wrote on many different topics, in various genres, to many people, and for diverse purposes. Heloise wrote only in the epistolary genre, to only a few people, and with a persuasive purpose, for which there were many Latin models to follow.

Nevertheless, Heloise and Hildegard used their education to resist, defy, and maintain uncompromising positions against male erudition that legitimated women's lives only at a physical level. Both women wrote about women's physical presence and how Church authorities tried to limit their movement educationally and spiritually. Although two famous medieval teachers, Jerome and Abelard, both known for their misogyny, devoted a large part of their teaching to women, composing religious and scholarly works at the request of women, Jerome and Abelard maintained that women should be educated so that they could rise above their sex.

The twelfth century marked the first time that women writers had a choice between writing in Latin and or in a vernacular. After the twelfth century, more women had access to the vernacular than to Latin, which required tutors, scribes, and convents, all of which were in decline.[25] In short, Latin came up against its own dominant practices in medieval culture. Because of its associations with classical Rome and the development of Christianity, and its long curricular status as the essential language of learning, Latin conferred prestige long after it was a natural language. Yet its institutional authority was slowly and successfully challenged in the thirteenth century by a more equitable language of power, the vernacular.

Notes

[1] Zieman, "Reading, Singing and Understanding," 97.
[2] Jerome, "Letter XXII."
[3] Ibid.
[4] Jerome. "Letter CVII."
[5] Mother Maria Caritas McCarthy, *The Rule of Nuns of St. Caesarius of Arles:*
[6] King, *Women of the Renaissance,* 175.
[7] Radegund, "Letter of Foundation."
[8] Baudonivia, *De vita sanctae Radegundis Liber II.*
[9] Waquet, *Latin or the Empire of a Sign*, 42.
[10] Wiethaus, "*Pulchrum Signum*?," 135.
[11] Ferrante, "The Education of Women in the Middle Ages," 34-35.
[12] Katharina M. Wilson and Glenda Macleod write,
Scanning women's writing by what one might think the simplest principle possible--the languages used--unveils the level of complexity facing any surveyor of medieval literature. Like men, women wrote in a wide assortment of languages; to understand the importance of this variety, however, one must recognize that linguistic choice for medieval writers, as

for some modern writers in multilingual areas, carried philosophical and political implications. 331

[13] Abelard, *Historia calamitatum*, 66.
[14] Ibid., 62. In *The Envy of Angels*, C. Stephen Jaeger argues that the twelfth century marks a major division between the old learning of the Church Fathers and the new learning that Abelard advocated:
> An entire system of education was caught in a conflict between a traditional kind of teaching that tended toward the acquisition of human qualities and a new kind that tended toward knowledge and rational inquiry....The clash between Abelard and Anselm of Laon exemplifies these tendencies strikingly. It is as if whatever forces of history shaped the general conflict designed Abelard and Anselm to embody it: they brewed the intellect and character of Anselm with an overbalance in favor of *mores* and eloquence (the products of the old learning), and then, like chemists performing an experiment, exactly reversed the proportions in brewing Abelard. Anselm and the type he represented may have lacked penetration and analytical sharpness, but they were masters of the discipline of living well. Abelard may have known a great deal and possessed a keenly analytical mind, but he was a failure at the discipline of life," an indictment is supported by Abelard's treatment of Heloise in the name of education. 236

[15] Abelard, 60.
[16] Ibid., 67.
[17] McNamer, *The Education of Heloise.*
[18] Clanchy, *Abelard: A Medieval Life*, 279.
[19] Hildegard, *Scivias*, 59.
[20] Clanchy, p. 14.
[21] Dronke, *Poetic Individuality in the Middle Ages,* 178-179.
[22] Newman, *Sister of Wisdom,* 25.
[23] Baird and Ehrman, eds. *The Letters of Hildegard of Bingen*, 7.
[24] Clanchy, *Abelard: A Medieval Life*, 47.
[25] See Sara S. Poor's discussion of the complexities of Latin and vernacular literacies in thirteenth-century women's writing in "Mechthild von Magdeburg, Gender, and the 'Unlearned Tongue.'"

Works Cited

Primary Sources

Abelard, Peter. *Historia calamitatum*, trans. Betty Radice. In *The Letters of Abelard and Heloise.* New York: Penguin, 1974.
Baudonvia. *De vita sanctae Radegundis Liber II,* ed.B. Krusch, *Monumenta Germanica Historia Scriptores rerum Merovingicarum* 2, 377-95.

Hildegard. *Scivias*., trans. Columba Hart and Jane Bishop. New York: Paulist Press, 1990.
Jerome, "Letter XXII," trans. W. H. Fremantle, 1892. http:www.ccel.org/ccel/schaff/npnf206.v.XXII.html.13 July 2005.
—. "Letter CVII," trans. W.H. Fremantle, 1892. http:www.ccel.org/ccel/schaff/npnf206.v.CVII.html.13 July 2005.
Radegund. "Letter of Foundation." In *Women Writing Latin: From Roman Antiquity to Early Modern Europe*, vol. 2, edited by Laurie J. Churchill, Phyllis Brown, and Jane E. Jeffrey, 11-13. New York: Routledge, 2002, 11-13.

Secondary Sources

Baird, Joseph L., and Radd K. Ehrman, eds. *The Letters of Hildegard of Bingen*, 3 vols. Oxford: Oxford University Press, 1998.
Brown, Phyllis, Linda A. McMillin, and Katharina M. Wilson, eds. *Hrotsvit of Gandersheim: Contexts, Identities, Affinities, and Performances*. Toronto: University of Toronto Press, 2004.
Churchill, Laurie, Phyllis Brown, and Jane E. Jeffrey, eds. *Women Writing Latin: From Roman Antiquity to Early Modern Europe*, 3 vols. New York: Routledge, 2002
Clanchy, M. *Abelard: A Medieval Life*. Oxford: Blackwell Publishers, 1997.
Dronke, Peter. *Poetic Individuality in the Middle Ages: New Departures in Poetry, 1000-1150*. Oxford: Oxford University Press, 1970.
Ferrante, Joan M. "The Education of Women in the Middle Ages in Theory, Fact, and Fantasy." In *Beyond Their Sex: Learned Women of the European Past*, ed. Patricia H. Labalme. 9-42. New York: New York University Press, 1984.
Jaeger, C. Stephen. *The Envy of Angels: Cathedral Schools and Social Ideals in Medieval Europe, 950-1200*. Philadelphia, Pennsylvania: University of Pennsylvania Press, 1994.
King, Margaret L. *Women of the Renaissance*. Chicago: University of Chicago Press, 1991.
Labalme, Patricia H., ed. *Beyond Their Sex: Learned Women of the European Past*. New York: New York University Press, 1984.
McNamer, Elizabeth Mary. *The Education of Heloise: Methods, Content, and Purpose of Learning in the Twelfth Century*. Lewiston, N.Y.: Edwin Mellen Press, 1991.
Mitchell, Linda, ed. *Women in Medieval Western European Culture*. New York: Garland Publishing, 1999.

Mother Maria Caritas McCarthy, *The Rule of Nuns of St. Caesarius of Arles: A Translation with a Critical Introduction*. Washington, D.C.: Catholic University of America Press, 1960.

Newman, Barbara. *Sister of Wisdom: St. Hildegard's Theology of the Feminine*. Berkeley: University of California Press, 1987.

Poor, Sara S. "Mechthild von Magdeburg, Gender, and the 'Unlearned Tongue,'" *Journal of Medieval and Early Modern Studies* 31.2 (2001): 213-50.

Radice, Betty, trans., *The Letters of Abelard and Heloise*. New York: Penguin, 1974.

Waquet, Françoise. *Latin or the Empire of a Sign*. Translated by John Howe. London: Verso, 2001.

Weithaus, Ulrike. "*Pulchrum Signum*? Sexuality and the Politics of Religion in the Works of Hrotsvit of Gandersheim Composed between 963 and 973." In *Hrotsvit of Gandersheim: Contexts, Identities, Affinities,and Performances*, ed. Phyllis R. Brown, Linda A. McMillin, and Katharina M. Wilson, 125-143. Toronto: University of Toronto Press, 2004.

Wilson, Katharina M. and Glenda Macleod. "Sounding Trumpets, Chords of Light, and Little Knives: Medieval Women Writers" in *Women in Medieval Western European Culture*, ed. Linda E. Mitchell, 331-344. New York: Garland Publishing, 1999.

Zieman, Katherine. "Reading, Singing and Understanding: Constructions of the *Literacy* of Women Religious in Late Medieval England." In *Learning and Literacy in Medieval England and Abroad,* ed. Sarah Rees Jones, 97-120. Turnhout, Belgium: Brepols, 2003.

Chapter Three

A Cultural "Novelty": Christine de Pizan, a Self-Educated Single Mom in Medieval France

Dorothée Mertz-Weigel

Christine de Pizan is considered by many to be the first feminist writer in medieval Europe because of the multiple volumes she dedicated to the defense of women.[1] Feminism and medieval times, a time "when womankind in general was held in singularly low esteem"[2] are usually not juxtaposed in the same mind frame, let alone in the same sentence. However, Christine's bringing up at the court, with the proximity of her father, his knowledge and education, as well as countless library resources, and despite her mother's wish for her to conform to more typical medieval girl's activities, such as spinning,[3] gave her the grounds to develop a mind of her own. Christine de Pizan might not have become famous, had she not had special circumstances in her life which brought her to writing. Most Christine de Pizan scholars emphasize the fact that the medieval author was ahead of her time. In this essay, using her work *The Book of the City of Ladies* as a focal point, I will argue that while she was clearly a woman of her times in many ways, Christine de Pizan's contributions as a feminist scholar set her apart,[4] but her novelty lies in the fact that she wanted to educate and empower all women through the example of her life intertwined in her writings.

Christine de Pizan's father was Tommaso di Benvenuto da Pizzano, a lecturer in astrology at the University of Bologna (1348) and later a physician. Tomasso left Bologna for Venice in 1357 where Christine was born. Shortly after her birth in 1365, he became the court astrologer of Charles V, and moved his family to Paris in 1368. Christine got married at fifteen, with Etienne du Castel, a young scholar from Picardie and of noble parents. Christine and Etienne were happily married, as Christine mentions in the *City of Ladies*[5] and gave life to three children. Unfortunately, ten years after their marriage, Etienne died, leaving Christine on her own to take care of her children, her mother, and two nieces who needed to find husbands. Also, Christine discovered that her husband had been a very poor economist and she was pursued by his creditors.

In order to support her family and take care of her debts, she retired to a study where she decided to dedicate herself to intellectual work and writing. Studies say that she was probably a copyist,[6] and that she most likely had other sorts of monetary funding. Indeed, even the most famous male poets of the time could not support their lives with writing only: "She must have had another source of income beyond whatever her husband left. Even Eustache Deschamps [a contemporary poet of Christine] could not support his living by writing alone. Careers such as these were simply not available to women at the beginning of the 15th century."[7] Interestingly, Christine de Pizan was destined to be a successful writer, despite the unfavorable conditions for women writers during her epoch: "Left a widow at the age of twenty-five and with a family to support and care for, she managed to make her way through exceptionally troubled times and achieve for herself a much-desired renown, an ambition she mentioned often in her writings."[8] Because she became very famous in France and abroad,[9] and was sponsored by financially rich patrons, she was able to support herself and her family successfully.

As Glenda McLeod says, "as a woman writer she was seen as an anomaly."[10] Men, in feudal times, held the monopoly on knowledge and writing, and were the ones who showed women the path to virtue and salvation.[11] It seems that women had no speech; women were not speaking for women in writing, and everything they had to do was dictated by men, especially men whose religious vows forbade them contact with women. By the time Christine wrote, women who had access to higher education were always either noble or religious, and there were a number of women who were influential in politics and religion, such as Catherine of Sienna (according to Wempel and Opitz.)[12] Since there were some literate women during her era, she was able to find an audience for her writing with them first. But, considering the small amount of literary testimonies by medieval female writers available, it is easy to guess that the access to expression for women was difficult and was limited to men.[13] Christine herself in one of her earlier works called *Mutation of Fortune* (ca. 1403) says: "How I, a woman, became a man by a flick of Fortune's hand/ How she changed my body's form/To the perfect masculine norm."[14] In other words, she needs to undergo a sex change and become a man in order to take on the responsibilities left by the death of her husband, but also to be taken seriously as a writer and included in the literary canon. Christine knew that from a literary point of view, she did not belong to her time, as she states in *Christine's Vision* (1405), through the mouth of Dame Opinion:

> 'In the times to come, more will be said of you than during your lifetime, for... you have lived in a bad time, when sciences are not held in great esteem...but after your death there will come a prince full of valor and wisdom who, through knowing your volumes, will wish that you had lived during his lifetime and would have liked to know you.'[15]

In the *City of Ladies* (1405), however, she completely assumes her female identity and does not need to undergo the same sex change in order to feel comfortable in her writing, as a female writer. According to Kevin Brownlee, "*Cité des Dames* definitely rejects the construct of gender change that had served as a kind of provisional solution to the problem of self-representation in the *Mutacion*."[16] Christine de Pizan's acceptance of her identity as a female writer is more assertive and open as her career progresses.

Thereby, Christine de Pizan, who created a new kind of writing by a woman was a novelty for the late Middle Ages. She created a new voice for herself and asserted her identity as female writer. She knew that knowledge was not as widely available to women as it was to men and mentions it in several of her works, such as *The Book of the City of Ladies*, and confirms the knowledge of the limitations imposed on her sex, which she wants to transcend.[17] In her works, she wants not only to give a literary voice to women, but she wants to give them a place and a role in the public sphere, and wants them to have access to education, just as men do, because they have the same intellectual abilities as men, as stated in the *City of Ladies*.[18] For instance, Christine de Pizan is also familiar with the various steps required for the assembly of books and wants to involve women in it:

> In her writings, Christine often refers to aspects of book production. In her biography of Charles V, for instance, she speaks of the scribes who were constantly at work copying manuscripts in the royal library. Although she is never referred to specifically as one of these scribes, that this is a sort of work that would have been available to women is confirmed by records of that time of women working as both copyists and illustrators. Such an apprenticeship would not only have given Christine a source of income and the range of knowledge that is evident in her writings but it would have taught her how to organize and to operate a workshop of her own.[19]

The fact that she could have managed a book production workshop of her own was also a way for her to involve other women in it. A workshop operated by a man would have probably been less likely to allow women in it. Copying manuscripts was consequently a way for women to earn some income, but illustrating them was another way, and Christine de Pizan, in the *City of Ladies*, refers to a person known as Anastasia who illustrated manuscripts:

> Regarding what you say about women expert in the art of painting, I know a woman today, named Anastasia, who is so learned and skilled in painting manuscript borders and miniature backgrounds that one cannot find an artisan in all the city of Paris—where the best in the world are found—who can surpass her, not who can paint flowers and details as delicately as she does, nor whose work is more highly esteemed, no matter how rich or precious the book is. People cannot stop talking about her. And I know this from experience, for she has executed several things for me which stand out among the ornamental borders of the great masters.[20]

Consequently, rather than an abnormality,[21] since there were a few other women writers, though mostly religious,[22] or other women involved in the production of books, Christine de Pizan was unique for her times, because she rarely spoke of God, which was the main accepted topic of writing for medieval women of letters, and she directed her attention on women, which was almost without precedent: "As a woman's view on life and society were almost without precedent, they indeed offer a novelty…Her own experience was the best she had to offer, and another woman's voice would not be heard in France for more than a hundred years."[23]

Writers of the fifteenth century were often sponsored by patrons, and Christine's particular problem, according to Charity Cannon-Willard "was to find a prince who would be willing to protect a woman writer, a novelty to say the least,"[24] and Christine de Pizan herself knew that her popularity was due to the fact that being a female writer was an innovation.[25] In Christine's case, the newness of her work as a woman writer helped her reputation spread rapidly and consequently helped her in finding sponsors. At first, she wrote ballads and other popular forms of poems for her times, and fortunately, as Brownlee says "After starting from a position of complete professional obscurity, by the year 1405 she was writing for the most prestigious patrons in France: the king, the queen, and the royal princes and princesses."[26] Consequently, she not only had one patron throughout her career but several who had specific requests for her.

Finally, she was the first female writer to be included in an all-male literary canon. This fact was recognized by Eustache Deschamps, whose ballad 1242 "responds to Christine's epistle with a series of epithets bestowing canonical status upon her as a woman writer, while at the same time stressing her uniqueness in this regard."[27] Not only was she a novelty, but she was also accepted in the all-male literary cannon by contemporary poets.

Christine de Pizan's uniqueness goes beyond the fact that she was a female writer. The topics treated in her works were also new. She was the most important defender of women's honor in medieval literature and this ideal is best presented in *The Book of the City of Ladies*. Her most famous work now, *The Book of the City of Ladies*, was also among her most popular works when she was alive with *The Book of Three Virtues* and especially *Othéa's Letter to Hector* (an introduction to the study of classical mythology), and was still read and later owned by the most renowned Renaissance ladies, such as Marguerite de Navarre. In *The Book of the City of Ladies*, Christine follows the medieval format of allegory used by her male contemporaries, with three ladies, Reason, Honesty and Justice who talk Christine into building a city for the most famous ladies of history. Christine presents the construction of this city as an allegory for a history of women. She wants to show that since the beginning of times, there have been numerous great women who were virtuous and wise. This work is a direct reaction to Jean de Meun's *Romance of the Rose* (1268-1280), one of the most popular vernacular works of the thirteenth to the fifteenth century. Christine's text especially attacks its misogynistic portrayal of women, as Judith Kellogg states: "In this text, Christine tackles the problem of misogyny head-on, offering an alternative view of history in which women's contribution as historical figures is fully recognized."[28] Also, this particular work was known not only in France but also in Europe: it was translated into Flemish in 1475 and into English in 1521.[29] This is very important, especially knowing that Christine de Pizan insisted in her writings on her desire to be remembered after her death: "This trait links her firmly to the new intellectual era that was spreading north from Italy to France in which the quest for fame was considered one of the legitimate objectives of life as opposed to the otherworldliness of the true Middle Ages."[30] She already knew she wanted her contribution as a historical figure to be fully recognized.

In 1405, when the *Book of the City of Ladies* was written, there were other such "catalogues" written in which women were discussed. One such book is by Boccaccio and is entitled *De claris mulieribus* (of Famous Women),[31] which Christine de Pizan quotes extensively in the *City of Ladies*. These other available catalogues were written by men and gave men's insights on women's life stories. Christine did not merely translate Boccaccio's work as a source for the history of women she includes in her work: instead of just listing famous women and their accomplishments, she connected them to the evolution of civilization and noted their contributions to it. She rewrote history and refashioned "traditional stories to highlight women's active role and fundamental contribution to society generally,"[32] and, "Her *Cité des dames* is among other things a bold rewriting of human history that shows women not only as models of moral uprightness, but also as active creators, builders and guardians of the institutions, intellectual traditions, social structures and beliefs cherished by the medieval world."[33] She was consequently deconstructing the conclusions of misogynistic ideas used by male writers, and, according to Brown-Grant, also seeking "to empower her female reader by valorizing key areas of women's experience, as opposed to the historical perspectives and examples adopted in [the works of her male predecessors.]"[34] This is where her pedagogical goal to educate women about their own contribution to history starts.

As a result, most of the reasons for this work's success are in one way or another related to the fact that Christine and her work were a novelty. Overall, nothing like Christine's work had been seen before, and the *City of Ladies* itself was highly original. The book's first innovation, as mentioned above, is that Christine rewrote history from a new perspective, that of women and their contributions to civilization throughout the years and centuries. The second one is that it is written by a woman for women. The third one is its open criticism of misogyny, and finally, the fourth one is that she made her work inclusive by writing it for and including in it women of all social statuses and religious faiths.

In the *Book of the City of Ladies*, Christine speaks as a woman, and describes herself as a learned woman of letters.[35] Interestingly, she does not have any example to draw from as a female writer, and consequently expresses her doubts: "[this work] has a much more extensive prologue in which she reveals her 'anxiety of authorship' in taking up a pen in the first place, given that she has no previous examples of women writers on whose literary authority she can draw."[36] Moreover, she intends this work to be didactic, in the tradition of the time, but intended it to be didactic for women, to instruct them on the accomplishments women have done throughout history, to give women the ways to disarm their adversaries and even triumph over them by claiming their rights.[37] She also wants for women to learn from the examples she gives, and perhaps change their minds on the possibilities women can have and have had over the course of history. Interestingly, according to Brown-Grant,

> the most striking divergence between Christine and her predecessors is that whereas Petrarch and Boccaccio share a pessimistic view of history, which they regard either as a process of decline or as a continuum of vice down

the ages, she argues that history has been marked by progress and that women have played a key role in the development of civilization.[38]

Consequently, Christine de Pizan's originality is not only in instructing others of her sex of the great achievements accomplished by women through the ages, but also in teaching everyone that progress has been made from the beginning of time. For Christine de Pizan, all of these developments are instructive and edifying. Moreover, for her female readers not to think that she is above them because of her literary knowledge: she "represents herself in the *Cité* as a receiver rather than a dispenser of wisdom, thereby appearing to place herself on the same level as her implied readers."[39] With this further step, Christine de Pizan helps the reader identify with the narrator, and consequently eases the involvement of the female reader in this new realm, which Christine conceptualizes as being entirely female.

In this new world that she is creating, there is room for the great accomplishments done by women of all times and all statuses, and for an open criticism of misogyny. Considering the history of women with which Christine is familiar, it is no surprise that she wonders why men keep criticizing women and giving them negative attributes, even for women such as Eve or Mary Magdalene. In other words, she herself is criticizing misogyny, which she witnesses in all works written by men. Not only did she have to suffer the misogynistic views of men in all works she read, but, according to Cannon-Willard, she also "had felt the sting [of it], not only in the debate over *The Romance of the Rose*, but even more unpleasantly during the first years of her widowhood."[40] In the *City of Ladies*, Christine wants to clean the (literary) history of women from all misogynistic views. It is a novelty to come to the defense of women because, according to Cannon-Willard, in the Middle Ages, the attacks against women were traditional.[41] Moreover, the first male author who degrades women that Christine mentions in the *City of Ladies*, Mathélous,[42] was a fervent admirer of Jean de Meun, and consequently represented all that Christine resented.[43] Christine de Pizan and all her female readers needed a work on which they could count, which did not perpetuate misogynistic ideas. They needed a work that was by a woman for women. Women needed to be reassured about the fact that learning was possible for women. This was necessary in part because they had been made to feel ambivalent about writing. Putting pen to paper was a possible source of improvement but could also cause permanent alienation.[44] Christine de Pizan herself, by refusing to mention other defenses of women written by male writers in the *City of Ladies*, stresses the novelty of her approach by opposing an overwhelming mass of negative opinions about women.[45]

Finally, as a woman talking to women, defending them against misogyny and consequently rewriting history with a female point of view, Christine knew her work would not be complete if she did not include women of all social statuses and religious faiths. Even though she has been criticized because she devoted most of her work to queens and princesses, one must remember, as Cannon-Willard points out, that at the time they were the most literate women, and consequently were the ones who were most likely going to read Pizan's works.[46] She has also been accused of prudishness "for upholding a high standard of virtue, yet the realism of her analysis demonstrates her awareness of the penalty society is capable of exacting from a young woman if she allows herself to be compromised."[47] However, even if Christine included the nobility to a greater extent, she managed to include all women in a spiritual way in her work and thereby made it more inclusive,[48] because,

> she concerns herself with the problems of women of all social classes, rather than addressing a specific group of women, and furthermore, she is concerned not only with prescribing for them a domestic and spiritual life...but also with encouraging them to stand on their own feet, to make some sort of contribution to society, to dominate the conditions of their lives that make or break them.[49]

She also presents an all-female canon in the *City of Ladies*. Among the writers that she names are three that are particularly well-educated and intelligent: Cornificia, Proba, and Sappho. Each of them is explicitly presented as having been praised by Boccaccio.[50] With this point, she is also trying to prove herself as belonging to this new canon, one that would involve women: "The significance of the *Cité* lies not in its anticipation of twentieth-century feminism but in the way in which Christine offers her female readership models of behaviour which, unlike those of Boccaccio's catalog, are meant to be accessible to all medieval women."[51] Finally, in the *City of Ladies*, she introduces the idea of a liberal education for women,[52] an education that would probably, one can imagine, have the *City of Ladies* as a starting point.

While Christine de Pizan was clearly a woman of her times in many ways, her contributions as a feminist scholar set her apart. She was a medieval woman because she was educated and well-read, just as many other noble women of her era, but she was also able to survive the troubles of widowhood without external help thanks to her education and her writing. The novelty came not only with her gender in the profession she chose, but also with the introduction of new, feminist ideas in her literature, made to empower all women through education against the misogynistic ideas and practices of the moment, with her own life as the most empowering model of self-education for all women.

Notes

[1] Régnier-Bohler, *Voix littéraires, voix mystiques,* 454. " Et c'est bien la première féministe des lettres françaises que nous entendons ici" (And this really is the first feminist of French literature we hear here, *translation mine.)*
Altman, McGrady, *Christine de Pizan: A Casebook*, 81-146.
In the second part of the volume edited by Barbara K. Altman and Deborah L. McGrady, four scholars explain the "profeminine" agenda of Christine de Pizan from different perspectives. Rosalind Brown-Grant shows how "Christine challenged accepted views of women's nature and role in medieval society" (3), Roberta L. Krueger "demonstrates that Christine understands women's management of financial resources as a key to their well-being" (3), Thelma Fenster "notes the absence of the typical romance heroine" (3), and Judith L. Kellogg "explores the innovative configurations of space in Christine's *Cité des dames*" (3). See also Rose Rigaud, *Les idées féministes de Christine de Pizan* (Neufchâtel: Attinger, 1911; Geneva: Slatkine Reprints, 1973). Earl Jeffrey Richards says, in his introduction to his translation of *The City of Ladies* that « Christine was a highly respected and widely disseminated voice on the status of women » (xxiv) and that "Christine's repeated appeals for peace, not surprising in an age so wracked by civil strife as the late thirteenth and early fourteenth centuries in France, take their place beside her incessant plea for the recognition of women's contributions to culture and social life as the most remarkable features of her work" (xxvi).
Overall, Christine the Pizan's contributions deal with the topics of philosophy, politics, religion, and the lyric tradition.
[2] Cannon-Willard, *Christine de Pizan: Her Life and Works*, 15.
[3] Ibid., 33.
[4] In her writings, Christine de Pizan was a defender of women, engaged herself in the political problems of France of her time, was also part of the first literary debate ever (the debate over the *Romance of the Rose* by Jean de Meun), and was considered by her own contemporaries as the first important female writer.
[5] Pizan, *City of Ladies*, 147.
[6] Piponnier, *L'Univers féminin: Espaces et Objets*, 418.
[7] Cannon Willard, *Christine de Pizan: Her Life and Works*, 44.
[8] Ibid., 15.
[9] Christine de Pizan's patrons were mostly highly ranked political figures such as John, Duke of Berry, Philip the Bold, John the Fearless, Louis of Orleans and his wife, Valentina Visconti, Charles VI and his wife Isabella of Bavaria.) Many of her works were read by her contemporary countrymen and women, but they were also translated into different languages during her lifetime. *The City Of Ladies* was

translated into English in 1521 and in Flemish in 1475. (Richards, *City of Ladies*, xxix.) Contemporary male writers, such as Eustache Deschamps, recognized her as a talented author, worth of belonging to the literary cannon.

[10] McLeod, *The Reception of Christine de Pizan from the Fifteenth through the Nineteenth Centuries*, ii.
[11] Delarun, *Regards de Clercs*, 31.
[12] Wemple, *Les Traditions Romaine, Germanique et Chrétienne*, 212, and Opitz, *Contraintes et Libertés*, 320.
[13] Régnier-Bohler, *Voix Littéraires, Voix Mystiques*, 450.
[14] Pizan, *Mutation*, 110-2.
[15] Pizan, *L'Avision-Christine*, 144-145.
[16] Brownlee, *Christine de Pizan: Gender and the New Vernacular Canon*, 101.
[17] Régnier-Bohler, *Voix Littéraires, Voix Mystiques*, 453.
[18] Pizan, *City of Ladies*, 92.
[19] Cannon-Willard, *Christine de Pizan: Her Life and Works, 45.*
[20] Pizan, *City of Ladies,* 85.
[21] As Glenda McLeod states it, "If we continue to think of her as a literary rarity, an isolated figure without precedent, province, or immediate survival, we continue to take her work out of context." McLeod, *The Reception of Christine de Pizan*, iii. Although Christine de Pizan might not be an isolated figure in her work, and spoke of common medieval themes such as love, marriage and the home, as McLeod states it, her ideas about women were a novelty for the time.
[22] Suzanne Fonay Wemple states that careers in education, administration and literature were more accessible to women who were willing to live a celibate life. Wemple, *Les Traditions Romaine, Germanique et Chrétienne,* 212.
[23] Cannon Willard, *Christine de Pizan: Her Life and Works*, 51.
[24] Ibid.
[25] Ibid, 164.
[26] Brownlee, *Christine de Pizan: Gender and the New Vernacular Canon,* 99.
[27] Kellogg, *Transforming Ovid: The Metamorphosis of Female Authority*, 106.
[28] Ibid., 129.
[29] Ibid.
[30] Cannon-Willard, Christine de Pizan, 211.
[31] Brown-Grant, *Christine de Pizan and the Moral Defence of Women,* 129.
[32] Kellogg, *Transforming Ovid: The Metamorphosis of Female Authority*, 188-9.
[33] Ibid., 191.
[34] Brown-Grant, *Christine de Pizan and the Moral Defense of Women,* 132.
[35] Pizan, *City of Ladies*, 35.
[36] Brown-Grant, *Christine de Pizan and the Moral Defense of Women,* 140.
[37] Moreau, *City of Ladies,* 13.
[38] Brown-Grant, *Christine de Pizan and the Moral Defence of Women,* 155.
[39] Ibid., 140.
[40] Cannon-Willard, *Christine de Pizan: Her Life and Works,* 138.
[41] Ibid., 73.

[42] According to Christine de Pizan, Mathéolus wrote a book that discussed respect for women. She read it and went on for a while but then put it down because "the subject seemed to me not very pleasant for people who do not enjoy lies, and of no use in developing virtue or manners, given its lack of integrity in diction and theme..." and this same book also makes her wonder "how it happened that so many different men—and learned men among them—have been and are so inclined to express both in speaking and in their treatises and writings so many devilish and wicked thoughts about women and their behavior" (Pizan, *The City of Ladies*, 3-4).
[43] Cannon-Willard, *Christine de Pizan: Her Life and Works*, 138.
[44] Moreau, *City of Ladies*, 16.
[45] Brown-Grant, *Christine de Pizan and the Moral Defence of Women*, 141-2.
[46] Cannon-Willard, *Christine de Pizan: Her Life and Works*, 147.
[47] Ibid.,151.
[48] Brown-Grant, *Christine de Pizan and the Moral Defence of Women*, 134.
[49] Cannon-Willard, *Christine de Pizan: Her Life and Works*, 146.
[50] Kellogg, *Transforming Ovid: The Metamorphosis of Female Authority*, 102.
[51] Brown-Grant, *Christine de Pizan and the Moral Defence of Women*, 173.
[52] Pizan, *City of Ladies*, 155.

Works Cited

Primary Sources

Pizan, Christine de. *Le Livre de la Cité des Dames*. Translated by Eric Hicks and Thérèse Moreau. Paris: Stock, 1986.

—. *L'Avision- Christine*. Ed. Sister Mary Louise Towner (Washington, D.C., 1932).

—. "Mutation." *The Writings of Christine de Pizan*. Translated by Nadia Margolis, edited by Charity Cannon Willard, 110-112. New York: Persea Books, 1994.

Secondary Sources

Altman, Barbara K., and Deborah L. McGrady, eds. *Christine de Pizan: A Casebook*. New York: Routledge, 2003.

Brown-Grant Rosalind. *Christine de Pizan and the Moral Defence of Women: Reading beyond Gender*. Cambridge: Cambridge University Press, 1999.

Brownlee, Kevin. "Christine de Pizan: Gender and the New Vernacular Canon." In *Strong Voices, Weak History: Early Women Writers and Canons in England, France and Italy,* edited by Pamela Joseph Benson

and Victoria Kirkham, 99-120. Ann Arbor: The University of Michigan Press, 2004.
Cannon Willard, Charity. *Christine de Pizan: Her Life and Works.* New York: Persea Books, 1962.
Delarun, Jacques. "Regards de Clercs." In *Histoire des Femmes en Occident: II Le Moyen Age,* edited by George Duby and Michelle Perrot, directed by Christiane Klapisch-Zuber, 31- 54. Paris: Plon, 1991.
Duby, George and Michelle Perrot, eds. *Histoire des Femmes en Occident: II Le Moyen Age.* Christiane Klapisch-Zuber, Dir. Paris : Plon, 1991.
Duby, George. *France in the Middle Ages 987-1460 : From Hugh Capet to Joan of Arc.* Juliet Vale Transl. Oxford: Blackwell, 1991.
Fenster, Thelma S. "Strong Voices, Weak Mind? The Defenses of Eve by Isotta Nogarola and Christine de Pizan, who Found Themselves in Simone de Beauvoir's Situation." In *Strong Voices, Weak History: Early Women Writers and Canons in England, France and Italy,* edited by Pamela Joseph Benson and Victoria Kirkham, 58-98. Ann Arbor: The University of Michigan Press, 2004.
Kellogg, Judith L. "Transforming Ovid: The Metamorphosis of Female Authority." In *Christine de Pizan and the Categories of Difference,* edited by Marilynn Desmond, 181-194. Minneapolis: The University of Minnesota Press, 1998.
Klapish-Zuber, Christiane. "Introduction." In *Histoire des Femmes en Occident: II Le Moyen Age,* edited by George Duby and Michelle Perrot, directed by Christiane Klapisch-Zuber, 11-23. Paris: Plon, 1991.
McLeod, Glenda K., ed. *The Reception of Christine de Pizan from the Fifteenth through the Nineteenth centuries: Visitors to the City.* The Edwin Mellen Press: Lewiston, 1991.
Opitz, Claudia. "Contraintes et Libertés (1250-500)." In *Histoire des Femmes en Occident: II Le Moyen Age,* edited by George Duby and Michelle Perrot, directed by Christiane Klapisch-Zuber, 277-335. Paris: Plon, 1991. French Edition.
Piponnier, Françoise. "L'Univers féminin: Espaces et Objets." In *Histoire des Femmes en Occident: II : Le Moyen Age,* edited by George Duby and Michelle Perrot, directed by Christiane Klapisch-Zuber, 343-355. Paris : Plon, 1991.
Régnier-Bohler, Danielle. "Voix Littéraires, Voix Mystiques." In *Histoire des Femmes en Occident: II Le Moyen Age,* edited by George Duby and Michelle Perrot, directed by Christiane Klapisch Zuber, 443-500. Paris: Plon, 1991.

Wemple, Suzanne Fonay. "Les Traditions Romaine, Germanique et Chrétienne." In *Histoire des Femmes en Occident: II Le Moyen Age*, edited by George Duby and Michelle Perrot, directed by Christiane Klapisch-Zuber, 185-216. Paris: Plon, 1991.

CHAPTER FOUR

"BUT TILL SOME HOUSEHOLD CARES ME TIE, / MY BOOKS AND PEN I WILL APPLY": EARLY MODERN WOMEN'S WRITINGS AND THE DEBATE ON FEMALE EDUCATION

ULRIKE TANCKE

In a letter to her sister that precedes her poem collection *A Sweet Nosegay* (1573), Isabella Whitney self-consciously comments on her role as a writer:

> Had I a husband, or a house,
> and all that 'longs thereto
> Myself could frame about to rouse,
> as other women do:
> But till some household cares me tie,
> My books and Pen I will apply.[1]

Whitney here conceptualizes writing as an activity that a woman can engage in only when it is detached from the everyday, down-to-earth materiality of her life.[2] Her statement prompts a number of questions as regards women's writing and female education in the early modern period: To what extent did women who wrote and/or had literary interests defy the conventional roles attributed to them? What is the relationship between educated femininity and the material conditions of women's lives? To what degree can female learning be perceived in terms of emancipatory possibilities, and what do women's attitudes to education tell us about female subjectivity in the period more generally?

A close analysis of the passage from Whitney's *Nosegay* suggests some rather disturbing answers. Whitney's stress on the material underpinnings of her writing is both striking and paradoxical. Whether she conceptualized the security provided by a household as a desirable condition or as a constraint, she certainly expresses an unmistakable awareness of the importance of the material for her writing. Her sentence suggests that only a woman who *lacks* the material backup of a house is able to write–after all, she is exempt from patriarchal control. Yet this literal reading occludes the extraordinarily precarious position of the (woman) writer in the early modern period. For men and women alike, authorship entailed financial insecurity, as literary production was increasingly determined by market relations. Specifically, for a woman to write was to incur suspicion. In a culture which associates female writing with usurpation of a male prerogative and hence loss of feminine virtue, writing makes a woman sexually disreputable. She figures as a threat to social cohesion and hence triggers the very anxieties that the burgeoning proto-consumerist culture elicits. Thus the tension in Whitney's poem focuses the wider implications of (women's) writing in the period. For a woman, writing always equals self-cancellation, as it causes the elimination of her physical and material or her social identity. Either way, it is an inherently dangerous and necessarily detrimental activity–and this is the hidden reality behind Whitney's seemingly carefree affirmation of her life choices.

My observations on Whitney's comments on female writing can be extended to and shed interesting light on early modern women's attitudes to education more generally. Obviously, the issue is particularly topical in early modern England because of the professed egalitarian tenets that sixteenth-century humanism had attributed to education as prerequisite for the formation of a balanced individual. Having said that, in spite of its allegedly universalist agenda, humanism had not brought about equal educational opportunities for men and women alike. Apart from the obviously discriminatory factor that certain subjects were deemed unsuitable for women, the education of (upper-class) females–that is, of the minority who were educated on terms similar to those of male academia at all–was exclusively in the hands of male teachers, and the recommended curriculum featured male authors and a restricted set of genres and texts that were considered appropriate for women.[3] Juan Luis Vives's remark in his *Plan of Studies for Girls* (1523) is telling as concerns the degree of male control that was thereby ensured. In his chapter on the teaching of writing, he declares the sole purpose of women's writing to be "that she may write down with her fingers anything that the tutor may dictate"[4] and hence become a passive receptacle for male learning.[5]

It is obvious that women's education–to the extent that it was a reduced version of its male equivalent, modified to accord with the principles of feminine virtue (the proverbial "chaste, silent and obedient" ideology) and restricting women to subservient roles–denied them access to the individuality that the masculine subject sought, and to the transcendence that he believed himself capable to achieve through reason and learning–one of the cornerstones of the modern self. Moreover, education also had a distinctly material dimension, in that it came to be perceived as a marketable asset in preparation for a professional career.[6] Early modern women were thus at a double disadvantage, because the existing educational opportunities forbade the development of a feminine subjectivity on a par with the masculine version, and because a professional identity was not one of their socially acceptable roles. And yet, there was a visible and persistent urge among women to have a share of the male privilege that was education, which, of course, went along with a sensitive understanding of the discriminatory nature of contemporary education. This essay analyses the female critique of educational politics in early modern England in a variety of women's writings. Rather than examining female-authored texts explicitly concerned with the debate on education–such as pamphlet literature–I focus on less-studied instances of this critique that occur "in passing", in women's textual interrogations of selfhood, identity and relationships.[7] The writings reveal the women's dissatisfaction as well as their strategies to counter their sense of intellectual deprivation with complementary tactics.

In 1617, Lady Grace Mildmay composed a written account of her life.[8] As a member of the landed elite of Tudor England, she had been married at a young age to Anthony Mildmay, who had gained the favor of Elizabeth I and, as an ambassador and royal commissioner, was largely absent from the family home.[9] In spite of the conventional patriarchal setup of her married life, Lady Mildmay thus enjoyed a considerable degree of autonomy as regards everyday household management and decision-making, and this discrepancy is clearly visible in her autobiographical writing. Drawing on the popular genre of the advice book, her narrative is interspersed with advice and admonitions to her daughter and grandchildren and to posterity more generally. The overall impression that the tone of her writing conveys to the reader is one of stability and contentment; above all, Mildmay displays a firm rootedness in her religious beliefs, which allows her to present a homogeneous personality at ease with herself. Yet she makes a brief, almost submerged reference to her lack of formal education, which disrupts this apparent homogeneity. She concludes the introductory part of her autobiography:

> Heartily praying every faithful reader thereof to accept my good meaning therein and give a patient, mild answer with meekness, not looking for eloquence, exact method or learning which could not proceed from me who have not been trained up in university learning.[10]

At first glance, the passage may be taken to suggest that Mildmay played on her lack of formal education to give herself some leeway for dilettantism. If we assume that she did believe herself to be capable of writing authoritatively, she might have used this self-diminishing remark to protect herself from patriarchal sanction and to maintain feminine modesty despite entering the masculine realm of public speech, whilst keeping intact her authorial voice. On the other hand, even if it is not made explicit, one may speculate that there is in the passage an underlying tinge of regret about not having had the chance to acquire "university learning." Yet, crucially, her observations do not prompt her to openly question the social structures responsible for her missed educational opportunities. We cannot tell whether Mildmay lacked the political insight to perceive them as a socio-culturally imposed disadvantage, or whether she did not dare to utter unveiled criticism in a potentially public arena. There certainly is a danger of imposing an anachronistic feminist consciousness on Mildmay, which would presumably mirror our own concerns rather than faithfully correspond to the attitudes she actually held.[11] If she was indeed dissatisfied with not having had access to a university education, this feeling is submerged in her overall self-presentation as a virtuous woman who counter-balances the lack of appreciation accorded to her writing with her right to provide guidance to subsequent generations. Moreover, she seems to explore her creative and intellectual potential by shifting it to the culturally acknowledged, acceptably "feminine" fields of music or embroidery[12] and immersing herself in medical care for her household and the wider community. Tellingly, her depictions of her everyday activities reveal a pervasive dialectic of submissiveness and incipient independence:

> Also every day I spent some time in playing on my lute and setting songs of five parts thereonto and practised my voice in singing of psalms[.] ... Also every day I spent some time in the herbal and books of physic and in ministering to one or other by the directions of the best physicians of mine acquaintance[.][13]

Her creative pursuits are both innovative–she writes her own "songs of five parts" to the music she plays on her lute–and reliant on tradition, as when she recites psalms. Similarly combining independent learning and imitation, she teaches herself with the help of herbology manuals and offers medical care to her community, but also acts on the directions of established (male) medical authorities.[14] As her medical services would have provided her with some extent of public power,[15] they allowed her to transcend the spatial restrictions imposed on women. Yet, at the same time, they are firmly rooted in the patriarchal, feudal hierarchy, as Mildmay depended on "male" medicine and relied on the capital provided by her estates to fund her activities. Clearly, her immediate subordination under male authority, be it God's ("and ever God gave a blessing thereonto"[16]) or that of allegedly more experienced, professional men, qualifies her self-determination, to some extent at least. However, to read her account simply as an example of a gentlewoman's stereotypical and conformist leisure activities and generally expected skills is simplistic. It is undisputable that her medical activities in particular "supplied a creative and intellectually challenging outlet for [her] ... energy and talents",[17] allowing her as it did to enter into correspondence and exchange experiences with other (male!) practitioners. Whether medicine was a genuine passion for Mildmay, or whether she merely resorted to this field in order "to satisfy an intellectual curiosity for which she could perhaps find no other fulfillment"[18] is a question that we cannot answer with any certainty and that, I would argue, even misses the crucial point. Whatever her initial motivation, her medical knowledge as well as her musical and artistic interests functioned as vehicles for her urge to create something of herself, if within a sanctioned arena. Although her medical activities draw on male precedents, their very existence proves wrong the radical feminist claim that "women who strive to emulate the art of men are merely reasserting old stereotypes and perpetuating their subjection by a patriarchal culture".[19] What is more, Mildmay goes on to admit to her desire to produce "works of mine own invention without sample of drawing or pattern before me".[20] Even though she is referring to conventional feminine pursuits ("... for carpet or cushion work and to draw flowers and fruits to their life with my plumett upon paper"[21]), there is a clear sense of emergent creativity and confident sense of self. The fact that Mildmay's creative pursuits extended only to socially acceptable fields need not be regarded as a restriction that suffocated her self-expression. Her own account strongly suggests that she derived genuine satisfaction from it.

This significant point also applies to the straightforward expression of discontent with patriarchal culture in the autobiographical poem by middle-aged gentry woman Martha Moulsworth. In *The Memorandum of Martha Moulsworth, Widow* (1632), she voices a plea for female education that is far more pronounced than Mildmay's passing remark. Little is known about her life, except from what she relates in her poem:

She was married three times, to prosperous upper middle class men, yet remained childless (her children, by her first and last husband, died early[22]). Moulsworth opens her chronological account of her life by presenting herself as part of the male academic tradition when she elaborates on the education she received from her father, Robert Dorsett:

> By him I was brought vpp in godlie pietie
> In modest chearefullnes, & sad sobrietie
> Not onlie so, Beyond my sex & kind
> he did wth learninge Lattin decke [my] mind[.][23]

It was clearly highly unusual for a woman in the late sixteenth century–even more so for a non-aristocratic woman–to be taught Latin, the key component of humanist education for men.[24] Moulsworth is certainly aware of the fact that her education bordered on the transgressive and construes herself as an exception. Yet at the same time she neutralizes this threat by mentioning her "godlie pietie", "modest[y]" and "sobrietie"–all of these being traits that are clearly in tune with the contemporary ideal of virtuous femininity. Moreover, she immediately undercuts her self-assured stance with a poignant qualification:[25] "Butt I of Lattin haue no cause to boast / ffor want of vse, I longe agoe itt lost".[26] Again, ambiguity is the organizing principle of her presentation of self: she *is* yet *is not* a woman of learning "[b]eyond [her] sex and kind". Her self-description establishes a dialectical simultaneity that is "too complex to be reduced to simple either/or polarities".[27]

The extent to which Moulsworth's balanced, straightforwardly coherent identity is artificially invented, in the attempt to reconcile her conflicting experiences with the demands her society directed at her, is highlighted by a close look at historical records. Robert Dorsett died in 1580, when Martha was less than three years old–hence he is most unlikely to have had the direct impact on her education that he is credited with in her poem.[28] Why, then, did Moulsworth so bluntly disregard historical facts? Quite possibly, she may have taken this poetic liberty to match the picture she creates of herself as an equal participant in masculine culture.[29] She depends on her father's imaginary presence because he legitimizes her own participation in patriarchal culture. In psychoanalytic terms, the identification with the father makes possible her entry into the patriarchal symbolic order. Conversely, it necessitates the all-out denial of the maternal: tellingly, she does not mention her mother at all in her poem. As this omission might indicate, Moulsworth's transition to the patriarchal symbolic is not quite as straightforward as it might seem.

In the following passage of the poem, she explicitly voices her concern with women's place in patriarchal society:

> ... the muses ffemalls are
> and therefore of Vs ffemales take some care
> Two Vniuersities we haue of men
> o thatt we had but one of women then
> O then thatt would in witt, and tongs surpasse
> All art of men thatt is, or euer was[.][30]

Moulsworth's plea for women's education has attracted considerable attention and has been hailed as attesting to a proto-feminist consciousness.[31] Clearly, her demand for equal access to educational opportunities was revolutionary at the time, especially with its explicit move beyond the primary educational site for women, the home, into the exclusively male domain of the universities. Moulsworth's distinct sense of self-worth comes across in a particularly pronounced fashion when she boldly asserts not only women's equality, but even their superiority in the academic realm.

And yet, reading her strongly opinionated claims as instances of proto-feminism falls short of recognizing their complexities. For a start, even though these lines sound like a revolutionary manifesto, they are not, in fact, a public utterance – there is no evidence that Moulsworth had a distinct audience in mind when writing her poem, or even intended it for publication.[32] Moreover, ambiguities appear if we consider the fact that Moulsworth invokes the muses and examine their connotations in early modern culture. With their multi-faceted roles in classical mythology, the muses were somewhat equivocal figures, offering artistic inspiration, tinged with sexual lure, but also threatening destruction.[33] Moulsworth, by contrast, presents them as a kind of female support group. She thereby reinterprets the muses, endowing them with a distinctly feminine significance that stretches beyond their traditionally passive role as the source of inspiration for the male artistic genius.[34] As Moulsworth portrays it, for the female writer, the presence of the muses is a way of escaping her "anxiety of authorship." However, in contrast to this positive reading, their mythological associations point to a disturbing flipside: they could easily represent the monstrous "other" of virtuous femininity. Given the general unease towards female literacy, the muses as a support group for writing women ultimately constitute a threat to the patriarchal order, with its dependence on virtuous females.[35] Hence for a woman to write is to deviate from the patriarchal, heterosexual norm; it is "sexually suspect, for to write [is] to find support from women, not men".[36] By referring to the muses, Moulsworth places herself in an insecure position socially, as she puts her own reputation under threat.

Moulsworth's uneasy stance prevails as she qualifies her surprisingly progressive attitude, contrasting her unusual plea with the futility of female education in the face of a social reality that values very different qualities in women. In the margins of her poem she soberly and somewhat ironically remarks that "Lattin is nott the most marketable mariadge mettall"[37]–in her own case, she "longe agoe itt lost"[38] when she got married and had to concentrate on her domestic duties. She is clearly aware of the view in her day of marriage as a means of transmitting property when she comments wryly on the economic transactions which dominated her own (as it did most middle- and upper-class) marriages: "Had I no other portion [than command of Latin] to my dowre, / I might haue stood a virgin to this houre"[39]–i.e. the material conditions and constraints of her life (financial security and the corporeal) are predominant. Strikingly, Moulsworth's remarks appear free of regret; although there is a sense of stoical acceptance or even resignation, she counters this with dry humor and ironic sarcasm. She is obviously aware of the financial precariousness of spinsterhood, but it seems that it was not only out of necessity and social pressure that she embraced married life. When she states: "I haue long since Bid virgin life ffarewell",[40] she conveys a surprisingly frank sense of (sexual) enjoyment.[41] Obviously, her emphasis on the joys of married life is surprising given the demonization of female sexuality that prevailed in early modern culture.

This presents us with yet another instance of ambiguity in Moulsworth's account of her life. On the one hand, social pressures to marry put an end to her personal development through education, i.e. she had to succumb to the patriarchal expectations that confined a married woman to the home. On the other hand, it was through marriage that she could, presumably, explore another facet of her self, namely experience her own corporeality as involving pleasure and enjoyment. The general impression of calm equilibrium that the *Memorandum* conveys suggests that Moulsworth was able to construct a sense of coherent selfhood in spite of the disappointments and constraints she presumably encountered. As she views herself and/or wants herself to be viewed, she has never been an object of trade between or the property of men, but always a self-determined individual making her own life choices.[42] Conversely, she is able to present herself in such a way because her poem also allows for a conventional, "safe" reading in accordance with patriarchal norms. She does not express open rebellion, but there are submerged hints at her sense of independence.

The problematic relationship between knowledge and virtue and the ways in which it enables and restricts women's access to learning is also an issue in gentry woman Elizabeth Joscelin's *The Mothers Legacy to her Vnborn Childe* (1624), an advice manual composed when she was expecting her first child and gripped with a sense of foreboding as regards her possible death in childbirth, which did occur shortly after. As the granddaughter of a bishop, Joscelin received an extensive home education, which she continued in the first years of her marriage to Tourell Joscelin.[43] It is thus doubly poignant that, in her *Legacy*, Joscelin voices her views on women's education in a way that is so tangled and self-contradictory that it is hard to overlook her unease. Outlining the education she deems fit for her child, should it be a daughter, she states that:

> I desire her bringinge vp may bee learninge the Bible as my sisters doo.[,] good huswifery, writing, and good work[.] other learninge a woman needs not though I admire it in those whom god hathe blesst wth discretion[,] yet I desire it not much in my own hauinge seen that sometimes women haue greater portions of learninge then wisdom wch is <n> of no better vse to them then A Maynsayle to [a] fly boat wch runs it < > vnder water, but wheare learning and wisdom meet in a virtuous disposed woman she is the fittest closet for all good^nes^[,] she is like a well ballancet[h] ship that may bear all her sayle[,] she is? indeed I should shame my selfe if I should go about to prays her more[.][44]

Joscelin hovers uneasily between praising female education and denigrating it as being of secondary importance compared with virtue.[45] Her expressed admiration for learned women betrays her own renunciation of learning as being presumably not entirely genuine. Her closing remark, condemning excessive praise of learned women, ends the subject with an abruptness that smacks of self-curtailment. It prompts the question what exactly she would need to be ashamed of–is she embarrassed about her own lack of learning, or is there something "shameful" about a learned woman as such?

At a closer look, however, Elizabeth Joscelin employs a strategy that enables her to not simply defend learned women, but to conceive of them in a comprehensive way. In stating that learning ought to go along with virtue, she combines the progressive demand for women's education with the patriarchal expectations of feminine virtue, rather than having the one exclude the other. This alignment opens up the opportunity for female learning in the first place, because it allows the woman who pursues knowledge to move within the patriarchal order, even if only on its fringes. In that, Joscelin's notion of educated womanhood moves beyond the standard account of female education in the period. A superficially similar simultaneity of praise and rejection of female learning occurs in a male-authored text, Richard Mulcaster's advice book *Positions Concerning the Training up of Children* (1581). Mulcaster refers to women who write, stating that "[their] excellencie is so geason [uncommon, amazing], as they be rather wonders to gaze at, then presidentes to follow".[46] For him, the learned woman can be integrated in the patriarchal social order only if she is treated as an exception–and as an exception which should not trigger emulation, but from which a truly virtuous woman should strive to set herself apart.

By contrast, Joscelin's simile of an educated *and* virtuous woman as a ship sailing under full sail is a potent image that hints at her balancing act: While a ship is usually referred to as "she", it belongs to the male domain of trade, travel and discovery.[47] Joscelin portrays the learned and virtuous woman as an ideal figure who has managed to negotiate the conflicting demands of her intellectual interests and the patriarchal constraints. For her, a woman needs to negotiate extremes not in order to preserve a position of power that is rightfully hers, but to conform to the patriarchal ideal of feminine virtue. Joscelin's virtuous woman is characteristically self-enclosed ("the fittest closet for all good^nes^"). The spatial dimension of her ideal feeds into the conventional alignment of feminine virtue and domesticity. The virtuous woman is like a "closet," she is self-contained and keeps her "learning and wisdom" within the confines of her own subjective realm.[48] At first glance, this confinement is clearly debilitating, insofar as it restricts her in a double sense, in terms of geographical space and literary genre. Yet it simultaneously opens up a specific sphere that is reserved for knowledge. In a sense, of course, enclosure and learning are a contradiction in terms: learning, even if it takes place in a physically restricted space, opens up the woman's inward self to the outside world, at least on the intellectual level. Hence even if enclosure may not seem to be a particularly liberating tactics and has potentially oppressive implications, it still has some value simply by virtue of constituting a workable alternative. I would suggest we read this ambiguity as another instance of at least partially successful negotiation: if learning potentially places women in a morally ambiguous position, their response can neither be to uncritically accept this danger, nor to radically oppose it. For women, to pursue learning but to restrict it to the confined closet space is a strategy to circumvent sanction by struggling to combine transgression and subordination.

The common thread that has emerged from my readings of early modern women's attitudes to education is a profound and pervasive sense of contradiction and ambiguity, as their statements oscillate between proto-feminist self-assertion and adherence to convention to the point of self-curtailment. At first glance, this seems to leave us at an impasse. The women appear to be prime examples of the new historicist assumption that subversion is inevitably met with containment and hence plays in the hands of the dominant ideology, so that the powers-that-be remain all-powerful.[49]

However, at a closer look, the texts suggest that these parameters are clearly simplistic as regards early modern women's senses of self. The focal concern of the writings I have studied, the debate on education, can be taken as exemplary field in which their attitudes are played out and negotiated and hence allows for observations that apply to early modern women's senses of self in more far-reaching and comprehensive ways.

Admittedly, the pervasive "chaste, silent and obedient" ideology and the patriarchal power structures undeniably restrict the women's speech. The agency that can be discerned in their writings is tentative and small-scale; it is often ambiguous and equivocal, predicated on the acceptance of contradiction and imperfection and ultimately based on the dominant discourses in which the women are situated and/or situate themselves. Yet this is not to say that the women's writings simply reaffirm their marginal status. Rather, if we want to adequately grasp their understandings of self, we have to abandon the notion of women as being at the margins of the patriarchal order, the perennial exception to the patriarchal norm. Alternatively, their position can be contextualized more fruitfully if we turn the idea of marginality on its head. If we take early modern women's writings seriously, as writings from the margins of the dominant discourse, their ways of identity formation need not be read as exceptions to a dominant and normative model, but can in fact open up a different, even generally applicable, paradigm of subjectivity. The strategies by which they achieve this subjectivity are intrinsically dialectical: the women writers accept patriarchal constraints but simultaneously express themselves creatively; or, conversely, they transgress patriarchal discourse but simultaneously neutralize their transgression. To repeat the central argument of my foregoing readings: early modern women engage in delicate balancing acts; negotiating compromise and reconciling conflicting desires, painful and continually threatened, is the crucial trajectory of their identity formation.

This insight is a sobering reminder that there is no unproblematic balance for women, no reassuring "middle way" which, once it has been achieved, guarantees a secure sense of self. The cornerstones of their subjectivity are contradiction and ambiguity and the ongoing struggle for an inevitably contested compromise; there is no fixed and stable speaking position. However, far from reading this as a disillusioning condition, I would argue that the very ambiguities and instances of precariousness in their writings constitute a specifically female strategy of self-definition. They construct a self whose civilized moderation and delicate balance counters the traditional alignment of women with uncontrolled physicality and irrationality. Shaping identity via this carefully crafted yet unstable compromise foreshadows and simultaneously destabilizes the (male, Enlightenment) rationalism that came to dominate modes of self-knowledge beyond the seventeenth century, thus situating women both within and at a critical distance from the thought of the day.

Notes

[1] Whitney, To her Sister Mistris A.B., *A Sweet Nosegay*, 37ff.)

[2] In an interesting way, she seems to both foreshadow and contradict Virginia Woolf's seminal observations in her famous essay *A Room of One's Own* (1928). Whitney stresses, as does Woolf, the need for the woman writer's intellectual capacities not to be smothered by her everyday chores; yet she replaces Woolf's demand for material security ("a woman must have money and a room of her own if she is to write fiction" (Woolf, *A Room*, 4)) with a renunciation of the material.

[3] For a more comprehensive of the issue, see Charlton, Women and Education.

[4] Vives, *Plan of Studies*, 141.

[5] Even if Jacob Burckhardt's claim that "[t]he education of the women in the upper classes was essentially the same as that of the men" (Burckhardt, *Civilization*, 280) may not be altogether misguided as regards the content of their learning, the conclusion he draws is grossly beside the point in the light of statements such as Vives's. Burckhardt emphasises the crucial connection between education and subjectivity which was at the core of the humanist veneration for learning. According to Burkhardt, "[t]he educated woman of that time strove, exactly like the man, after a characteristic and complete individuality" (Burckhardt, *Civilization*, 281). What cannot be accepted about Burckhardt's verdict is the alleged aim of a 'characteristic and complete individuality' shared by both men and women.

[6] Cf. Brotton, *The Renaissance*, 40f.

[7] The examples I will quote are, by their very existence, counter-evidence to Anne M. Haselkorn and Betty Travitsky's observation that "we do not find a large number of women enacting or expressing a consciousness of this contradiction [between the new educational opportunities and women's oppression], much less a resentment of it" (Haselkorn and Travitsky, *Renaissance Englishwoman*, 25).

[8] Mildmay's writings have only recently been compiled to resemble a modern-day, roughly chronological autobiography (Pollock, *With Faith and Physic*).

[9] Cf. Pollock, *With Faith and Physic*, 4ff.

[10] Mildmay, *Autobiography*, 25.

[11] Linda Pollock makes a highly significant, more general point to this effect. In her epilogue to Mildmay's writings, she argues that there might well be "a disjuncture between the existence of structural disadvantage and the perception of it. ... If certain structures were not perceived to be 'oppressive,' can we label them as such? ... [B]y concentrating on structures that we, as twentieth-century historians, have deemed oppressive, we risk overlooking those that early modern women themselves lamented. Giving women a history of their own is not enough; allowing them minds of their own undistorted by our ideological agendas is as important" (Pollock, *With Faith and Physic*, 144).

[12] Mildmay, *Autobiography*, 35.

[13] Mildmay, *Autobiography*, 35.

[14] In the sixteenth century, medical practice was not yet entirely the domain of qualified doctors. Although a 1512 act had restricted medical practice to Oxford and Cambridge graduates, the law was amended in 1542 to exempt from these restrictions "divers honest persons, as well men as women, whom God hath endowed with the knowledge of the nature kind and operation of certain herbs, roots and waters, and the using and ministering to them to such as be pained with customable disease" (quoted in Sim, *Tudor Housewife*, 86). Obviously, this allowed women some leeway to apply their own medical knowledge, independent of male authority.

[15] "Her services were publicly recognized and so would have enhanced her already privileged status within the community and may also have bestowed on her a form of public power. That the élite dispensed medical care in any case would reinforce the social structure–their succour to the needy helped legitimize their entitlement to rule" (Pollock, *With Faith and Physic*, 108).

[16] Mildmay, *Autobiography*, 35.

[17] Pollock, *With Faith and Physick*, 108.

[18] Ottway, *Desiring Disencumbrance*, 163.

[19] Rich, When We Dead Awaken, 38.

[20] Mildmay, *Autobiography*, 35.

[21] Mildmay, *Autobiography*, 35.

[22] Moulsworth, *Memorandum*, 71f.

[23] Moulsworth, *Memorandum*, 27ff.

[24] Exceptions include Queen Elizabeth I and gentlewoman and dramatist Elizabeth Cary.

[25] Cf. Evans, A Silent Woman, 151.

[26] Moulsworth, *Memorandum*, 37ff.

[27] Evans, Deference and Defiance, 108.

[28] Cf. Evans, Silent Woman, 152.

[29] Robert Evans observes: "The father whom Moulsworth loved so much seems to have been partly a creation of her own imagination, her invention; he was partly a mythical being invested with a great deal of psychic importance for her" (Evans, A Silent Woman, 52).

[30] Moulsworth, *Memorandum*, 31ff.

[31] For example, Bebe Barefoot claims that "[h]er radical wish for a women's university is the first hint of her budding feminism and move toward a new identity. Indeed, she has much more in common with modern feminists than with Renaissance women" (Barefoot, Martha Moulsworth/Poet, 76. However, I will argue that Barefoot's is an all too idealistic (because anachronistic) reading of Moulsworth.

[32] In fact, the only personal ties that she had at the time of writing, it seems, were to her stepdaughter Elizabeth Thorowgood, whom she was obviously close to and named in her will as executrix of her estate (cf. Depas-Orange, Moulsworth's Life 8). Presumably, the *Memorandum* was intended for a private audience, if at all.

[33] Cf. Seigneuret, *Dictionary*, 112ff.

[34] Cf. Wilcox, "Memorandum", 27. A reinterpretation of the muses similar to Moulsworth's occurs in Aemilia Lanyer's *Salve Deus Rex Judaeorum*, when she presents them in one of her dedicatory poems as "sacred sisters ... / Whose godly labours doe avoyde the baite / Of worldly pleasures" (Lanyer, Salve Deus, 49).

[35] "Those who are hostile toward women of learning associate the muse of poetry with ambiguous gender identity. A woman who invokes the muse is, at best, a slut, and at worst, a lesbian rapist" (Teague, Early Modern Writers, 176). Frances Teague is probably not overstating her case: Lynette McGrath quotes Ben Jonson as saying, in "An Epigram on the Court Pucell," that a female poet must "publicly enact a 'tribadic lust,' by forcibly raping her female muse and [thereby] moving outside the control of heterosexuality" (McGrath, *Subjectivity*, 4).

[36] Teague, Early Modern Writers, 179.

[37] Moulsworth, *Memorandum*, 38f.

[38] Moulsworth, *Memorandum*, 38.

[39] Moulsworth, *Memorandum*, 39f.

[40] Moulsworth, *Memorandum*, 42.

[41] Cf. Evans and Wiedeman, *"My Name Was Martha"*, 23.

[42] This lends support to Natalie Zemon Davis's observation that, in the early modern politics of marriage, "a strategy for at least a thread of female autonomy may have been built precisely around this sense of being given away ... [W]omen sometimes turned the cultural formation around, and gave themselves away" (Davis, Boundaries, 61).

[43] Cf. Metcalfe, Introduction, 4.

[44] Joscelin, *Mothers Legacy*, 54ff.

[45] "Joscelin presents us with the phenomenon of an educated woman in the same moment as she opposes women who have benefited from education, with the very existence of her narrative working against her own ostensible views. In short, the legacy that Joscelin furnishes is a vexed and uneven gift, one that simultaneously celebrates female production and publication and moves repressively against women's authorial activities. ... These discontinuities are typical of the genre of the mother's advice book; they also point to the unstable locations of seventeenth-century women themselves, as they looked to define themselves in relation to embattled ideological polarities." (Wray, *Women Writers*, 52).

[46] Mulcaster, *Positions*, 163.

[47] With thanks to Julia Paulk, who pointed out the gender implications of this symbolism to me. For a more detailed discussion of early modern ship imagery, which sheds interesting light on Joscelin's use of the motif, cf. Breitenberg, *Anxious Masculinity*, 194.

[48] Kim Walker reads the image of the closet as paradigmatic for women's access to learning in the period: "The spatial isolation of the closet is frequently called on by women writing in even the most marginal and ostensibly private genres. Her writing figuratively bounded by the confines of this retired chamber, the woman herself may become an enclosure, implicitly bounded and sealed, for knowledge" (Walker, *Women Writers*, 26).

[49] As Stephen Greenblatt argues in his seminal essay "Invisible Bullets", power creates its own subversion in order to solidify itself: "[T]he subversiveness which is genuine and radical ... is at the same time contained by the power it would appear to threaten. Indeed the subversiveness is the very product of that power and furthers its ends" (Greenblatt, Invisible Bullets, 23f.).

Works Cited

Primary Sources

Joscelin, Elizabeth. *The Mothers Legacy to her Vnborn Childe*. 1624. Ed. Jean LeDrew Metcalfe. Toronto: University of Toronto Press, 2000.

Lanyer, Aemilia. Salve Deus Rex Judaeorum. 1610. In: *The Poems of Shakespeare's Dark Lady. Salve Deus Rex Judaeorum by Emilia Lanier*. Ed. A. L. Rowse. London: Jonathan Cape, 1978.

Mildmay, Lady Grace. *Autobiography*. 1617. In: *With Faith and Physic. The Life of a Tudor Gentlewoman. Lady Grace Mildmay 1552-1620*. Ed. Linda Pollock. New York: St Martin's Press, 1993.

Moulsworth, Martha. *The Memorandum of Martha Moulsworth, Widow*. 1632. *Critical Matrix. The Princeton Journal of Women, Gender, and Culture* 10 (1996): 20-22.

Whitney, Isabella. *A Sweet Nosegay, or Pleasant Posy: Containing a Hundred and Ten Philosophical Flowers*. 1573. Eds. Nick Broyles et al. Bozeman: Montana State University.
http://www.montana.edu/wwwwhitn/whitney.html (accessed 20 May 2007).

Secondary Sources

Barefoot, Bebe. Martha Moulsworth/Poet. *Critical Matrix: The Princeton Journal of Women, Gender, and Culture* 10 (1996): 75-77.

Breitenberg, Mark. *Anxious Masculinity in Early Modern England.* Cambridge: Cambridge University Press, 1996.

Brotton, Jerry. *The Renaissance. A Very Short Introduction.* Oxford: Oxford University Press, 2005.

Burckhardt, Jacob. *The Civilization of the Renaissance in Italy.* 1860. Trans. S. G. C. Middlemore. Ed. Irene Gordon. New York and Toronto: Mentor / The New American Library, 1960.

Charlton, Kenneth. Women and Education. In: *A Companion to Early Modern Women's Writing.* Ed. Anita Pacheco. Oxford: Blackwell, 2002. 3-21.

Davis, Natalie Zemon. Boundaries and the Sense of Self in Sixteenth-Century France. In: *Reconstructing Individualism. Autonomy, Individuality and the Self in Western Thought.* Eds. Thomas C. Heller, Morton Sosna and David E. Wellbery. Stanford: Stanford University Press, 1986. 53-63.

Depas-Orange, Ann. Moulsworth's Life and Times. *Critical Matrix: The Princeton Journal of Women, Gender, and Culture* 10 (1996): 7-10.

Evans, Robert C. A Silent Woman Speaks: The Memorandum of Martha Moulsworth, Widow. *Yale University Library Gazette* 69.3-4 (1995):149-162.

—. Deference and Defiance. The "Memorandum" of Martha Moulsworth. In: *Representing Women in Renaissance England.* Eds. Claude J. Summers and Ted-Larry Pebworth. Columbia and London: University of Missouri Press, 1997. 175-186.

Evans, Robert C. and Barbara Wiedemann, eds. *"My Name Was Martha." A Renaissance Woman's Autobiographical Poem.* West Cornwall: Locust Hill Press, 1993.

Greenblatt, Stephen. Invisible Bullets. In: *Shakespearean Negotiations. The Circulation of Social Energy in Renaissance England.* Berkeley and Los Angeles: University of California Press, 1988. 21-65.

Haselkorn, Anne M. and Betty S. Travitsky, eds. *The Renaissance Englishwoman in Print. Counterbalancing the Canon.* Amherst: The University of Massachusetts Press, 1990.

McGrath, Lynette. *Subjectivity and Women's Poetry in Early Modern England. "Why on the ridge should she desire to go?"* Alsdershot: Ashgate, 2002.

Metcalfe, Jean LeDrew. Introduction to *The Mothers Legacy to her Vnborn Childe.* Toronto: University of Toronto Press, 2000. 3-27.

Mulcaster, Richard. *Positions Concerning the Training up of Children.* London, 1581.

Ottway, Sheila. *Desiring Disencumbrance. The Representation of the Self in Autobiographical Writings by Seventeenth-Century Englishwomen.* Groningen, 1998.

Pollock, Linda. Commentary to *With Faith and Physic. The Life of a Tudor Gentlewoman. Lady Grace Mildmay 1552-1620.* New York: St Martin's Press, 1993. 1-22, 92-109, 143-150.

Rich, Adrienne. When We Dead Awaken: Writing as Re-Vision. In: *On Lies, Secrets and Silence. Selected Prose 1966-1978.* New York: Norton, 1979. 33-49.

Seigneuret, Jean-Jacques (ed.). *Dictionary of Literary Themes and Motifs.* 2 vols. New York: Greenwood Press, 1988.

Sim, Alison. *The Tudor Housewife.* Phoenix Mill: Sutton, 1996.

Teague, Frances. Early Modern Writers and "the muses ffemall." In: *"The Muses Females Are": Martha Moulsworth and Other Women Writers of the English Renaissance.* Eds. Robert C. Evans and Anne C. Little. West Cornwall: Locust Hill Press, 1995. 173-179.

Vives, Juan Luis. *Plan of Studies for Girls.* 1523. Trans. Foster Watson. In: *Vives and the Renascence Education of Women.* Ed. Foster Watson. London: Edward Arnold, 1912. 137-149.

Walker, Kim. *Women Writers of the English Renaissance.* New York: Twayne Publishers, 1996.

Wilcox, Helen. "Memorandum" and "Milestone": Women's Studies and English Literature. *The European English Messenger* 6 (1997): 26-28.

Woolf, Virginia. *A Room of One's Own.* 1928. London: Penguin, 2004.

Wray, Ramona. *Women Writers of the Seventeenth Century.* Tavistock: Northcote House, 2004.

CHAPTER FIVE

CHEMISTRY BY A LADY FOR LADIES: EDUCATION IN THE ALCHEMICAL ARTS

SANDY FEINSTEIN

Marie Meurdrac's *La Chymie Charitable et Facile, en Faveur des Dames*, was first published in 1656, in Paris. A number of editions followed in a variety of places: Paris in 1666, 1674, 1687, and 1711; Lyon in 1680; six German editions (Frankfurt, 1674, 1676, 1689, 1712, 1738, and Erfurt, 1731); and one Italian edition (Venice, 1682).[1] From the book jacket, the first contemporary French edition (1999) appears to be based on the 1666 edition, though it is, in fact, an abridgement that samples from multiple editions, notably 1666 and 1687. Despite these numerous editions in three languages, Londa Schiebinger dismisses Meurdrac in a paragraph with the remark, "Within the context of medical cookery ... Meurdrac's work is not exceptional,"[2] never mind that the number of translations and editions together suggest that her work may well have been considered "exceptional" in its time. Although Schiebinger accurately summarizes the structure of Meurdrac's *Chymie*, she may be oversimplifying its genre and the context she claims for the text. Antonio Clericuzio acknowledges the work's pedagogic purpose in a footnote, even while categorizing it as a collection of medical and cosmetic recipes rather than a textbook course in chemistry.[3] Debus, identifies Meurdrac as among those "one could turn to for instruction," putting her in exclusive male company with "Clave, Arnaud, Barlet, Locques."[4] Meurdrac's book, then, may be both more and less than a medical cookery collection. From its organization to its "cosmetic recipes" described as "rare secrets," this book might be seen in the tradition of early modern alchemy, which, significantly, also included recipes that made it vulnerable to disparagement, specifically for its orientation to practice over theory[5]; Meurdrac's structure, however, also resembles classical natural histories, most notably Pliny's.[6] Thus, while duly citing illustrious, historical authorities from the ancients to her contemporaries, Meurdrac makes her work a teaching primer, with herself not merely as author, but, as we shall see, as a willing, active teacher.

Among the minor poet du Pelletier's many praise poems, one "To Miss Meurdrac on her Free and Easy Chemistry" that appears in the 1666 edition, accuses the ancients of keeping their secrets of nature hidden.[7] It goes on to compliment Meurdrac for making such knowledge accessible, easy even.[8] Though these are conventional compliments, my interest lies in the nature of the compliment: that Meurdrac be commended not for providing the mysteries of nature, but for making them easily available to others, namely that her act of publication itself is as a teacher who writes or a writer who seeks to teach.

This impression is further reinforced in the Preface, where Marie Meurdrac first of all justifies publishing her work. She explains that she initially wrote it for herself and thought about publishing it for two years. As she explains: it is not a woman's place to teach, though she may listen and learn, she should not show what she knows, for her silence is expected.[9] Here she speaks of teaching and learning, not of authorship or the authority of pen and print. She asserts that "the mind has no sex," perhaps the most well known sentence from her work[10]; she then goes on to say that if women were given the same opportunities as men, that is, if as much time and money were allotted to instruct them, then their achievements would equal those of men,[11] an assertion that echoes Christine de Pisan's argument two centuries earlier.[12] Despite the neglect of women's education, she claims that in her own time and that of her readers', there have been exceptional women who excelled in prose, poetry, languages, and philosophy, though she names none specifically.[13] Her prefatory remarks identify the need for her work in relation to the need for women to be educated at the same level as men, implying that her book is her attempt to redress the situation.

But equally interesting among the conventional modesty topos and apologia of the Preface is something different, something explicitly pedagogical: she will offer personal tutorials to those afraid to proceed on their own. Those who fear failure, should, she says, contact her, and she will explain the procedures in person and take care to demonstrate whatever her intended readers wish to learn.[14] In the sixth chapter on the composition of cosmetics, her final Preface reiterates this offer. Jean Jacques, annotator of the modern French edition, concludes from the introductory Preface that Marie Meurdrac had her own laboratory where she gave lessons.[15] Although private lessons in the Art were common in the seventeenth century, especially since iatrochemistry, or practical medical chemistry,[16] was banned from French university curricula, it is still difficult to know this for sure; welcome as the thought might be, the demonstrations of which there are records were provided by men, and those offered for free to the public at the "King's Garden" are unlikely to have included women in their audience. The likely exclusion of women, however, may well have been another motivation for both Meurdrac's book as well as for her offer to show women personally how to "make the operations I teach."[17]

Marie Meurdrac's chemistry, potentially, would not only have scandalized the male ruling class, as she makes clear[18] and the various poems by Pelletier reinforce, but she might also have disconcerted another group, those still more compelled by the mystery of alchemy than the testable methodology of chemistry. The tools of the trade that Meurdrac describes serve both professions. Meurdrac, though, has no pretensions to teaching anyone how to make gold from base metals; indeed, she pointedly omits discussion of gold and silver because, as she says:

> When I began this Book, I intended only to pass on my experiences. That is why in this part I omit the operations on gold and silver, not knowing their preparations at all, nor their utility in Medicine. I have seen several operations given the names "potable gold," "tincture of gold," and "silver oil," that I could not understand; nor could I be persuaded that bodies, if perfect and concentrated, are liquefiable. It is not that I condemn these operations because I am not able to imagine them; I would otherwise be rash as the blind, who, because they haven't seen it, are sure there isn't any sun. For the operations that follow, I assure you, are true and tested.[19]

While rejecting certain assertions regarding gold and silver, she is self-deprecating,[20] yet, simultaneously, she expresses her doubt with regard to the transmutation of metals themselves. Alchemy, as she engages it, is not for such a purpose but for another equally ambitious goal of the alchemist: deferring, if not defying, death through chemical remedies; correcting nature's work by offering cosmetic as well as medical remedies.

Alchemy, with its elusive elixir, was not about only one kind of change—elemental, brute metal to gold—it was a metaphor for multiple ideals of perfection, not least of which include immortality and eternal youth, as readers of Harry Potter's first adventure could explain. More to the point, alchemical texts were still being translated and published in France in the seventeenth century.[21] What distinguishes Meurdrac's approach is that she might appear to be publicizing that which is conventionally kept secret for initiates who were typically men.[22]

In her opening Preface and letter to the Countess de Guiche, Marie Meurdrac expresses her intention to challenge the conventions of secrecy, as the new natural philosophy also claimed to be doing. She might be seen to respond to Margaret Cavendish's frustration regarding the obscurity of language usage by natural philosophers, who "instead of making hard things easy, make easy things hard."[23] Unlike those natural philosophers to which Cavendish refers, however, Meurdrac would initially appear to be making "hard things easy" with a pedagogic methodology based on classical models. Like Anna Maria Von Schurmann before her, she appropriates the Aristotelian rhetorical convention of beginning with a definition of terms. She defines, for example, the basic and most significant ingredients of alchemy, Paracelsian iatrochemistry, and early modern chemistry: salts, sulfur, mercury, and sal ammoniac. She also defines various processes key to alchemy and chemistry, some of which are used in kitchen remedies as well—sublimation, fermentation, calcination, and distillation, among many others. And, like Pliny, she extols specific sources for palliatives in a systematic structure, for example in her discussion of honey, to which she alludes to Pliny directly.[24]

Marie Meurdrac is not, however, always clear. But her lack of clarity has little to do with her abilities as a writer, despite her claims. As with so many of the women writers of the period, she offers a gender specific apology. She introduces a rhetorically conventional defense as she anticipates the reaction to a woman publishing on this subject. In short, she expresses concern regarding how her work will be received. Despite her seemingly well-ordered structure and ability to use rhetorical conventions effectively, as well as her claim to scientific practice involving not only testing but the repetition of those tests, she shows herself to be an adept at the conventional rhetoric of alchemy, which means inevitable vagueness: in other words, she can be obscure in much the same way as many an alchemist before her. Her explanations of ingredients and processes share the traditional metaphors that characterize alchemical texts and make them subject to accusations of obscurity, among other things.

The beginning of Marie Meurdrac's work may suggest the contrary, a focus intent on being clear and easy to follow, starting, as she does in her first chapter, with a definition of chemistry, followed by a discussion of salts. But by the second sentence of the first paragraph, she has already reverted to one of the standard metaphors of alchemy, that of generation. She says, "Firstly, we will speak of Salt as of the Father of Generation, because it seems as if it contributes most to extraction."[25] Typically, the

"Father of Generation" is sulfur, not salt[26]; Meurdrac is ambiguous here, suggesting either that salt is "the Father of Generation" or is "like" the Father of Generation (sulfur). Thus she seems to conflate the two as the Father of Generation, and, in so doing, elide the old art of alchemy with the new science of chemistry.

Equally conventional and telling is the metaphor Meurdrac uses in her chapter on mercury, one of the most important ingredients in both alchemy and Paracelsian iatrochemistry. She begins the chapter with a discussion of origins, a variation of the metaphor she has used to describe salt. According to this chapter, chemistry partakes of the divine Trinitarian structure of the world; it provides a kind of pencil sketch, a shadowy insight into that divine world.[27] The image of salt as the Father of Generation now more clearly associates it with the Divine Father and Creation itself. These images are conventional in alchemy, what chemists will ultimately distance themselves from. But as Erica Harth points out, this "older discourse in which signifier and signified were mediated by metaphor, coexisted for a time in the seventeenth century with the discourse of Cartesian objectivity, in which the signifier claimed transparent representation of the signified."[28] And they co-existed in the same authors, even the same works. Meurdrac moves easily between methodical process and the language Harth identifies with the "old discourse," "characterized by metaphor, veiled allusions, hyperbole, and circumlocution," a language she argues as belonging with "the Renaissance episteme of resemblance," which is, in fact, the language of alchemy that existed well before and after the Renaissance.

We hear that discourse when Meurdrac asserts significantly, if cryptically,

> All the things which are in the world come from one and this one produces of it three: what can give us one idea of the adored mystery of the very sacred Trinity. Chemistry presents us a sketch, since she finds one trinity not only in every subject but in every principle.[29]

The image of the trinity describes the potential power of "la chymie" (understood as both alchemy and chemistry), and suggests that chemistry provides insight into the mystery of the sacred trinity by reflecting its very structure. This metaphor may also suggest Meurdrac's implicit awareness of the vexed history of alchemy with regard to the Catholic church that condemned alchemy as early as the Middle Ages: for it offers clarification of chemistry as a concept that embodies the most sacred rather than as a presumptuous ideal that overreaches the divine will in its search for earthly perfection. She elaborates on the way mercury, sulfur, and sal ammoniac reflect the divine order:

> The very subtle Mercury, the subtle Sulphur, and/or the volatile Ammoniac work together in the distillations, thus we see in every principle a very united Trinity, which three principles are products of one, and each a product of three.[30]

These characteristic metaphors, typical of alchemy, are as often implicit as well as explicit in Meurdrac's treatise. Her word choice when discussing mercury, for example, includes references that are alchemical commonplaces: she refers to its three "reigns,"[31] to its being "rendered very spiritual by the hand of the Artist,"[32] and that "married" it cannot be divided.[33] The idea of rule or reigns, the spiritual nature of the process, and the marriage of elements figure widely in alchemy and serve to reinforce the connection of the earthly art to God's perfection. Even so, Meurdrac is not unaware of the dangers of mercury: she warns her readers about its dangers, strongly advising against its use in cosmetics.[34]

Although Londa Schiebinger implies Marie Meurdrac's only interesting claim is that from which she took the title of her own first book, *The Mind has No Sex?*, the text itself elicits interest on a number of other levels and begs some questions: What does it mean for a woman to publish on alchemy or chemistry? What does it mean for a woman to be among the initiates in the secret art, especially given the vexed relationship alchemy has had with the church since the Middle Ages? What does it mean for a woman to appropriate the language of alchemy and offer what purports to be a pedagogical treatise specifically for women? What does it mean to have a woman offer a means for others to control health, beauty, life itself? Kathleen Perry Long has examined how in Early Modern France, alchemical images, verbal and visual, "often combined with images of monstrosity, offer a window into social, religious, political, and epistemological issues of the day," very specifically the sexual issues of the time.[35] Meurdrac's book appears to tame the monstrous in its claims and recipes for maintaining beauty and sustaining life, thereby opening the window wider and drawing attention to who controls the images and processes of alchemy.

This issue of ownership extends to the very few examinations we have of Meurdrac's work. Significantly, for our purpose, the first modern considerations of her work appear in chemistry education journals, the first in the *Journal of Chemical Education* (1970). This early treatment offers a very general description of the *La Chymie*, quotes her preface, and basically seeks to establish Meurdrac as the first female chemist.[36] Fifteen years later, in 1985, in another pedagogic chemistry journal, *Education in Chemistry*, the authors provide a summary of "Some Women Chemists" with Meurdrac heading the list, and, as will become typical, her preface is quoted. Unlike the earlier article, this treatment of Meurdrac concludes by making a very different argument regarding the author's science. While acknowledging its former popularity, the authors conclude, "The text is very alchemical in nature, so it has little relevance to modern chemists."[37] Four years later, Schiebinger would identify Meurdrac's book with the tradition of medical cookery.[38] Most recently, in 2001, after the publication of the 1999 Modern French translation, a new descriptive article appeared in *Ambix*: Lucia Tosi, an Italian historian of science, argues for Meurdrac as a feminist and Paracelsian chemist. She provides a cultural context for *La Chymie* and the most complete discussion of the author to date. Though Tosi cites information provided in the new edition, she says little about the edition itself, or its editor. The new edition is interesting, partly, for not being a particularly scholarly edition. Edited by former Emeritus Director and Professor of Research at CNRS, Collège de France, which published the book, Jean Jacques, began his career as a chemist studying the relations between estrogen's molecular structure and activity, followed by studies on fertile eggs and stereo-chemistry of liquid crystals.[39] He considered Marie's work as early chemistry and, it would seem, had the authority to do so. He identifies her work as "science-fiction," recognizing that it has little in common with the chemistry taught and practiced today[40]; yet, he acknowledges that the work offers what he calls an unpretentious example of therapeutic chemistry that bears witness to the new state of the scientific spirit beginning to manifest itself during that time in the seventeenth century.[41]

Neither Lucia Tosi nor Jean Jacques looks very closely at the rhetoric of the treatise, though both remark the many allusions to alchemists. They create a portrait of Marie Meurdrac extrapolated from the text and culture, since, as both concede—and as all other treatments have acknowledged—nothing is actually available concerning Meurdrac in her own time. Not surprisingly, then, all who have written on her agree that one problem concerns the identity of the author, not so much her sex, which she herself addresses, but *who* she is. Jean Jacques is blunt: "One knows hardly anything about the author of *La Chymie*" and that one is, therefore, "reduced to making deductions."[42] He credits the hypothesis that she was the sister of a noble lady whose memoirs appeared in 1681, a Madame de Guette who, before her marriage, was Catherine Meurdrac.[43] All the information known about Marie Meurdrac comes from her sister's *Memoirs* and *La Chymie*; there is not much in the way of credible biographical information, despite the popularity of *La Chymie*. Of course, biographical material is scant on male alchemists as well.[44] Those who revealed secrets, especially secrets that violated law or custom, works that might reveal presumption, sin, perhaps even congress with the devil, were best kept veiled by pseudonyms, anonymity, and vague biographies.

Historians of science have suggested the difficulty of making certain determinations regarding women's contribution to early modern science. They have asked, "What matters?" or "What Counts?" and considered the problematic nature of those contributions. I would argue that Marie Meurdrac's work lacks recognition in our time because as Falstaff says of Mistress Quickly, "she's neither fish nor flesh, a man knows not where to have her."[45] Perhaps contextualizing has its limits, which is to say, that even while putting this woman in her place, we still do not know where or how to have her, how or where she fits, and thus, like Falstaff, we may be "unjust." Tosi, for example, remarks the expressed similarity of intentions between Meurdrac's work and Christophle Glaser's *Traité de la Chymie*, first appearing in 1663—that both advertise reliable, practical, useful, tested information; though she then observes how "strongly" Meurdrac "departs" from Glaser's sequence, content, and emphasis.[46]

These very differences provide one source of the confusion: by combining numerous functions, the work has been considered as chemistry, *or* (not and) alchemy, *or* (not and) a recipe book of medicines and cosmetics. The multiplicity of appropriation, if not uses, partly distinguishes Meurdrac's work, and perhaps, up to the present time, accounts for its neglect. Put one way, the lack of conformity to one consistent discourse community and its genre conventions make it a difficult work to categorize, and, therefore, has perhaps even kept it from being appropriated by any one discipline in our own time. Put another way, while the work's (literal) originality has been recognized —in that it is thought to be the first chemistry by a woman—the actual originality of the work itself has been ignored. That originality may well be in those violations of generic expectations, in the multi-functionality of the work, as well as in its identification of women as its audience just ten years before the Académie Royale des Sciences was officially founded; this organization, like the Académie Française before it, would soon limit who was to be officially accepted and recognized as a scientist and who would not be—and women were among the latter.[47] Meurdrac's versatile form might have had something to do with the author's sense of audience as well as with her understanding of those who she rightly assumed would reject her contribution: whether the French academy of her own time or modern scholars centuries later whose genre categories would either dignify a work as chemistry or denigrate it as cookery. Its very hybridity, however, suggests the author's sense of audience and the realities of the period.

In her examination of "the largely untapped reserve of ... *positive* or *productive* instruction to which Medieval English readers turned for help in shaping (or fixing) themselves and the world around them," medieval scholar Lisa Cooper provides an important means for understanding Meurdrac's early modern contribution.[48] As she reminds us, well before the seventeenth century, there were numerous "medieval herbals, leech-books, surgical treatises, lapidaries, cookbooks...,"[49] some of which Meurdrac cites.[50] What Cooper explains with regard to medieval practical texts applies as well to the groundswell of such texts in the seventeenth century:

> ...on the one hand, practical literature lays claim to authority by pointing, at least implicitly, towards a past act that has met with success (this is, at any rate, the leap of faith a credulous reader must make). On the other hand, practical texts...are designed less to narrate the probable past than they are to represent the quite literally possible future, *if*—and this...is a key condition—their reader(s) should choose to follow directions.[51]

Unfortunately, we don't know who may have chosen to follow Meurdrac's directions. But we do know that her book was popular enough to be reprinted throughout the century and into the next. Apparently, it was not enough that there were similar texts with similar recipes by male writers in France or elsewhere; it didn't matter that there were also recipes books available. Marie Meurdrac's book continued to be reprinted throughout the second half of the seventeenth century, with new recipes added and some older ones omitted. The editions were not static, suggesting there may have been specific demands or concerns. Nor were the excised recipes particularly controversial; they may simply have been rejected as superfluous, or as not having accomplished the stated purpose, or as having failed in some other way: in production perhaps, rather than product. We may never know the reasons for the changes in editions, just as we may never know who tried these recipes, if anyone, and who actually sought out Meurdrac for a personal tutorial, or even her own still elusive identity.

Sarah Hutton claims that "The history of science is not just about the winners, it is about everything that went on, including some of the theories which to us seem strange, irrational, even defunct, like alchemy."[52] It is also, however, about the difficulty of disentangling very different approaches to science and to education. Alchemists wrote recipes in codes, a list of which appears in Meurdrac's work,[53] though she never resorts to the use of these codes in any of her recipes, the so-called kitchen chemistry that women could justifiably appropriate; indeed, she suggests that these symbols are part of the protected obscurity of the Art, as alchemy was known.[54] It is for the reader to decide what constitutes science: its products or methodology. If methodology, then Meurdrac's recipes for cures and cosmetics qualify her as a practicing scientist as well as a teacher of scientific practices that might serve not only women but the world as it was understood and experienced.

Notes

[1] Jean Jacques, *La Chymie Charitable & Facile, en Faveur des Dames*, 14, lists these editions; he does not mention the earliest edition of 1656, which appears in the WorldCat, http://firstsearch.oclc.org.ezaccess.libraries.psu.edu/, accessed PSU 15 October 2007.

[2] Schiebinger, *The Mind has No Sex?*, 113.

[3] Clericuzio, "Teaching Chemistry and Chemical Textbooks in France," 352., fn 47.

[4] Allen G. Debus, *The French Paracelsians: The Chemical Challenge to Medical and Science Tradition in Early Modern France* (Cambridge: Cambridge University Press, 1991), pp. 133-134.

[5] Clericuzio, 235.

[6] Meurdrac, *La Chymie,* the frontispiece of the 1687 edition foregrounds the equipment of alchemy: a flask and funnel, a possible distillation device; and it reveals a secret shelf of books and pots behind a curtain pulled back by a classically robed Lady—the icon of chemistry. (There is no kitchen.)

[7] "Puisqu'ils nous ont voilé d'une nuit très obscure." I am paraphrasing the modern French transcription of the edition by Jean Jacque, *La Chymie Charitable & Facile, en Faveur des Dames*, 22. The 1680 edition includes twice as many of the poet's sonnets to Marie, though not this one The translations into English are my own. All quotations hereon in will be cited by page number that corresponds to the French in the modern edition. The French will be quoted in the endnotes and cited as Meurdrac unless otherwise stated. I reproduce the capitalization of this modernized edition. When I quote directly from the original 1680 or 1687 editions, I retain their original spellings and capitalizations.

[8] Meurdrac, 22, "Et toi tu nous fais voir qu'il n'est plus difficile."

[9] Meurdrac, 17, "Dans ce combat je suis resté près de deux ans irrésolue; je m'objectais à moi-même que ce n'était pas la profession d'une femme d'enseigner; qu'elle se doit demeurer dans le silence, écouter et apprendre, sans témoigner qu'elle sait." For specifics, see, for example the Princess Elizabeth of Bohemia (1618-1680), who carried on an important intellectual correspondence with

Descartes and Anna Zieglerin, a controversial alchemist; Erica Harth, *Cartesian Women: Versions and Subversions of Rational Discourse in the Old Regime*, 64-122; and, April G. Shelford, "'Others Laugh, Even the Learned': An Erudit's View of Women and Learning in Seventeenth-Century France," 221-232.

[10] Meurdrac, 17, "que les Esprits n'ont point de sexe."

[11] Meurdrac, 17, "et que si ceux des femmes étaient cultivés comme ceux des hommes, et que l'on employât autant de temps et de dépenses à les instruire, ils pourraient les égaler."

[12] Christine de Pizan, *The Book of the City of Ladies*, Rev. Ed., Trans. Earl Jeffrey Richards (New York: Persea Books, 1998), I.27.i.

[13] Meurdrac, 17-18, "que notre siècle a vu naître des femmes qui pour la Prose, la Poésie, les Langues, la Philosophie et le gouvernement même de l'Etat, ne cèdent en rien à la suffisance et à la capacité des hommes."

[14] Meurdrac, 19, "ou qui craindront de ne pas réussir, je m'expliquerai de vive vox quand on me fera l'honneur de m'en communiquer."

[15] Meurdrac, Jean Jacques, 229 and cf. fn. 5.

[16] Iatrochemistry refers to chemistry intended specifically for medicinal purposes; Paracelsus is one of the earliest natural philosophers to be identified with this kind of alchemy and chemistry. See Clericuzio, 336-350, for discussion of the history of teaching medical chemistry and the controversies regarding its inclusion and exclusion from French and German universities, especially 343-47, for a discussion of the public lessons at the "Jardin du Roi."

[17] This second offer does not appear in the Preface to the sixth section of Jean Jacques' edition or in the 1687 edition; it appears, as follows, in the 1680 edition, 253, "Dans ma Preface je me suis offerte à montrer à faire les operations que j'enseigne; je le reïtere encore, & seray moy-mesme les choses dont on aura besoin.

[18] Meurdrac, 17.

[19] Meurdrac, 129, "Quand j'ai commencé ce Livre, je me suis proposée de ne point passer mes expériences. C'est pourquoi je supprime en cette Partie les opérations sur l'or, et sur l'argent, ne connaissant point leurs préparations, ni leurs utilités en Médecine. J'ai vu plusieurs opérations auxquelles on a donné le nom d'Or potable, de teinture d'or, d'huile d'argent, que je n'ai pu comprendre; ne me pouvant persuader que des corps si parfaits et condensés, fussent liquéfiables. Ce n'est pas que je condamne ces opérations pour ne les pouvoir pas concevoir; je serais aussi téméraire que les aveugles, qui assureraient qu'il ne serait point de Soleil, parce qu'ils ne le verraient pas. Pour les opérations qui suivant, j'assure qu'elles sont véritables, et expérimentées."

[20] Meurdrac, 129, "je n'ai pu comprendre; ne me pouvant persuader."

[21] See, for example, Long, "Salomon Trismosin and Clovis Hesteau de Nuysement: The Sexual Politics of Alchemy in Early Modern France." She considers the 1612 French translation.

[22] Jane Dee is a notable exception, supporting as she did her husband's experiments in natural philosophy. See Harkness, "Managing an Experimental Household: The Dees of Mortlake and the Practice of Natural Philosophy."

[23] Cavendish, *Observations on Experimental Philosophy*, 12.

[24] Meurdrac, 125.

[25] Meurdrac, 27, "Premièrement nous parlerons du Sel comme du Père de la génération, puisqu'il semble que c'est lui qui contribue le plus à la production."

[26] See, for example, Gareth Roberts, *The Mirror of Alchemy*, 86.

[27] Tosi, "Maria Meurdrac: Paracelsian Chemist and Feminist," especially, 74, regarding this passage, notes the specific allusion or influence of Duchesne and his *Traité de Matière*, among other alchemical allusions.

[28] Harth, *Cartesian Women: Versions and Subversions of Rational Discourse in the Old Regime*, 82.

[29] Meurdrac, 29, "Toutes les choses qui sont au monde proviennent d'un, et cet un en produit trois: ce qui nous peut donner une idée du mystère adorable de la très-sainte Trinité. La Chymie nous en présente un crayon, puisqu'elle trouve une trinité non seulement dans chaque sujet, mais dans chaque principe."

[30] Meurdrac, 30, "Le très subtil Mercure, le Soufre subtil, et l'Armoniac ou volatile passent ensemble dans les distillations, ainsi nous voyons dans chaque principe une Trinité très unie, lesquels trois principes sont produits par un, et chacun en produit trois."

[31] Meurdrac, 30, "les trois règnes."

[32] Meurdrac, 30, "et rendu par la main de l'Artiste très spiritual."

[33] Meurdrac, 31, "qu'il n'est pas en notre pouvoir de diviser entièrement ce qu'elle a conjoint."

[34] Meurdrac, 190, "Pour le Mercure, le Sublimé,…je conseille de ne s'en servir en aucune façon; outre qu'il effacent la beauté du visage par le long usage, ils produisent des maladies très fâcheuses, et quelquefois incurables."

[35] Long, "Salomon Trismosin and Clovis Hesteau de Nuysement: The Sexual Politics of Alchemy in Early Modern France," 10.

[36] Bishop and Deloach, "Marie Meurdrac—First Lady of Chemistry," 448, also remark that the work should be of equal interest to literary historians as well as historians of science, because, in describing Marie as an authentic savant, they claim that, therefore, her work also provides insight into the background of Molière's play, *Les Femmes Savantes*.

[37] Rayner-Canham and Frenette, "Some French Women Chemists," 176.

[38] Schiebinger, 113.

[39] Mémo Sciences, biographies of presenters (1999), http://www.memosciences.be/elchimie26.htm. See also John Caldwell and Nina Berova, eds., "Obituary: Jean Jacques."

[40] Meurdrac, Jean Jacques, 10, "La 'chymie' de Marie Meurdrac n'a pas grand-chose à voir avec la chimie (sans 'y') que l'on enseigne et pratique aujourd'hui."

The internal quotations around "chymie" may refer to the archaic spelling or suggest a qualification regarding the state of the chemical science itself, or both.

[41] Meurdrac, Jean Jacques, 11, "Le petit ouvrage de Marie Meurdrac nous fournit un exemple sans prétention de ce que pouvait être la chimie thérapeutique des années 1660, mais il apporte aussi un témoignage du nouvel état d'esprit scientifique qui commence à se manifester." Therapeutic chemistry is a reference to the iatrochemistry of the time.

[42] Meurdrac, Jean Jacques, 9, "On ne sait presque rien sur l'auteur de *La Chymie*.... On en est réduit aux déductions qui reposent...."

[43] Meurdrac, Jean Jacques, 9.

[44] We know more about those who satirized alchemy than about those who practiced it: the former include Chaucer, Jonson, Cavendish. It's no accident the authors of alchemy are known as Pseudo-Aquinas, Pseudo-Albertus Magnus, Troismoisin. See, for example, Charles Webster, *From Paracelsus to Newton*. In the seventeenth century, both Robert Boyle and Isaac Newton practiced alchemy.

[45] Shakespeare, *IHenry IV*, III.iii.127-128.

[46] Tosi, 73-74, should be commended for rehabilitating Meurdrac as a feminist Paracelsian chemist while recognizing the many influences in the treatise, including medicinal recipes, cosmetics, and alchemy. Clearly dependent on Jean Jacques' edition, Tosi seems to have been unaware of the earliest edition of Meurdrac's work, unmentioned in his introduction; the 1656 edition predates Glaser's 1663 work, and, therefore, suggests a different order of influence and departures.

[47] Schiebinger, 20-24.

[48] Cooper, "The Poetics of Practicality."

[49] Cooper, 493.

[50] Meurdrac, Jean Jeacques, see, for example, 58, 59, 65, 67, 75.

[51] Cooper, 504.

[52] Hutton, "Anne Conway, Margaret Cavendish and Seventeenth-Century Scientific Thought," 232.

[53] Unfortunately, I have not yet had the opportunity to examine the 1656 or 1666 editions for myself; I have worked from the original 1680 and 1687 editions. I thank Terry Barnett and Southwestern College for their generous loan of the 1680 edition and the Folger Library for access to the 1687 edition.

[54] Jean Jacques, 48, omits this chapter from his modern French edition; he uses ellipses to mark the omission. I take this quotation, therefore, from the 1680 edition, 38: "The philosophers have done all that they could not to make their operations public. Under specific symbols, they have hidden the names of the operations' substances and vessels, which has resulted in several secrets not having been practiced. That is why I wanted to explain them for the benefit of those who will read this book, in order to facilitate all kinds of operations and to keep them from looking elsewhere for explanations" ("Les Philosophes ont fait

tout ce qu'ils on pû pour ne pas rendre leurs operations communes. Ils ont caché sous de certains caracteres le nom de la matiere des operations, & des vaisseaux, ce qui a esté cause que plusieurs secrets n'ont pas esté pratiquez. C'est pourquoy j'ay voulu les expliquer en faveur de ceux qui liront ce Livre, pour leur faciliter toutes sortes d'operations, & pour les exempter de chercher ailleurs leurs explication.").

Works Cited

Primary References

Cavendish, Margaret. *Observations on Experimental Philosophy* (1668), 3-22, 46-53, 58-62, 74-87.
Conway, Anne. *The Principles of the Most Ancient and Modern Philosophy* (1690). Ed. and trans. Allison P. Coudert and Taylor Corse. Cambridge: Cambridge University Press, 1996. 1-70.
de Pizan, Christine. *The Book of the City of Ladies*, Rev. Ed. Trans. Earl Jeffrey Richards (New York: Persea Books, 1998)
Meurdrac, Marie. *La Chymie Charitable & Facile, en Faveur Des Dames.* 2nd ed. Lyon, 1680.
—. *La Chymie Charitable & Facile, en Faveur Des Dames.* 3rd ed. Paris, 1687.
—. *La Chymie Charitable & Facile, en Faveur Des Dames.* Ed. Jean Jacques. Paris: CNRS editions, 1999.
Shakespeare, William. *1Henry IV*. Riverside Shakespeare. 2nd ed. Ed. G. Blakemore Evans, et al. Boston: Houghton Mifflin, 1974.

Secondary References

Bishop, Lloyd D., and Will S. Deloach. "Marie Meurdrac—First Lady of Chemistry." *Journal of Chemical Education* 47 (1970): 448-449.
Caldwell, John and Nina Berova, eds., "Obituary: Jean Jacques." *Chirality* 13.9 (25 September 2001): fmvi. Wiley InterScience journal, http://www3.interscience.wiley.com.ezaccess.libraries.psu.edu/cgibin/fulltext/85512871/PDFSTART?CRETRY=1&SRETRY=0, accessed 24 September 2007, PSU.
Clericuzio, Antonio. "Teaching Chemistry and Chemistry Textbooks in France. From Beguin to Lemery." *Science and Education* 15.2-4 (March 2006): 235-255.

Cooper, Lisa H. "The Poetics of Practicality." In *Oxford Twenty-First Century Approaches to Literature: Middle English*. Ed. Paul Strohm. Oxford: Oxford University Press, 2007. 491-505.

Harkness, Deborah. "Managing an Experimental Household: The Dees of Mortlake and the Practice of Natural Philosophy. *Isis* 88.2 (1997): 247-262.

Harth, Erica. *Cartesian Women: Versions and Subversions of Rational Discourse in the Old Regime*. Ithaca: Cornell University Press, 1992. 64-122.

Hutton, Sarah. "Anne Conway, Margaret Cavendish and Seventeenth-Century Scientific Thought." In *Women, Science and Medicine 1500-1700*. Eds. Lynette Hunter and Sarah Hutton (Phoenix Mill, U.K.: Sutton Publishing, 1997), 218-234.

Long, Kathleen Perry. "Salomon Trismosin and Clovis Hesteau de Nuysement: The Sexual Politics of Alchemy in Early Modern France." *L'Esprit Créateur* 35.2 (1995): 9-21.

Mémo Sciences Conference (1999), http://www.memosciences.be/elchimie26.htm, accessed 24 September 2007.

Rayner-Canham, Geoffrey W., and H. Frenette. "Some French Women Chemists." *Education in Chemistry* 22.6 (November 1985): 176-178.

Roberts, Gareth. *The Mirror of Alchemy*. Toronto: University of Toronto Press, 1994.

Schiebinger, Londa. *The Mind has No Sex?* Cambridge: Harvard University Press, 1989.

Shelford, April G. "'Others Laugh, Even the Learned': An *Erudit's* View of Women and Learning in Seventeenth-Century France." *Proceedings of the Western Society for French History* 24 (1996): 221-232.

Tosi, Lucia. "Maria Meurdrac: Paracelsian Chemist and Feminist," *Ambix* 48 (2001): 69-82.

Van Schurman, Anna Maria. *Whether a Christian Woman Should Be Educated and Other Writings*. Ed. and trans. Joyce Irwin. Chicago: University of Chicago Press, 1998. 1-56.

Webster, Charles. *From Paracelsus to Newton*. Cambridge, 1982; rpt. New York: Barnes and Noble, 1996.

CHAPTER SIX

THE LIBERATORY POSITIONING OF BRITISH FEMALE RHETORIC: BATHSUA MAKIN'S *AN ESSAY TO REVIVE THE ANTIENT EDUCATION OF GENTLEWOMEN*, MARY WOLLSTONECRAFT'S *THE EDUCATION OF DAUGHTERS*, AND LUCY WILSON'S *THE EDUCATION OF WOMEN*

JULIA E. KIERNAN

The texts of Bathsua Makin, Mary Wollstonecraft, and Lucy Wilson exemplify the differing rhetorical strategies exercised by British women in support of female education from the early modern to pre-Victorian period. A close reading of these texts, with emphasis upon economic class, demonstrates the changing constraints of patriarchal British society in terms of female and male constructions of morality, marriage, and motherhood. A comparison of these texts indicates a development within this genre of writing that is disruptive while linear, specifically in terms of class. Thus, these texts indicate seventeenth- and eighteenth-century assumptions that only upper class women are to be educated; the disjuncture occurs when one moves to the nineteenth century and emphasis turns away from economic privilege towards not simply a focus on equality between genders, but between classes. The writings of Makin, Wollstonecraft, and Wilson, while divergent in respect to audience, authorial voice, and perceived credibility, offer a unique look into a pattern of proto-feminist and feminist rhetoric concerning the education of women over three centuries in the British Isles.

In the periods wherein the texts of Makin, Wollstonecraft, and Wilson were written and disseminated, educational choices were governed by what men wanted women to be.[1] Despite the strength and forthrightness of these women's arguments, they existed within a minority. Within the debate concerns over the content of female education erupted: one side argued that education should prepare women as pleasing ornaments for their husbands; the other contested that the female sex should be trained in domestics, as good mothers and heads of households.[2] Nancy Weitz Miller argues "rhetoric has long been recognized as a fundamental means of securing authority, and in an effort to keep them in a submissive position, women had long been excluded from exercising their power of speech."[3] Thus, the very fact that the texts of Makin, Wollstonecraft, and Wilson exist makes them worthy of study. If we recognize that their circulation was most likely limited, especially among female readers because of their lack of literacy, the similarity and tradition of rhetoric found among these texts make them a striking source of inquiry.

Seventeenth-century English society was at best ambivalent toward women who attempted to enter what was perceived as a male arena of life, specifically education through writing and reading.[4] In the eighteenth century most advocates of female education were primarily concerned with middle class women. Browne in *The Eighteenth Century Feminist Mind* articulates "by the end of the [eighteenth] century, women's right to better education was generally accepted, although people had different views about what this better education might be, and women themselves could express a wide range of opinions about it."[5] However, my research shows that such acceptance was only—grudgingly—accepted among members of the upper and middle classes. Even in the nineteenth century, where we would expect progression towards the obtainment of female rights and privileges in respect to education, working class girls were included in state provision of elementary education *only* in the latter part of the century; further, this education emphasized virtues of good housewifery and domestic management.[6] This is hardly the "better" education that Browne implies, an analysis of Makin's, Wollstonecraft's, and Wilson's texts will illustrate women struggled to establish their right to an education throughout three centuries.

Little biographical information remains on the life of Bathsua Makin, which is an unfortunate historical pattern of most women in the early modern period. However, Jean Brink reports that Makin was a middle class woman whose writing career spanned approximately sixty years. Her first publication occurred in 1616, and in the mid-seventeenth century she was tutor to Princess Elizabeth, daughter to Charles I. In 1649 Makin gained the patronage of Lucy, Countess of Huntington, and wrote *An Essay to Revive the Antient Education of Gentlewomen*; however, this tract was not published until 1673 when Makin would have been seventy-three years old,[7] and its popularity and dissemination are unclear. In this publication Makin dismisses the common male objection to female education, explaining that such education is evident in biblical, classical, and historical traditions. Makin offers these as proof that in the past women have been educated and, thus, education should be maintained as a natural pursuit of women.[8]

Mary Wollstonecraft, the daughter of a tradesman, acquired basic education in a small school in England. Similar to Makin, Wollstonecraft worked for a period as a schoolmistress.[9] In 1786, Wollstonecraft wrote a short tract entitled *Thoughts on the Education of Daughters*. In this text Wollstonecraft views education as a means to develop character and to produce strength in body and mind; she advocates a national system of coeducation. However, while her name has become synonymous as a symbol for the unwomanly woman,[10] such a voice is not heard in *Thoughts on the Education of Daughters*. Instead the education that Wollstonecraft discusses in this text is aimed at procuring a feminine and ladylike disposition. Thus, I would like us to consider that while Wollstonecraft has argued persuasively for universal female educational advancement and formal education, this is not the case in *Thoughts on the Education of Daughters*, and for this reason it differs from the arguments of Makin and Wilson. This may be one reason why there is little contemporary popularity surrounding this text and why it has not been as heavily theorized by feminist scholars as Wollstonecraft's two *Vindications*.

Now I turn to Lucy Wilson about whom very little is known. Wilson's pamphlet *Women and Education* is housed in the University of Huddersfield archives; it is assumed to have been given as a lecture at the Huddersfield Mechanic's Institution. It is quite short, only two pages long; however, it puts forth the same arguments of Makin's and Wollstonecraft's much longer texts. Because the Mechanic's Institute existed from 1843-1884, we can place Wilson's text within this timeframe. This text and the Institute itself are important due to Huddersfield's distinction of having been the first British institution organized and managed for the education of young women of the working classes. Opened in 1846, the Institute had classes in reading, writing, dictation, arithmetic, spelling, grammar, geography, history, and sewing. The preamble of the Institutes' rules and regulations explains "its object being to provide for females of this town and neighbourhood, increased facilities for improvement by means of Evening Classes, a Library, Addresses, and much other methods as may appear suitable for importing a sound, moral, and secular education" (Huddersfield). And while this information does not cast light on the personality of Lucy Wilson, the Institute records indicate that George Wilson, a working class subscriber, donated money from 1857-1871; further, in 1860-61 a Miss Martha Wilson was elected as officer of her class, and in 1863-1864 a Miss Mary Jane Wilson was elected as class officer. This information indicates that the Wilson family had an ongoing relationship with the school. Additionally I have recently uncovered a correspondence between Helen Taylor, a nineteenth-century woman's suffrage advocate and woman's rights activist, and Lucy Wilson that occurred in March of 1881 concerning the topic of female education. Finally, while Peter Gosden offers biography concerning Wilson's personal and professional endeavors he makes no direct mention of her contributions to the Huddersfield Mechanics' Institute.

Strategies

While the arguments of these three texts are quite similar in rhetorical content, with emphasis upon morality, marriage, and motherhood, the strategies each author uses to persuade are divergent. Miller explains that because of hostile environments, women writers had a difficult time establishing credibility.[11] Therefore, many works of women display a range of strategies to create an authoritative ethos. Makin uses strategies that align her with female and male audiences; she writes to a female patron, but under the persona of an English gentleman. The first lines of her text read: "To all Ingenious and Virtuous Ladies, more especially to her Highness the Lady Mary, eldest Daughter to his Royal Highness the Duke of York."[12] Thus the first move Makin makes is towards a female audience, but six paragraphs down a further plea is made:

> I hope I shall not need to beg the patience of Ladies to peruse this Pamphlet: I have bespoken and do expect your Patronage; because it is your Cause I plead against an ill custom, prejudiced to you, which Men will not willingly suffer to be broken. I would desire Men not to prejudge and cast aside this Book upon the sight of the Title. If I have solidly prove', what I do pretend to, and fairly the Objections brought against my Assertions, and if I have proposed something that may be profitable to Man-kind, let it not be rejected.[13]

In this second passage Makin recognizes her patron, but in doing so she also acknowledges a male audience. Makin, lest she be considered female because of the subject matter, prepared for such a misreading by asserting in the same passage: "I am a Man myself, that would not suggest a thing prejudicial to our Sex."[14] This affirmation of "male authorship" is perhaps one reason why the text remains available to modern readers.

Wilson's strategies are quite different from Makin's. Her female authorship is disclosed in both the inclusion of her name and the probability of its oral deliverance.

> Men would soon cease to be indifferent to women's education if they would but realize how heavily they weight themselves in the race of life by decreeing that from and to all time their mothers shall be ignorant; how much habits of inaccurate observation and reasoning have been acquired by them unconsciously as they learnt to speak and to walk, habits which enormously retard them in the pursuit of truth and knowledge.[15]

In this passage Wilson blames men for not only the ignorance of women, but the breakdown of national social systems. She is alluding to men's incapacity to interpret the implications of uneducated women. Wilson explains that men have failed to "realize"—to see and comprehend—the imperial errors within their logic. Specifically she blames this lack of intellectual foresight, "inaccurate observation and reasoning," on the male laws which declare that "mothers shall be ignorant." In this passage Wilson points to the collapse of British unity and control as intimately linked to female ignorance, which "retards" not simply women in the "pursuit of truth and knowledge," but the men who are raised by these "ignorant" mothers, in consequence to the whole nation.

Wollstonecraft, unlike Makin and Wilson, is explicit about the purpose of her text, indicating that her authorship would not have been problematic or at least as problematic as Makin—who wrote when women were not authorized to write—or Wilson—who as a working class woman had very little authority in any male dominated sphere. In the eighteenth century, women, at least those of the middle and upper classes, were not as constrained in terms of textual production as those of earlier generations. Further, Wollstonecraft's class position enabled her to write and publish texts concerning female education in ways that were still not viable to the working class women of the nineteenth century. Wollstonecraft's preface to *The Education of Daughters* articulates,

> In the following pages I have endeavored to point out some important things with respect to female education. It is true, many treatises have been already written; yet it occurred to me, that much still remained to be said. I shall not swell these sheets by writing apologies for my attempt. I am afraid, indeed, the reflection will, by some, be thought too grave; but I should not make them less so without writing affectedly.

However, while Wollstonecraft's method of presentation assumes authority she demonstrates female modesty, thus drawing attention away from the radical nature of her text. In this passage womanly virtue is attempted through an "endeavoured" "attempt," through offered "apologies" for this "attempt," and through the fear that the text will be read as "too grave"—too unwomanly.

Audience

Appeals to audience in these three texts are tied to class and class-based home environment. Such constraints fall in line with Hunt's research that positively correlates learning experience and class.[16] The differing strategies of Makin, Wollstonecraft, and Wilson indicate each author consciously shaped her arguments for a specific class-based audience. Makin's strategies of address are directed towards upper and middle classes, explicit in her awareness of her audiences' access to personal time: "My design is upon such Persons whose leisure is a burden."[17] Similarly, Wollstonecraft speaks to an audience, both male and female, also accustomed to this luxury: "Very frequently, when the education has been neglected, the mind improves itself, if it has leisure for reflection, and experience to reflect on."[18] The similar usage of the word "leisure" is of importance as neither author questions women's access to it. Wilson offers a divergent perspective,

> To the poor man the full development of all his powers is of greater personal moment than to the rich...We constantly hear that among the poorer classes it is their wretched homes that drive men to drink, and drink that drives them to crime. It cannot, then, be wise to ensure wretched homes to these men by leaving the presiding genii of those homes densely ignorant.[19]

This nineteenth-century text makes no allusion to leisure; instead, Wilson details the life of the "poor man," members of British society whose "burden" is not the "leisure" suggested by Makin, but "wretched homes," "crime," and the fate of being labeled "densely ignorant." In all three narratives the authors claim that the education of women has been ignored, yet the similarity between Wilson's and Wollstonecraft's texts in terms of "neglect" is divergent; there is no moment of Wollstonecraft's "reflection" for the working class man (or woman). In fact Wollstonecraft's repetition of the word "reflect" insinuates a calmness and peace not evident in the "wretched homes" of the working class. The texts of Makin and

Wollstonecraft indicate a level of natural entitlement; the reader's class is both apparent and expected.

The problem with synthesizing these texts is that they are not uniform in terms of argument; they often deal with issues quite differently. For instance, Makin and Wollstonecraft address a middle to upper class mixed gender audience while Wilson is speaking to a working class male audience. Consequently we see similarity and disparity in audience appeal. Positive relationships are most easily drawn between Makin and Wollstonecraft, due to similarity in their readership. The following two passages, written a century apart, utilize related rhetoric, organization, and word choice. Makin posits,

> I hope I shall by this Discourse persuade some Parents to be more careful for the future Breeding of their Daughters. You cark and care to get great Portions for them, which sometimes occasions their ruin. Here is a sure Portion, an easy way to make them excellent. How many born to good Fortunes, when their Wealth has been wasted, have supported themselves and Families too by their Wisdom?[20]

And Wollstonecraft echoes,

> If what I have written should be read by parents, who are now going on in thoughtless extravagance, and anxious only that their daughters may be *genteelly educated*, let them consider to what sorrows they expose them; for I have not over-coloured the picture. [21]

Both women narrate a scenario wherein all goes wrong, despite access to "good Fortunes," "Wealth," and "extravagance." These passages are a warning to the wealthy, an omen of educate-your-daughters-or-else. The use of "Discourse [to] persuade some Parents" is a move towards female education and a dismissal that women's education will lead to downfall, which is not pragmatic in terms of maintaining family wealth and investment. Makin and Wollstonecraft are pointing to the shortsightedness of moves to "cark and care" for daughters, in securing a "genteel" education, but there is a reality that frivolous education will "expose" them to sorrow. There is great disparity of argument from these in Wilson's text,

> I am not saying to you, Delegates of the Mechanics Institutions of the county, things that are too high to concern the people whose interests you represent. I have said that there is no sex in education, neither is it the peculiar birthright of any social class.[22]

In this passage there is no mention of "parents," but a direct beseechment of the male "Delegates of the Mechanics Institutions." Wilson makes connections between class issues and gender asking her working class audience to note the disparity of education between the classes, which these men would view as unfair, and extend this class argument into all facets of education. Wilson's text is divergent from Makin's and Wollstonecraft's because she is speaking to a group of people whose own education is questionable to the upper classes; she is pushing her audience to relate inequality of classes to inequality of sexes. Further, Wilson expounds upon the simplicity of her argument: "I am not saying to you...things that are too high to concern the people whose interests you represent"; this is an attempt to unite the audience in terms of class, and across sexes.

Thus, we see difference in the moves these women make in persuading their audiences into supporting female education. Makin and Wollstonecraft appeal to personal motives of securing wealth and by extension family name, while Wilson is pushing her audience toward the attainment of equality between the rich and poor *and* between men and women. However, Wilson also offers her audience the same argument of the possibility of unforeseen sorrow that arises in the Makin and Wollstonecraft texts.

> I will not plead for it to-day on the ground that we need it for ourselves, that we shall be better and happier if we have it, but that you will be better and happier if we have it, that your way through life would be smoothed and expedited in countless ways.[23]

All three authors point to a dim future if women fail to enter into proper schooling; Makin and Wollstonecraft point to the demise of the daughter and her family, while Wilson describes this same fate in terms of men and by extension the nation. All three suggest that if women are properly educated the life of individual and collective men, women, and families will "be smoothed and expedited in countless ways."

Morality

Morality is intimately tied to religion and virtue. In order to be considered virtuous, a characteristic expected of all good women, behavior was to conform to religious law and standards. Makin, Wollstonecraft, and Wilson all wrote in periods when women who took part in rhetorical endeavors were viewed as immoral; this assumption is tied to the biblical writings of St. Paul that dealt specifically with speaking within the church, but were and have been extended into a plethora of rhetorical venues. Views concerning reading, writing, and education were closely tied to morality;[24] because women were perceived as naturally deficient in both moral and intellectual virtue they were denied education. Further, women who aspired to intellectual knowledge were suspected of harboring the same moral weakness that led to Eve's disobedience.[25] Makin, whose text would have been most morally subversive of the three due to period of publication, acknowledges the problems that many men would have had with sanctioning female education: "To offer to the World the liberal Education of Women is to deface the Image of God in Man, it will make Women so high, and men so low like Fire in the Hose-top, it will set the whole world in a Flame."[26] But she also points to the moral benefits that education will impart upon women: "I acknowledge the great end of Arts and Tongues is the better to enable us to know God in Jesus Christ."[27] Makin is the only one of these authors to make connections between religion, virtue, morality, and education, which comments upon the period *An Essay to Revive the Antient Education of Gentlewomen* was written, rather than the oblivion of Wollstonecraft and Wilson to these relationships.

All three texts address linkages between education and morality. Despite the differences in class argument, there is similarity in that each woman is speaking to a Christian audience wherein systems of morality would have been universal. Morality, unlike education, was attainable to both sexes, and as a result men and women were expected to possess it in some level of equality. Because moral improvement was coveted in both men and women, Makin uses this argument to align morality with education, "So Men, by liberal Education, are much bettered, as to intellectuals and morals."[28] Similarly, Wollstonecraft explains heightened morals as a consequence of education: "Amusing employments must first occupy the mind; and as an attention to moral duties leads to piety, so whoever weighs one subject will turn to others, and new ideas will rush into the mind."[29] In Wilson's pamphlet morality is held up against wealth, which illustrates not a shift in morality, as the rich were always seen as more virtuous due to their income, but an alignment between the obtainment of morality. Men could acquire morality through capitalist endeavors and women through intellectual processes, both of which would serve to ultimately benefit the working class, pushing them towards higher morality and consequently a higher class position.

> Is money-making and bread-winning, for which it is worth while to educate men, the only occupation useful to the race?...If an educated woman promotes directly the moral and intellectual progress of the race, is

she not as valuable, has not her education produced as good a return as if she had been a man and had brought money?[30]

What is interesting in these three passages is the placement of the word moral. In Makin's and Wilson's tracts it is tied to intelligence; Makin speaks of "intellectuals and morals" while Wilson addresses the "moral and intellectual progress of the race." These authors play upon the union of morality and intellect, implying that one cannot occur to capacity without the other. Conversely, Wollstonecraft associates morality with piety, relying upon religious connection rather than intellect. This places Wollstonecraft's text in the contextual past, rather than moving towards a new way of defining morality as tied to intellect—the result of education. Both Makin and Wilson explicitly refer to the role education plays in the moral and intellectual progress of women and, by effect, the nation; Makin accomplishes this through a connection to men's "liberal Education," Wilson through a comparison of men's education that leads to "money-making and bread-winning" and women's place in "moral and intellectual progress."

Marriage & Motherhood

One of the arguments against the education of women was that the female sex didn't need knowledge because their lives existed only within the domestic sphere. Miller explains that when education was granted to women, it was directly related to household duties and was dependent upon its ability to help women insure the well being of the family. The intellectual education of men (languages, geography, history, etc.) if granted to women would result in a deficiency of the performance of household duties and direct competition between men and women in the public arena, acts which would pervert the social order, acts perceived as supreme disobedience.[31] Despite this contention Makin, Wollstonecraft, and Wilson all argue that men want their wives to be educated. What is noteworthy about this argument is that while the audiences of these women are dissimilar in respect to class, they all draw upon a reality that men, especially those who are educated and members of the upper class, desire educated wives. Makin explains,

> As some Husbands, debauched themselves, desire their Wives should be chast, their Children virtuous: So some men, sensible of their own want, (caused by their Parents neglect) will choose a learned Woman, in whom they may glory, and by whose prudence their defect may be supplied.[32]

In this passage Makin is pointing to the stability that a "learned Woman" brings to a "debauched" and "defect[ed] man." Her argument is covert in that she appeals to corrupted men, who are most likely not members of the upper and middle classes (as these men would face pressures throughout life to maintain their virtue). She is insinuating that marriage to a good woman will inevitably lead to "glory" and success; while making class distinctions she is also positing that marriage to a "learned Woman" leads to class mobility. Wollstonecraft, who is addressing only the upper and middle class, echoes Makin's reasoning: "few men seriously think of marrying an inferior."[33] Because her audience is accepting of marriage between equals as conventional practice, readers of the lower classes might want to emulate such actions in order to rise in socio-economic status. Similarity, Wilson uses the *Times*, a text that would have served as a symbol of class status, to establish her argument for the education of women.

> It is…on the assumption that [women] will marry that I assert that it will be worth while to give them the highest mental culture…We learn from the *Times* newspaper…that a girl should aim at fitting herself, not to be married, not to discharge the grave responsibilities that marriage brings with it, but to get married, to attract momentarily some man not much wiser than herself, and who would, therefore, consider her perfect when endowed with "a little history, a little conversational French, and music enough to amuse his evenings.[34]

Wilson identifies female education in terms of social hierarchies and explains that education will give women the "highest mental culture," implying upward class mobility. She also makes the same move towards intellectual equality within a marriage as Wollstonecraft's "few men seriously think of marrying an inferior" in the statement, a woman should seek out "some man not much wiser than herself." Each author is suggesting that if men, particularly those of the upper classes, choose wives who are intellectual equals, then there is a demand for educated women. Further, if working class men want their daughters to marry up, they need to accommodate this with "the highest mental culture." All three authors use the same argument in respect to motherhood: if men want their sons to rise in status, mothers, because "none have so great an advantage of making most deep impression on their Children,"[35] should be put in the position, through education, to aid in this mobility.

Conclusion

An analysis of these texts points to rhetorical similarity in three women's advocation of female education, arguments which spanned three centuries of British female publication. The writings of Makin, Wollstonecraft, and Wilson exemplify how these women used their class position to demonstrate the changing constraints of patriarchal society's views of morality, marriage, and motherhood. These texts suggest both connect and disconnect between three historical perspectives of female education, specifically in terms of class. While the seventeenth and eighteenth-century arguments are confident in the entitlement of women's education, the later nineteenth-century text has no claims to class privilege. The writings of Makin, Wollstonecraft, and Wilson illustrate a carry over in the rhetoric that surrounds the education of women, but an articulation of very different assumptions about such education.

Acknowledgements

I would like to offer many thanks to Hilary Haigh and her fellow archivists at the University of Huddersfield, without their patience this publication would have been impossible. I also offer sincere appreciation to Carol Mattingly who encouraged and fostered my research.

Notes

[1] Browne, *The Eighteenth Century Feminist Mind*, 116.
[2] Ibid., 104.
[3] Weitz Miller, "Ethos, Authority, and Virtue," 273.
[4] Ibid., 273.
[5] Browne, *The Eighteenth Century Feminist Mind*, 118.
[6] Lewis, *Women in England 1870-1950*, 91.
[7] Brink, Bathsua Reginald Makin, 313-321.
[8] Weitz Miller, "Ethos, Authority, and Virtue," 280.
[9] Flexner, *Mary Wollstonecraft*, 19.
[10] Kersey, *Classics in the Education of Girls and Women*, 163.
[11] Weitz Miller, "Ethos, Authority, and Virtue," 272.
[12] Makin, An Essay to Revive, 2.
[13] Ibid., 3.
[14] Ibid., 3.
[15] Ibid., 2.
[16] Hunt, *Lessons for Life*, xiv.
[17] Makin, An Essay to Revive, 22.

[18] Wollstonecraft, *Thoughts on the Education of Daughters*, 94.
[19] Wilson, The Education of Women, 2.
[20] Makin, An Essay to Revive, 29.
[21] Wollstonecraft, *Thoughts on the Education of Daughters*, 77.
[22] Wilson, The Education of Women, 2.
[23] Ibid., 1.
[24] Browne, *The Eighteenth Century Feminist Mind*, 102.
[25] Weitz Miller, "Ethos, Authority, and Virtue," 276.
[26] Makin, An Essay to Revive, 2.
[27] Ibid., 10.
[28] Ibid., 4.
[29] Wollstonecraft, *Thoughts on the Education of Daughters*, 27.
[30] Wilson, The Education of Women, 1.
[31] Weitz Miller, "Ethos, Authority, and Virtue," 273.
[32] Makin, An Essay to Revive, 21.
[33] Wollstonecraft, *Thoughts on the Education of Daughters*, 76.
[34] Wilson, The Education of Women, 1.
[35] Makin, An Essay to Revive, 19.

Works Cited

Primary Sources

Huddersfield Female Educational Institute. Rule Book. http://www.hud.ac.uk/cls/archives/fei/feirule.htm.

Makin, Bathsua. An Essay to Revive the Antient Education of Gentlewomen, in Religion, Manners, Arts & Tongues, with An Answer to the Objections against this Way of Education. http://www.pinn.net/~sunshine/book-sum/makin1.html.

University of Huddersfield. 1846 - 1883: Female Educational Institute Formed. http://www.hud.ac.uk/uni_history/18461883_female_edu_institute.html.

Wilson, Lucy. Date of publication unknown. The Education of Women. Leeds. Housed in University of Huddersfield Archives.

Wollstonecraft, Mary. 1974. *Thoughts on the Education of Daughters*. London: Garland Publishing.

Secondary Sources

Brink, Jean R. 1991. Bathsua Reginald Makin: "Most Learned Matron," *Huntington Library Quarterly*. 54.4:313-26.

Browne, Alice. 1987. *The Eighteenth Century Feminist Mind*. Detroit: Wayne State University Press.

Flexner, Eleanor. 1972. *Mary Wollstonecraft*. Baltimore: Penguin Books Inc.

Gosden, Peter. 2004. *Oxford Dictionary of National Biography*. Oxford: Oxford University Press.

Hunt, Felicity. 1987. *Lessons for Life: The Schooling of Girls and Women, 1850-1950*. Oxford: Basil Blackwell.

Kersey, Shirley Nelson. 1981. *Classics in the Education of Girls and Women*. Metuchen, N.J.: The Scarecrow Press, Inc.

Lewis, Jane. 1984. *Women in England 1870-1950: Sexual Division & Social Change*. Sussex: Wheatsheaf Books.

Miller, Nancy Weitz. 1997. "Ethos, Authority, and Virtue for Seventeenth-century Women Writers: The Case of Bathsua Makin's Essay to Revive the Antient Education of Gentlewoman (1673)." In *Listening to Their Voices: The Rhetorical Activities of Historical Women*, ed. Molly Meijer Wertheimer. Columbia, South Carolina: University of South Carolina Press.

CHAPTER SEVEN

FEMALE EDUCATION IN NINETEENTH-
CENTURY GERMANY:
CAROLINE DE LA MOTTE FOUQUÉ
AND THE REJECTION OF BOURGEOIS MODELS
OF DOMESTICITY

KARIN BAUMGARTNER

> Women can, of course, be educated, but their minds are not adapted to the higher sciences, philosophy, or certain of the arts. These demand a universal faculty. Women may have happy inspirations, taste, elegance, but they have not the ideal. The difference between man and woman is the same as that between animal and plant. The animal corresponds more closely to the character of the man, the plant to that of the woman. In woman there is a more peaceful unfolding of nature, a process, whose principle is the less clearly determined unity of feeling. If women were to control the government, the state would be in danger, for they do not act according to the dictates of universality, but are influenced by accidental inclinations and opinions. The education of woman goes on one hardly knows how, in the atmosphere of picture—thinking, as it were, more through life than through the acquisition of knowledge. Man attains his position only through stress of thought and much specialized effort.[1]

This quote from Hegel's *Philosophy of Right* (1821) sums up the general view of women's potential for education around 1800. While it seemed clear that women *could* be educated and might achieve great accomplishments like Dorothea Leporin or Dorothea Schlözer,[2] for example, the consensus was that women missed their true calling if they strived for formal knowledge and education. Pedagogical tracts attempted to confine women to the newly emerging domestic sphere, and advised parents to teach their daughters those skills that would make them better wives and mothers. As the eighteenth century gave way to the early nineteenth century and the Napoleonic Wars (1806–1814), women's education, particularly in the Protestant regions of Germany, was infused by nationalist sentiments and the economic needs of the emerging bourgeoisie.[3]

The educational tradition most frequently studied for nineteenth-century Germany is the one encapsulated by the bourgeois Woman's Movement founded in 1865 by Louise Otto-Peters and Auguste Schmidt. The goals of the movement were educational opportunities for girls and professional and (limited) job opportunities for unmarried women and widows. Yet these middle class educators never seriously questioned the separation of men and women into a public/male and domestic/female sphere, but rather sought to elevate the domestic sphere in public appreciation.

The focus of this chapter will be on an educational tradition that was erased by the German Woman's Movement and its focus on the middle classes. In 1810, the Prussian aristocrat Caroline de la Motte Fouqué (1773-1831) published a comprehensive social and political theory that focused not on women's roles in the bourgeois family (or a version thereof in the public sphere), but on women's fundamentally indispensable functions in the state. Basing her arguments on Romantic philosophy and Enlightenment political theory that drew analogies between the state and the family, Fouqué imbued the role of the mother with far-reaching civic and political duties. In Fouqué's theory, the welfare of the state was no longer dependent solely on the royal father figure, but equally dependent on the mother. Women's education, therefore, was of utmost importance to Fouqué, since women required training to fulfill their divinely ordained functions in the social sphere where opinions about public matters were shaped. For this reason, Fouqué thought little of educating women in the skills necessary to run a bourgeois household; rather, as the title of her second pedagogical tract stated, women needed to be trained for "society" ("die grosse Welt"). In doing so, Fouqué fused two models of aristocratic femininity—the mistress of a feudal household (most often found on a country estate) and the highly educated, politically savvy female salonière of the ancient régime—to create a woman who moved equally well in the public and the domestic sphere. In Fouqué's theory, this woman was tasked with creating a public sphere where the political will of (educated) men and women would be articulated. Fouqué's idealist political vision was soon set aside by social, political, and economic developments that displaced the educated salonière in favor of the more domestic bourgeois mother and wife.[4] Educational models, as the one proposed by Fouqué, point, however, to the multiplicity of gendered discourses in circulation at the time.

After a brief overview over of the most common ideas on women's education in circulation around 1800, the chapter will focus on Betty Gleim and Caroline Fouqué, two radically different, yet equally outspoken proponents of women's education. Gleim, a middle class woman from Bremen, was arguably the most important pedagogue in the early nineteenth century, while Caroline de la Motte Fouqué is mostly known for her marriage to famous writer Friedrich de la Motte Fouqué.[5] The main points in this essay are that, from the beginning, there were a number of differing views among the German cultural elite about the scope of women's education. Second, citizenship and female education were fused in the views of early educators, a view from which the German Woman's Movement later retreated. Third, the displacement of women into a segregated domestic sphere was not universally supported, and the writings of *conservative* German women like Fouqué point to the fact that the emerging polarized gender stereotypes were interpreted in radically different ways.

In the late eighteenth century, three competing visions about the purposes of education were in conflict. One view, symbolized by Theodor Gottlieb von Hippel (1741-96), claimed that education was tasked with producing the rational citizen. In this view, woman's education was crucial, as she would, in turn, educate the next generation. This discourse, rooted in Enlightenment philosophy, held that gender differences were accidental and constructed, and accordingly Hippel wrote: "Citizens need to be educated for the state without regard to gender differences, and what women need to know as mothers and homemakers can be left to special instruction."[6] In her essay "Properties and Principles Necessary for Happiness in Marriage" (1791), Emilie Berlepsch also claimed that women should be educated for their very complex roles as wives and mothers.[7] Like Hippel, she de-emphasized women's biological functions in favor of intellectual and moral capacities, and women's essential rationality as human beings. Another, entirely utilitarian, approach was framed by Joachim Heinrich Campe, who did not dispute women's essential rationality nor did he question women's ability to be scholars, artists or writers. Rather, he (like the philanthropinists) argued that women's biology destined them for childbearing and household duties, and women needed to be educated for precisely these functions. A third group was focused exclusively on women's roles as mothers. The French Revolution, and later the Napoleonic Wars, had brought women's roles as mothers (and educators) of the nation to the fore, and women were made responsible for shaping the citizens of the emerging German nation.[8] Betty Gleim and Caroline de la Motte Fouqué belonged to this third view.

The redefinition of women as *mothers* was part of a fundamental restructuring of the sexual economy. No longer was sexual stratification based on brute force, rather the polarization of sexual characteristics was yoked to anthropological arguments. The chief architect of the new system of polar sexual stereotypes was Wilhelm von Humboldt, who argued against both utilitarian and civic approaches.[9] Rather, education was to serve the self-actualization of the (male) individual. Since self-actualization was gendered for Humboldt, women who were neither citizens nor truly human, could not participate in the educational enterprise on which Humboldt would later embark as the founder of Berlin's Humboldt University.[10] Accordingly, during his tenure at the educational administration of Prussia in 1809-1810, Humboldt made no provisions for girls' formal education beyond the elementary level.[11] As a consequence, William Rasch argues, advocating for female education would prove difficult for women, as their biology seemed to pre-dispose them against self-actualization and citizenship.

German women, nevertheless, turned to education in an effort to improve their social standing. In 1785, Karoline Rudolphi formed a girls' boarding school near Hamburg and, in 1807, she published her educational ideas as *Paintings of Female Education* [*Gemälde weiblicher Erziehung*].[12] Betty Gleim (1781-1821) followed with an educational treatise in 1810 in which she proposed a systematical approach to girls' education. Less sentimental than Rudolphi, Gleim passionately argued that girls were first and foremost human beings and as such, should be given the chance to develop their true human nature through education.

Gleim wavered between neo-humanist and enlightenment arguments. On the one hand, she claimed the neo-humanist discourse of Humboldt when she defined the purpose of education as a path to self-actualization and called for co-education.[13] On the other hand, she employed the utilitarian discourses of the eighteenth century when calling for women's education so that those women who did not find husbands and widows would not become a burden on their families. Although she suggested a broad curriculum for girls that included languages, mathematics, the natural sciences and physical education, she emphasized that particular attention should be paid to women's vocation as wives and mothers.

Like Humboldt, Gleim's concern was for the growing civil servant class. Gleim's educational plans were explicitly tailored to the needs of this quickly expanding segment of society. Educated men needed wives who could run their homes with intelligence, self-sufficiency, and financial savvy. These wives, stepping onto the stage of public leisure that had earlier been reserved for the aristocracy, needed to be able to participate in the social life of their home towns, educate their children, and help their husbands form strategic alliances while keeping the family's often limited finances sound.[14] For this reason, Gleim incorporated a healthy lifestyle, cooking, and accounting into an essentially humanist curriculum, and demanded professional choices for the many unmarried and widowed women who had become a burden on the nuclear families of the civil servant class.[15]

The most important aspect of Gleim's educational plan for women consisted in her recognition of women as citizens. The Napoleonic occupation of large parts of Germany between 1806 and 1812 had helped Germans think about the home front and the duties of all citizens to the state, and Gleim specifically addresses the need for women to instill nationalist sentiment in children.[16]

Caroline de la Motte Fouqué argued from a radically different angle in her pedagogical text *Letters about the purpose and the direction of female education* [*Briefe über Zweck und Richtung weiblicher Bildung*] (1810). While earlier texts (Berlepsch, Hippel) had argued for women's universal humanity, and Gleim sought to straddle the gulf between utility and self-actualization, Fouqué insisted on women's fundamental biological and mental difference from men. Like the idealist philosophers, she argued that woman was not only *determined* by nature, but woman herself *was* nature. Like nature, woman was able to unite polar opposites, and create harmony and love from chaos and strife.[17] Giving the ruling gender ideology a new twist, Fouqué turned Humboldt's definitions of gender polarity into a shield that protected women against confinement within a limited sphere of activity. In effect, Fouqué argued that woman's vocation, her "Bestimmung," did not need to be reinforced through training as so many other educators had argued. Rather, Fouqué claimed that nothing could be alien to nature, and since woman was nature, nothing should be alien to her. For this reason, there was no reason to exclude women from any field of knowledge:

> Why should beings, sublime enough to understand nature intuitively, destined to gather the many human endeavors into a common focus, into the heart of a closed entity, into the center of a family circle, why should they, by necessity, turn away from that which has been painstakingly researched or created by intuition.[18]

Based on women's divine roles as embodiment of nature, the acquisition of knowledge was imperative for Fouqué. Accordingly, she argued that women needed to interrupt their household duties for regular hours of study and contemplation, because women lagged so far behind men in general knowledge.[19]

Women's inferior education was of particular concern to Fouqué and she returned to this point repeatedly. In an article from 1812, "A word of warning" ["Ein Wort der Warnung"] she called the overall dismal education of young girls a "hodgepodge of modern methods superficial enough to evaporate immediately." She argued that girls did not learn to sharpen their wits, which resulted in ill-conceived marriages and unhappy women forced to renounce their best qualities,[20] a concern Betty Gleim shared.[21] Most important for Fouqué (and also for Gleim) was that the absence of education for girls produced young wives and mothers unable to interact socially, or take charge of their families and their lives.[22] Keeping women in ignorance, then, Fouqué declared, jeopardized the very foundation of the state: the family. What was worse, women retreated from the sphere of sociability owing to their limited understanding of civic matters and deprived the state of their particular insights.[23] In "A word of warning" and "Call to Germany's women" ["Ruf an die deutschen Frauen"] (1813), Fouqué argued that the lack of education for women had contributed directly to Napoleon's military victory over Prussia in 1806 and the fall of the Holy Roman Empire in the same year.

At this point, it is necessary to define more clearly, what "family" connoted in the early nineteenth century as it is one of the key terms in Fouqué's philosophical frame. Around 1800, various interpretations of "family" co-existed, yet had in common that family always meant a patriarchal arrangement with a beloved, yet feared father at its helm. Sometimes a family was conterminous with a household, meaning that a (sometimes extended) kin group shared a dwelling. A family could, however, also mean a dynasty or a (blood) lineage most often in the context of an "important" or "illustrious" family. In political theory, Enlightenment thinkers used the family to draw analogies between political absolutism and familial patriarchy and compared the absolute ruler to the father, and his subjects to children.[24] In contrast, Jean Jacques Rousseau posited the family as the opposite to the state, a natural and uncorrupted refuge in a politically and morally corrupt world.[25] Rousseau's glorification of the family as a social space untouched by political and moral corruption gained prominence with the French Revolution and elevated the roles of bourgeois women whose functions as mothers were tied ever more tightly to the domestic sphere.

Fouqué yoked family, education, and female citizenship together in a radical way. Drawing on various theoretical strands, she argued that women were the center of a family circle that went far beyond the domestic sphere to include extended social circles: "Inside [the family circle] is the world, our nation, honor, and women's sublime activities."[26] In the same vein, aristocratic women were at the center of more public families that might include the court, as in the case of the queen. In her thinking, Fouqué differed significantly from bourgeois educators, male and female, for whom citizenship and political participation did not become a universal demand (for males at least) until the revolution of 1848/49. Many looked at politics as the prerogative of a Francophile aristocracy that was to be avoided by God fearing German men and women.[27] Caroline Fouqué, in contrast, argued as a member of the Prussian aristocracy who had (limited) access to the Prussian political center in Berlin, and this background allowed her to think of the public sphere as the sphere of sociability and locate it inside the family. It was there, under the direction of educated women, where members of the cultural elite would come together to form consensus and express their political will.[28] Employing the "family" as the location of the public sphere allowed Fouqué to combine the new ideologies of complementary gender attributes with a traditional political system.

For women to fulfill their important functions, Fouqué suggested co-education.[29] This would allow girls to partake in the educational advantages enjoyed by boys. More importantly, it would teach girls to develop the self-esteem, and sense of identity and confidence she saw in boys.[30] As a focus of female study, Fouqué suggested the environment (encapsulated in fields such as astronomy, geography, and history) and taught in such a way that internal connections between the various fields would become apparent.[31] Overall, Fouqué argued that the difference between the two genders should not be in their *access* to the outside world, but in the way each *processed* this world. While man's path led him to focused study of one or two individual disciplines, woman's vocation led her to understand all of nature by intuition, or in Fouqué's words, through sensibility.

While Gleim had worked out a complex curriculum that included a detailed list of "feminine" subjects (needlework, accounting, cooking), Fouqué remained more abstract and theoretical in her text. Although she included cooking in her curriculum, it would be used to teach girls chemistry, herbology, and even medicine.[32] Beginning with the tangible, Fouqué suggested, allowed girls to acquire empirical knowledge without the need for the type of university-level education that was unavailable to them.

Like Gleim, Fouqué rejected women scientists and artists. She called such women unhappy hybrids, who violated nature's preordained order. Such singular pursuits took women away from tasks Fouqué considered more important, such as their roles as mothers. And, indeed, Fouqué's pedagogical text culminated in the assertion that woman's true vocation lay in her role as mother. This exclusive focus on the mother imploded the traditional dichotomous gender system on which Humboldt's gender theories were predicated, and, in her theory, Fouqué replaced the male-female dyad with the mother-child dyad. Toward that end of *Letters about the purpose and the direction of female education*, she wrote,

> It is certain mothers must be compared to that Indian tree that drops its branches to the ground to form new roots. These new saplings remain interdependent on the mother tree and in turn, give strength to the mother tree as they receive energy back. This is the only way creation moves toward its purpose in nature.[33]

Fouqué envisioned a world structured by parthenogenesis where male influence and participation was entirely eradicated. The shaping of the world, i.e., the human condition, was the continual and exclusive task of women. Since *history* ("Geschichte") in the German language is related to fate ("Geschick"), the theoretical leap from women constructing the "world" to women making history was, therefore, a small one for Caroline Fouqué.[34]

This early pedagogical text was well received by critics and one reviewer recommended the text to his female readers as a lodestar for all women who sought to combine sense and sensibility.[35] Fouqué's insistence on love as woman's true nature dovetailed well with the bourgeois gender ideology of separate spheres. During the next fifteen years Fouqué took seriously the role for woman in the public sphere as she had outlined in *Letters*. She attempted to influence the fate of her native Prussia by publishing political pamphlets against Napoleon, blueprints for the reorganization of the Prussian state in the post-war era, novels about the French Revolution, and a large number of historical novels that featured educated, independent women characters. In 1826 Fouqué returned to the topic of female education. Deeply disappointed with the level of public life in Prussia, she published an instructional manual entitled *The Women of High Society. An Instructional Manual for Those Entering the Sphere of Sociability* [*Die Frauen in der großen Welt. Bildungsbuch beim Eintritt in das gesellige Leben*]. While earlier Fouqué had warned against the scholarly inclined "blue-stocking"—one of the two types of miseducated women in contemporary literature—this manual sought to rehabilitate the other type of miseducated woman: the salonière.³⁶ The book educated the women of the upper classes on becoming the centers of their social circles in order to acculturate men who were rapidly assuming the roles of gatekeepers to the public sphere. Throughout the manual, she challenged the middle class view that the public sphere should be reserved exclusively for male discourse. With her customary dry wit she wrote,

> In fact, I do not observe that reasoning over coffee goes any deeper than reasoning over tea, or that emotions are stronger, thoughts are more determined, and wishes are more particular at a fair or a casino-ball in the provinces than in the opera or at court.³⁷

In this passage, male (coffee) and female (tea) forms of sociability are equated as are bourgeois (fair) and aristocratic (court) venues, and they are deemed equally lacking. Fouqué proposed instead that all women must assume leadership roles in their social circles in order to raise the general civic spirit. Overall, the manual is a testimony to Fouqué's distrust of the new bourgeois morality that removed the bourgeois daughters from the public sphere and she argued that public life (and implicitly the state) would do better if women were given the necessary skills to navigate the public realm successfully.

The manual abandoned all claims to self-actualization in the neo-humanist tradition of Humboldt. Rather the text is part social analysis, part training manual for women as indicated by its title "Bildungsbuch" ("training manual"). For Fouqué, there was no need to "awaken, develop, and shape the individual faculties of the child" as Gleim had demanded,³⁸ because nature had already given women a unique insight into those faculties. Rather woman's purpose was clear: since humans were social beings, women were to be the mistresses of this social sphere and bring together the disparate interests of men so that a cohesive civic spirit could emerge.³⁹ Accordingly, the manual begins by postulating that identity is constructed discursively.⁴⁰ Individual and national identities are, therefore, best formed in the capital where different outlooks must necessarily compete.⁴¹ The lack of social interaction, in contrast, leads to inertia, apathy, and political ossification. The text rejects the tenet that young women were corrupted in the urban centers where they came into contact with French ideas and manners, and Fouqué mocked as absurd the view that entire classes and genders were threatened by duties required from them by birth and social station.⁴²

The manual promoted only those skills that aided women in their roles as social engines. Academic subjects are no longer mentioned, and the arts are summarily dismissed. Earlier, Fouqué had advised against the reading of novels; here she recommended that women should read widely so that they expanded their limited horizons and learned about society.[43] Dancing was acceptable, while painting (as a solitary occupation) was not. Fouqué discouraged female friendships—these kept women away from the larger social circles—but encouraged inter-generational relationships between women so that historical memory could be preserved. The strategies employed by debutantes to snatch a husband are mocked, but friendships between men and women, in particular husbands and wives, are encouraged as the glue that will keep the social circle viable. Overall, Fouqué attempted to instill in her (female) readers the conviction that women were indispensable for a healthy public sphere, and that the latter was foundational to the state. State politics, she wrote, were no different than the negotiations in a social circle; in its original form, the politics of the monarch were nothing more than social interactions at the highest level.[44]

These later educational ideas were radically out of step with the ruling gender and class ideologies. Since the Napoleonic Wars, Prussia had concentrated on liberalizing its feudal economy without, however, modernizing the legal framework and allowing for a direct relationship between citizens and the state.[45] Fouqué's advocacy for a public sphere and her claim that women should play an important role in this space received a cool reception both from her bourgeois male reviewers and from the Prussian court. For the former, she embodied a reactionary political class that stood in the way of modernization, and for both, Fouqué overstepped the boundaries of gender in calling for a public role for educated women. Upon her death in 1831, the literary critic Varnhagen von Ense, an erstwhile friend, called her a female Don Quixote for misjudging the winds of change and adhering to her notions of enlightened absolutism and a feudal social system.[46] Varnhagen's assessment proved prophetic: Fouqué's educational ideas—her insistence on women's roles in the public sphere, her definition of family as an extended kinship group that ultimately included the monarch, and her claim that women's nature could not be contaminated by knowledge—did not have a lasting impact. Rather, women's education became subject to the bourgeois quest for (male) political representation and economic liberalism.

The officially sanctioned German historiography considers 1865 the beginning of the German Women's Movement. Although some scholars have pushed the beginning date back into the early 1840s,[47] the voices generally considered are mostly middle class.[48] In general, the German aristocracy is summarily dismissed as a reactionary force.[49] There is little awareness of the positions carved out by aristocratic women who subscribed to an essentially pre-modern life style far into the nineteenth century.[50] Texts such as those by Caroline de la Motte Fouqué point to the diversity of views on women's education and the nature of the public sphere. For thinkers like Fouqué, gender polarity provided the foundation for women's civic roles in the sphere of sociability, her critique of middle class values, and her appreciation of the family. Unapologetically, she claimed the public sphere and the realm of politics for educated upper class women in a way that would not be possible until the twentieth century for the daughters of the bourgeoisie.

Notes

[1] Georg Wilhelm Friedrich Hegel, *Philosophy of Right*, 144-45.

[2] Dorothea Christiane Erxleben, born Leoporin (1715-1762) was the first woman to receive a medical degree in Germany (1754), in *Allgemeine Deutsche Biographie* 6: 334-335. Dorothea von Rodde-Schlözer (1770-1825) received her doctorate from the University of Göttingen in 1787 in *Allgemeine Deutsche Biographie* 29: 1-2.

[3] James Albisetti argues that women's education was mainly a discourse in Protestant regions. Catholics did not see a need to redefine the role of women as they already had a long tradition of learned women in convents. Albisetti, *Schooling German Girls and Women*, 9.

[4] Compare Mary Jo Maynes who argues that the nineteenth century exalted middle class female domesticity "by economic change that split morality off from the economic realm, by technological change that enlarged workplaces and separated them from the home, and by political changes that elevated claims made about 'public life' and citizenship and made it important to set boundaries around who could participate in such supposedly universal public life and who was excluded." Maynes, "Class Cultures and Images of Proper Family Life," 202.

[5] Friedrich de la Motte Fouqué (1777-1843), a descendent of a famous Huguenot family, was the author of Romantic poetry, romances, novels, plays and epics. He is best known for the novella *Undine*.

[6] Theodor Gottlieb Hippel, *Über die bürgerliche Verbesserung der Weiber*, 133. All translations, unless otherwise noted, are mine.

[7] Emilie Berlepsch, "Über einige zum Glück der Ehe nothwenige Eigenschaften und Grundsätze," 101.

[8] Maria Blochmann, *"Laß dich gelüsten nach der Männer Weisheit und Bildung." Frauenbildung als Emanzipationsgelüste 1800-1918*, 12.

[9] Two influential articles on sexual difference were published in 1794 and 1795 by Humboldt. Wilhelm von Humboldt, "Über den Geschlechtsunterschied und desssen Einfluss auf die organische Natur," in *Wilhem von Humboldt: Werke*, I: 268-95; Wilhelm von Humboldt, "Über die männliche und weibliche Form," in *Wilhem von Humboldt: Werke*, I: 296-337.

[10] William Rasch, "Mensch, Bürger, Weib: Gender and the Limitations of Late 18th-Century Neohumanist Discourse," 27.

[11] Albisetti, *Schooling German Girls and Women*, 15.

[12] For information on Karoline Rudolphi (1754-1811), see Carl Wilhelm Otto August von Schindel, *Die deutschen Schrifstellerinnen des 19. Jahrhunderts*, 228-34.

[13] Betty Gleim, *Erziehung und Unterricht des weiblichen Geschlechts. Ein Buch für Eltern und Erzieher*, II: 5-142.

[14] Gleim, *Erziehung und Unterricht*, I: 97-100. See also Maynes, "Class Cultures and Images of Proper Family Life," 218 and Sibylle Meyer, "The Tiresome Work of Conspicuous Leisure: Duties of the Wives of Civil Servants in the German Empire (1871-1818)," 156-65.

[15] Gleim, *Erziehung und Unterricht*, I: 78. The often-insufficient salaries of the husband/provider prevented many families from taking in destitute relatives as had been possible in the agrarian household where additional labor was always needed. See David Kertzer, "Living with Kin," 40-72.

[16] Gleim, *Erziehung und Unterricht*, I: 5 and I: 7. On the home front, see Karen Hagemann, "Heldenmütter, Kriegerbräute und Amazonen. Entwürfe, patriotischer' Weiblichkeit zur Zeit der Freiheitskriege," 195

[17] Caroline de la Motte Fouqué, *Briefe über Zweck und Richtung weiblicher Bildung*, 9.

[18] "Wie sollten Wesen, erhaben genug, die unmittelbaren Eingebungen der Natur zu verstehen, ausersehen, die mannigfachen Strebungen der Menschen in einen gemeinsamen Brennpunkt, in das Herz eines geschlossenen Ganzen, in das Innere eines Familienkreises, zusammen zu ziehn, wie sollten diese sich von dem notwendig abwenden müssen, was Menschen mühselig erforschen, oder ebenfalls durch höhere Eingebung erzeugt haben," Fouqué, *Briefe*, 13-14.

[19] Fouqué, *Briefe*, 79.

[20] Fouqué, "Ein Wort der Warnung," 1343.

[21] Gleim, *Erziehung und Unterricht*, I: 103.

[22] Fouqué, "Ein Wort der Warnung," 1350.

[23] In contrast, Gleim rejected women's entry into the public sphere categorically. However, in my opinion, this rejection was equally based on gender prescriptions as on bourgeois notions that the public sphere contaminated the independent middle class citizen. Gleim's goal for women was, ultimately, independence. Gleim, *Erziehung und Unterricht*, I: 104.

[24] Bengt Sørensen, *Herrschaft und Zärtlichkeit*, 48.

[25] Sørensen, *Herrschaft und Zärtlichkeit*, 55-57.

[26] "Innerhalb [des Familienkreises] liegt die Welt, das Vaterland, die Ehre, wie die erhabenste Wirksamkeit der Frauen," Fouqué, *Briefe*, 97.

[27] See, for example, Amalie von Helvig, who exhorted men to fight against the French occupation only to return to an apolitical domestic sphere.

[28] For a definition of the public sphere, see Jürgen Habermas, "The Public Sphere," 49.

[29] Co-education of boys and girls often happened informally in the Enlightenment household where sisters shared in the instruction of their brothers. Johann Heinrich Pestalozzi (1746-1827) was one of the first to champion the concept in his school in Burgdorf. See Gleim's discussion of Pestalozzi, II: 5; 14-35. See also the German philosopher Fichte who advocated co-education in his *Reden an die deutsche Nation*.

[30] Fouqué, "Ein Wort der Warnung," 1349.

[31] Fouqué, *Briefe*, 104.

[32] Fouqué, *Briefe*, 100-01.

[33] "Es ist gewiß, eine Mutter ist jenem indischen Baume zu vergleichen, der seine Zweige wieder in die Erde senkt und darin Wurzeln fassen läßt, damit sie als selbständige Wesen, in steter Wechselwirkung mit dem alten Stamme, diesem neuen Kräfte geben und die seinen zurückempfangen mögen. So nur geht die Bildung der Welt fortschreitend ihrem Ziel entgegen," Fouqué, *Briefe*, 114.

[34] "Geschick," see Grimm, *Deutsches Wörterbuch*, 5: 3870-74.

[35] *Zeitung für die elegante Welt* 227 (1810): 1801-02.

[36] Albisetti, *Schooling German Girls and Women*, 11.

[37] "Allein, ich sehe doch auch nicht, daß die Raisonnements am Kaffeetisch tiefer gingen, als die am Theetisch, eben so, daß die Gefühle kräftiger, die Gedanken concentrierter, daß Wollen bestimmter sei auf einem Kirmeßfest oder einem Cassino-Ball (sic) in der Provinz, als in Opern und Schloßsälen," Fouqué, *Die Frauen in der großen Welt*, 17-18.

[38] Gleim, *Erziehung und Unterricht*, I: 8.

[39] Fouqué, *Frauen*, 162-65 and 186.

[40] Fouqué, *Frauen*, 9.

[41] Fouqué, *Frauen*, 10.

[42] Fouqué, *Frauen*, 12-13.

[43] Fouqué, *Frauen*, 72-73. Susanne Barth argues that Fouqué is one of the few writers who demanded freedom in the choice of reading materials for girls. Barth, *Mädchenlektüren. Lesediskurse im 18. und 19. Jahrhundert*, 139.

[44] Fouqué, *Frauen*, 106.

[45] Reinhart Koselleck, *Staat und Gesellschaft in Preußen, 1815-1848*, 78.

[46] Varnhagen von Ense, *Biographische Porträts*, 123-24.

[47] See Renate Möhrmann, "Vorwort," *Frauenemanzipation im deutschen Vormärz*, 9.

[48] Möhrmann and Maynes are clearly aware that they are describing women's emancipation from a bourgeois point of view and deplore the scarcity of proletarian texts and artifacts for the first half of the nineteenth century.

[49] See, for example, Wolfram Siemann, *Vom Staatenbund zum Nationalstaat. Deutschland 1806-1871*.

[50] For a description of aristocratic life style choices, see Christa Diemel, *Adelige Frauen im bürgerlichen Jahrhundert*.

Works Cited

Primary Sources

Fouqué, Caroline de la Motte. *Briefe über Zweck und Richtung weiblicher Bildung*. Berlin: Hitzig, 1810.

—. "Ein Wort der Warnung," *Zeitung für die elegante Welt* 168/169 (1812): 1339.

—. *Ruf an die deutschen Frauen. Die Einnahmen zum patriotischen Zwecke*. Berlin: Julius Hitzig, 1813.

—. *Edmund's Wege und Irrwege. Ein Roman aus der nächsten Vergangenheit*. Leipzig: Gerhard Fleischer der Jüngere, 1815.

—. *Die Frauen in der großen Welt. Bildungsbuch beim Eintritt in das gesellige Leben*. Berlin: Schlesinger's Buch- und Musikhandlung, 1826.

Gleim, Betty. *Erziehung und Unterricht des weiblichen Geschlechts. Ein Buch für Eltern und Erzieher*. Leipzig, G.J. Göschen, 1810.

Secondary Sources

Albisetti, James. *Schooling German Girls and Women*. Princeton: Princeton University Press, 1988.

Allgemeine Deutsche Biographie, ed. Historic commission of the Bavarian academy of sciences and the Bavarian state library. http://mdz1.bib-bvb.de/~ndb/adb_index.html.

Bath, Susanne. *Mädchenlektüren. Lesediskurse im 18. und 19. Jahrhundert*. Frankfurt: Campus, 2002.

Berlepsch, Emilie. "Über einige zum Glück der Ehe nothwenige Eigenschaften und Grundsätze." *Neuer Teutscher Merkur* 2 (1791): 63-102.

Blochmann, Maria W. *'Laß dich gelüsten nach der Männer Weisheit und Bildung.' Frauenbildung als Emanzipationsgelüste 1800-1918*. Pfaffenweiler: Centaurus, 1990.

Campe, Joachim Heinrich. *Vätherlicher Rath für meine Tocher. Ein Gegenstück zum Theophron*. Edited by Ruth Bleckwenn. Reprint of 1796 edition. Paderborn: M. Hüttemann, 1988.

Dawson, Ruth P. "The Feminist Manifesto of Theodor Gottlieb von Hippel (1741-96)." In *Amsterdamer Beitrage zur Neueren Germanistik*, 10: 13-32. Amsterdam: Rodopi, 1980.

Diemel, Christa. *Adelige Frauen im bürgerlichen Jahrhundert. Hofdamen, Stiftsdamen, Salondamen 1800-1870*. Frankfurt am Main: Fischer, 1998.
Fichte, Johann Gottlieb. *Reden an die deutsche Nation*. Osnabrück. Edition Simile, 1973.
Habermas, Jürgen. "The Public Sphere." *New German Critique* 3 (1974): 49-55.
Hagemann, Karen. "Heldenmütter, Kriegerbräute und Amazonen. Entwürfe, patriotischer' Weiblichkeit zur Zeit der Freiheitskriege." In *Militär und Gesellschaft im 19. und 20. Jahrhundert,* ed. Ute Frevert, 174-200. Stuttgart: Klett-Cotta, 1997.
Hegel, Georg Wilhelm Friedrich. *Philosophy of Right*. Transl. S. W. Dryde. Kitchener: Batoche Books, 2001.
Helvig, Anna Amalie von. *An Deutschlands Frauen von einer ihrer Schwestern*. Leipzig: Vogel, 1814.
Hippel, Theodor Gottlieb von. *Über die bürgerliche Verbesserung der Weiber* [1793]. Frankfurt am Main: Syndikat, 1977.
Humboldt, Wilhelm von. *Werke*. Edited by Klaus Giel and Andreas Flitner. Stuttgart: Cottasche Buchhandlung, 1960.
Jacob Grimm and Wilhelm Grimm, ed. *Deutsches Wörterbuch*.16 vols. Leipzig: S. Hirzel, 1854-1960.
Kertzer, David I. "Living with Kin." In *Family Life in the Long Nineteenth Century 1789-1913,* ed. David I. Kertzer and Marzio Barbagli, 40-72. New Haven: Yale University Press, 2002.
Koselleck, Reinhart. "Staat und Gesellschaft in Preußen, 1815-1848." In *Moderne deutsche Sozialgeschichte*, ed. Hans Ulrich Wehler, 55-84. Cologne: Kiepenheuer & Witsch, 1976.
Maynes, Mary Jo. "Class Cultures and Images of Proper Family Life." In *Family Life in the Long Nineteenth Century 1789-1913,* ed. David I. Kertzer and Marzio Barbagli, 195-226. New Haven: Yale University Press, 2002.
Meyer, Sibylle. "The Tiresome Work of Conspicuous Leisure: Duties of the Wives of Civil Servants in the German Empire (1871-1818)." In *Connecting Spheres: Women in the Western World, 1500 to the Present*, ed. Jean H. Quataert and Marilyn J. Boxer, 185-193. New York: Oxford University Press, 1987.
Möhrmann, Renate, ed. *Frauenemanzipation im deutschen Vormärz. Texte und Dokumente*. Stuttgart: Reclam, 1978.

Müller, Adam. *Die Elemente der Staatskunst. Sechsunddreißig Vorlesungen.* Berlin: Haude & Spenersche Verlagsbuchhandlung, 1808-1809.

Nave-Harz, Rosemarie. *Die Geschichte der Frauenbewegung in Deutschland.* Hannover: Bundeszentrale für politische Bildung, 1997.

Rasch, William. "Mensch, Bürger, Weib: Gender and the Limitations of Late 18th-Century Neohumanist Discourse." *German Quarterly* 66.1 (1993): 20-33.

Rudolphi, Karoline. *Gemälde weiblicher Erziehung.* Heidelberg: Mohr und Winter, 1815.

Schindel, Carl Wilhelm Otto August von. *Die deutschen Schrifstellerinnen des 19. Jahrhunderts.* Leipzig: Brockhaus, 1825.

Siemann, Wolfram. *Vom Staatenbund zum Nationalstaat. Deutschland 1806-1871.* Munich: Beck, 1995.

Sørensen, Bengt Algot. *Herrschaft und Zärtlichkeit.* Munich: Beck, 1984.

Varnhagen von Ense, Karl August. *Biographische Porträts.* Leipzig: Brockhaus, 1871.

Zeitung für die elegante Welt 227 (1810): 1801-1803.

Chapter Eight

The Education of a Young Creole: The Countess of Merlin's Memoirs

Claire Emilie Martin

Abandoned by her parents in 1789 to the care of her maternal great-grandmother, the young Cuban aristocrat María de las Mercedes de Santa Cruz y Montalvo, Condesa Merlin, found herself reunited with her family in Spain twelve years later. Her childhood, spent in the tropical paradise of the Spanish colony, became the "petite histoire" (to use Sylvia Molloy's term) of a Cuban Creole in search of an identity in her first autobiographical narrative *Mes douze premières années* published in 1831. The book became a huge success among the Parisian literary circles. Merlin's autobiography was indeed as exotic as the beautiful Creole author herself, by then an acclaimed "bel canto" artist and hostess to one of the most famed salons in Paris. The countess claimed among her friends George Sand, the Baron Rothschild, Rossini, the Count d'Orsay, Lord Palmerston, General Lafayette, Victor Hugo, Musset, Lamartine, Balzac and María Malibrán, among many others.[1] Assured of an interested readership eager for tales that dealt with the inner life, Merlin's first account of her childhood became a blueprint for the public act of writing her life in subsequent volumes. In these volumes, entitled *Souvenirs et Mémoires de Madame la Comtesse Merlin, publiés par elle meme*, (1836), she embedded the polemic about women's education and women's role in society stemming from the Enlightenment, and in particular, from the writings of Jean-Jacques Rousseau.

Shortly after leaving her beloved Cuba in 1801, in an excess of sentiment, Merlin exclaimed: "Especially Rousseau and his writings caused great turmoil in my head. The praise and even criticism I had heard about them inflamed my desire to know all of his works, and when I thought about my marriage, one of the greatest pleasures that I envisioned ensuing from it was the possibility to read *The New Heloïse* or the *Confessions*" (112).[2] The young Mercedes who had been denied an education because of her sex and the leniency of her carefree upbringing, looked upon marriage not so much as a romantic ideal of love fulfilled, but as a key to the library of the *philosophes*. Using this early and intriguing confession in her autobiographical *Mes douzes premières années*, I propose a fresh reading of Merlin's reconstruction of the self based on Rousseau's much debated theories on the education of women in his *Emile; ou de l'education* (1761) and *Julie; ou la nouvelle Héloïse* (1761). My contention is that the same ambiguities attributed to Rousseau's female characters and to his contemporary readers can be found in Merlin's textual autobiographical persona. I will explore then two aspects of the reconstruction of the self that capture this ambivalence in regards to book learning and women's access to formal education as well as the motivation of the development of women's intellect. Merlin will explore these issues within the retelling of the education she never fully received, and the rewriting of a motherless childhood associated with Rousseau's theories of women's education and the role of parents in the intellectual development of the child with particular attention to the relationship with the mother.

The Making of an Education

Resisting some of Rousseau's prescriptive notions on womanhood, the countess nevertheless embraced the ideal of marriage and maternity, but nonetheless she firmly protected her right to an education and the pursuit of a public and engaged intellectual and political persona. In her memoirs, Merlin dedicated dozens of pages to a historical overview of Napoleonic Spain and advanced a harsh and seemingly objective analysis of the mistakes committed by the Spanish crown. Clearly, she saw no limitations, no demarcation line separating the writing of the inner life and writing outside of the domestic sphere. In Merlin's view, an unfinished education and an obedient nature did not preclude incisive observations about the world. Women's intellectual curiosity and talents could and should not be confined to "feminine" endeavors.

Some forty years after the publication of Mary Wollstonescraft's *Vindication of the Rights of Woman (1792)* and *Maria or the Wrongs of Woman (1798)*, Merlin, in a reassuringly less radical manner and certainly less ambitious stance, advocates for the right of women like herself to earn a living through access to education. By then, women writers abounded, but the utopian society of equality for both men and women under the law that Wollstonecraft had fashioned in her *Vindication* was very much an unrealized dream.

From Wollstonecraft to Mme de Roland and Mme. D'Epinay, many educated women endured an uneasy relationship with Rousseau's writings and stance on women's position in society. They alternately admired his understanding of the female soul and despised his most strident misogynistic tendencies. Mary Seidman Trouille, in *Sexual Politics* explains this unsettling tension:

> Even if their views on women and their political and literary activities seem incompatible with Rousseau's sexual politics (as in the case of Staël, Wollstonecraft, and Roland), his women readers still identified with him and with the characters of his novels because they expressed, on an existential level, their deepest aspirations and longings—for ideal love, self-fulfilling motherhood, and domestic felicity. In an age of loveless marriages and widespread adultery, they saw Rousseau as the champion of a new moral order in which women could play a central role. By nursing their babies themselves (instead of sending them away to wet-nurses, as had long been the custom), by devoting themselves to their husbands and children and to domestic and charitable tasks, they hoped to create stronger affective ties within their families, thereby fostering the moral regeneration of society envisioned by Rousseau and by other moral reformers of the period. Far from being considered a trap, the ideals of motherhood and enlightened domesticity advocated by Rousseau seemed to offer a new dignity to women, regardless of their socio-economic status.[3]

The dialogue among critics about the nature of Rousseau's thought and relationship to women will not be silenced any time soon as it fuels the intense debate on the eighteenth-century construction of womanhood viewed through the lens of XXI century feminist thought.[4] These ever-evolving views on the nature and destiny of woman in Rousseauean thought provide a fecund theoretical underpinning to the exploration of Mercedes Merlin's reconstruction of the self. As we shall see, she neither wholly succumbed to the idealized version of womanhood nor was she duped by the trappings of gallant salon society. Rather, Mercedes Merlin successfully transposed her feelings into her narrative making good use of her enlightened intellectual prowess in an intense battle to gain selfhood. She remained aware of her initial lack of education but over came her intellectual shortcomings by hosting the most brilliant minds of the time in her salon. In her writings, she honed her skills as an astute observer and a sentimental writer in line with the literary fashion of the time and the works of her admired Rousseau.

A Cuban Childhood

Paradise, the locus of unfettered freedom and lazy pleasures was found in Merlin's great-grandmother's home. In this literal garden, Mercedes spent her first eleven years in a state of absolute innocence brought to an end by her father's unexpected return. Before her departure for Spain, the young Mercedes described her life in the following terms: "Life went on sweetly, but in complete indolence. I found myself without guidance and always surrounded by society. I did not learn anything and I hardly knew how to write ... I was not inclined to studying and nobody had tried to instill in me this talent. But I wanted to learn, and in spite of a lack of formal education, I observed everything around me."[5] Young Mercedes was afforded the "natural" environment that led: "to the cultivation of the native propensities of the human being... The role of education is to provide the best possible conditions for permitting the innate propensity to filter through, to express itself and develop."[6] Whether this autobiographical interpretation of her first years' lack of education derives from her later acquaintance with Rousseau's writings or with a "natural" disposition from within her colonial milieu, it's difficult to ascertain. However, her reminiscing about her first few years fits perfectly with what Rousseau called the "The Age of Nature" (the second stage from two to ten or twelve). During this stage children receive "negative education" that fosters the development of physical qualities and the five senses not the mind left undisturbed until later.

Mercedes' father, described in terms of his extreme youth and lack of parental discernment, (definitely not tutor material in Rousseauean terms) decided to marry her in Cuba to avoid taking her to Europe and to a life in which she would certainly need some resemblance of an education. Thus, marriage in the context of America is identified with ignorance or, more appropriately, with the rejection of a useless education in the context of the natural environment that represents the colony. However, Merlin's apparent acceptance of her father's plan ran against her own feelings: "My precocious and ardent imagination was already in flight towards the unknown; I felt tormented by the desire to learn, and I arrived at the conclusion that the active faculties of my soul were in prompt need of development."[7] Education (even the most cursory one) was dependent on her role as future spouse and mother. In her study of *Emile*, Helen Evans Misenheimer notes that Rousseau: "obviously feels that in Sophie he has formed emotionally, physically, and morally the perfect feminine counterpart for his beloved Emile. Sophie is intellectually satisfactory, morally adjusted and physically fit. She is sexually eager while modestly restrained."[8] In a much-cited passage, Rousseau falters: "I wanted to paint an ordinary woman, and by means of elevating her soul I have troubled her reason; I have lost my way. Let us retrace our path. Sophie has only a natural goodness in an ordinary soul; all that she possesses more than others is the result of her education."[9] Of course, the vexatious problem is that Sophie is a literary construction, and the women who read Rousseau were flesh and blood, endowed in many instances of extraordinary talents and "innate propensities" that begged to be nurtured. Like many of those women readers and admirers of Rousseau, Merlin decided that she was ready to receive the instruction denied her and so she sought it herself as an act of rebellion and defiance that betrayed the dominant role that her emotions and feelings exerted upon her. She thus embraced the pre-romantic credo espoused by Rousseau in his *Confessions* that "Feeling always came before thought with me," but nevertheless explored the intellectual opportunities afforded to her.[10]

Later on in the narrative, Merlin suffered a second abandonment when she was taken to the convent and all communication with her family was interrupted and even forbidden as a punishment for her actions and to keep inopportune thoughts at bay regarding her imminent voyage to Europe.[11] Mercedes escaped a few days later with the help of a young nun who would become the subject of the second part of the first narrative entitled "The story of Sor Inés." Like Fénelon and Diderot, Rousseau pronounced himself against convent education for girls since it separated them from their families and a moral education at home from enlightened parents.[12] The countess rendered a devastating criticism of conventual life and in her cell, Merlin faced for the first time in her young life the absence of physical freedom in addition to the deprivation of her solitary communion with the American nature, the place where her meager learning had mainly occurred.

Once in Spain, in a passage highly charged with her identity as a Creole, Merlin compares the Andalusian winter to her native land: "...I sighed thinking about that virgin and powerful vegetation, whose rich profusion continuously renews itself without effort. Many times, during my play time, I entertained myself by doing experiments and scattering on the soil all sorts of seeds to find that they had germinated the following day."[13] Cuba, her garden and her great-grandmother, Mamita, represented for the older Mercedes the site of youthful experimentation and observation, of instruction without tutors, of physical freedom, of unconditional love and happiness. The voyage to Europe signified the violent rupture with that childhood in a way echoing Rousseau's own remembrance of that fateful incident with Mlle Lambercier when he was eleven: "Thus came to an end the peaceful calm of my early life. From that time I ceased to enjoy a simple happiness, and even today I feel that the memory of childhood's charms stops here."[14]

Spain, where her biological mother resided, became a surrogate mother and learning took the aspect of a chore. Only the discovery of her mother's library produced an intellectual awakening: "...we were allowed to read a great number of novels, such as those by Richardson, Mme. de Genlis, Mme. de Staël, &,&. For a while, I was undecided between my enthusiasm for the Greeks and the Romans, and the vivid interest that Delfine, Corine [sic] and Malek-Adel inspired in me."[15] The selection of books bore an uncanny resemblance to Rousseau's: first his mother's romances that he devoured with his father, and then, his paternal library filled with the classics. In his *Confessions*, Rousseau reminisced: "My thoughts were constantly occupied with Rome and Athens. I might almost say that I lived with their great men."[16]

Certain books had been forbidden, but the young Mercedes was inescapably attracted to them: "I directed my quick steps towards the shelves where I would find the books I was looking for, without daring to even glance to the place where the works that I truly coveted were; and if per chance my indiscreet hand touched them, an involuntary terror made me retreat it as if I had touched upon a burning piece of coal."[17] Knowledge burns the unsuspecting hands, not yet prepared to receive their often-troubling message. It is in this context that Mercedes Merlin evoked Rousseau and his absolute hold on her imagination in the quote mentioned at the beginning of this article.[18]

Mary Seidman Trouille, among many others, is highly critical of Rousseau's stance on the education of women. She remarks that for Rousseau,

[W]omen were generally far inferior to men in intellectual and creative potential and so should not attempt to emulate them in their studies or in their literary and artistic endeavors. Since the roles and intellectual capabilities of the two sexes were in his view so different, he opposed coeducation, as well as the use of the same program of studies for girls and boys. In *Emile*, he argued that the education of girls should be geared toward practical, domestic matters, because such training best prepared them for their future role as housewives and because girls were (in his view) less capable than boys of abstract thought. Although he conceded that 'the art of reflection is not totally foreign to women,' he insisted that 'they should have but a cursory introduction to the analytical sciences' (IV: 791)."[19]

To follow the prescriptive model of a girl's education, a young girl had to avoid novels on the basis of their corrupting values and the "false romantic illusions" they encouraged in their unformed minds. At eighteen, Sophie had read only two books (Fénelon's *Telemaque* and a manual on household management). In contrast, at twelve, Merlin was reading the tragedies of Racine in the original French. Like Sophie, Merlin had "natural taste, artless talents, unschooled judgment".[20] On the other hand, Julie, in *Julie; où la Nouvelle Heloïse*, had a broader education guided by Saint-Preux which contradicted Rousseau's educational designs on the ideal woman, Sophie. Many critics have explained this apparent contradiction on the basis of the heroines' difference in social class. Merlin's education, I maintain, borrowed from both models as she sought to fulfill her life in blissful domesticity without relinquishing the meaningful quest for knowledge.

A motherless childhood

As Mercedes grew into a young woman, her ambivalence about her role as a wife, mother, and *salonnière* was subtly displayed in her life story. The seemingly flattering portrait of her own mother, the aristocratic and distant Teresa Montalvo y O'Farrill, complicates the already richly textured mother-daughter plot. Like the "orphaned" Emile, Mercedes' childhood is marked by the physical and emotional absence of the mother. The maternal breast denied to her (her wet nurse was a slave) robbed Mercedes of the nurturing embrace and the nourishing milk she evidently felt entitled to and that remained beyond her textual reach.

Mercedes' loss of her parents and in particular, her mother was not felt in all of its amplitude until much later, and would become a determining factor in her education and her life choices. Again, the mother's absence (the great-grandmother takes her place) not only influences the education she was to receive as befitting a girl of her class at the end of the XVIII century, but also made of her a pariah and a rebel, a dutiful daughter and a free-spirited artist.

Teresa Montavo y O'Farrill embodied the woman Rousseau wrote against and exhibited all the prejudices and conventions of her class. Mercedes subtly hinted at her disappointment when she was finally reunited with her mother. Just before the awaited meeting, her father concocted a cruel charade to test his wife's maternal instinct by presenting her daughter among a group of young women. Fearing perhaps the failure of such a test, he desisted. Merlin assured the reader that her mother surely would have known in her heart that she was her daughter. She then added:

"Besides, my exterior was perhaps no better that the others; but I did not resemble anyone, and would have been betrayed, without doubt, by a certain native air, if I can explain it that way, that distinguished me from the other girls."[21] When she finally met her mother, she described her feelings as a sweet malady: "...I almost fainted: I reclined my head, and for the first time I felt the maternal breast."[22] Her mother's first acts were to identify her qualities and deficiencies in regards to the education befitting a young aristocratic woman: Mercedes could sing but her voice was untrained, she could write but had horrible calligraphy; her education lagged behind her younger brother and sister. The task of making this stranger a lady was given priority and it separated her once more from her mother due to the distance between her study rooms and the salons where her mother presided: "In isolating us thus, my mother had wanted to avoid all foreign influence in our moral education, and to preserve, while guiding us according to her conscience, an absolute mastery over our impressions."[23] In addition to her physical and emotional isolation from her mother, Teresa and all her entourage showed a marked preference for Mercedes' sister Paquita, plunging the young girl into long bouts of depression.

Her mother's presence is remarkably faint in the three volumes that constitute her memoirs. Teresa Montalvo's willing absence from her daughter's childhood illustrate the failure of the Rousseauean model of enlightened motherhood in emotional, moral and intellectual terms. Merlin herself would endeavor all her life to embody that model of motherhood that she so admired in Rousseau's writings. Mercedes referred plaintively to one of the few physical objects that remained after her mother's death, a portrait: "[S]he has disappeared. Nothing is left of her; and so many perfections, so many virtues have left on this earth not even the trace of tenuous colors on a piece of ivory!..."[24] Such a devastating assessment of the fleeting passage of her mother on earth, and obviously in her life, points to the undercurrent of filial conflict and regret that Merlin harbors towards the mother who abandoned her as an infant. However much she desired to conjure up her image in her memoirs, Teresa only was made concrete in one or two episodes closely linked to death retold as part of Mercedes' desperate attempts to bond with her mother. Surely the most pathetic instance occurred when Mercedes recounted how she saved her mother from a fiery death. Upon seeing her dress in flames she threw herself on top of her mother and extinguished the fire with her own body in an act of self immolation: "Merciful God! What had I done to deserve such joy?... From that day on, a new bond united me to my mother."[25] In spite of these assertions there is no textual evidence of such a rapprochement, and the reader is left wondering about the honesty implicit in the retelling of the past.

In the reinvention of her life story, Merlin erased the wound of the maternal desertion and applied the soothing balm of her great-grandmother's unconditional love. Over and over again in her narratives she's compelled to return to the natural, unspoiled and unschooled world of her paradise lost. The family portrait of "mamita," her surrogate mother, is heightened by the passing of time and the act of reinventing her life on paper. The love and harmony that surrounded these happy memories hid the painful betrayal of her parents' abandonment -which was supposed to last only six months and extended to twelve years. Mamita is seen through the veil of love, her wrinkles smoothed by the tears that Mercedes sheds while remembering her idyllic past in Cuba. Taken at face value, her reconstructed childhood pointed to a paradise where familial love and freedom reigned. Her recollection of childhood was shrouded in white gauze, literally and metaphorically. Her "mamita" wore only white and her hair was completely silver. Later on, in her encyclopedic *La Havane* (1844), Merlin would describe to her friend George Sand the women of Havana in the same chromatic terms: always dressed in flowing, nightgown –like, ethereal white dresses. "Mamita" and the women of Havana were infantilized through their dress in a perpetual state of childhood indolence that contrasted fiercely with the life of the "salonnière" that Merlin led in Paris during the 1820s, 30s and 40s.

The unnamed illness that ravaged Teresa while her daughter was pregnant with her first child provided the textual space on which to graft the resolution to the mother-daughter plot and the Rousseauan maxims of motherhood. Teresa Montalvo died just a few days before Mercedes gave birth to a baby girl after a difficult childbirth. When Mercedes emerged from her near death experience, she immediately demanded to breastfeed her child: "I wanted to feed her; but either because of my excessive youth or my nervous and excitable nature I was not able to fulfill this act and my child languished and I was slowly dying."[26] Unable to feed her daughter, she is repeatedly told by her doctor and her husband that she has to give up her dream for her baby's sake and hire a wet nurse: "No, never, never. I rather die! But I did not know what I wanted, poor madwoman, because I was going to let my daughter die!"[27] When the wet nurse finally arrived, the baby gorged on the plentiful milk, and the scene produced a torrent of tears in the mother who witnessed her daughter's happiness and satiation at another woman's breast. Even though it was never invoked, the absence of the maternal breast in Mercedes' life was painfully present in the scene reproducing the gnawing memory of the mother's abandonment.

As a child of her age seeped in her aristocratic roots, Mercedes Merlin naturally gravitated towards a more intellectually engaged life that would be fulfilled in her famous salon in the Rue de Bondy and in the writings that made her famous. Rousseau's works left on her as an author and a new woman a profound mark that helped fashion her reconstruction of the self, and in a strange way reconcile both visions of women portrayed by the author who had captured so vividly the aspirations and limitations of XVIII century women in his female characters Sophie and Julie.

Notes

[1] For the most extensive and fascinating book-length study of Merlin's works, see Adriana Méndez Rodenas' *Gender and Nationalism in Colonial Cuba*.

[2] All the translations from Merlin's works in the original French are mine.

[3] Seidman Trouille, *Sexual Politics*, 4. While exploring the literature dealing with Rousseau's overwhelming influence over his women readers, Helena Rosenblatt notes in her study on the author's misogyny: "We are encouraged [by some feminist critics] to assume that these women [Rousseau's readers] must have been reacting emotionally, and not rationally, to his writings…it is suggested, for example that rather than responding to Rousseau's thought with their intellects, women were "seduced" by the picture Rousseau drew of them in his novels" (95).

[4] Helena Rosenblatt cites Mira Morgenstern, Jean Bethke Elshtain, Lori Jo Marso, Gita May among those critics who have given a more nuanced view of Rousseau's much accepted misogyny.

[5] *Mémoires*, 78.

[6] Sahakian, 33. Interestingly, the same argument was made by Sor Juana Inés de la Cruz in 1690 when the Church forced her to give up her studies.

[7] *Mémoires*, 39.

[8] Mesenheimer, 57.

[9] As cited in Helen Evans Mesenheimer's study, 64.

[10] Boyd, *The Educational Theory*, 9.

[11] *Mémoires*, 49.

[12] Book V of *Emile; ou de l'education*.

[13] *Mémoires*, 100.

[14] Boyd 17.

[15] *Mémoires*, 110.

[16] Boyd, quoted in his *The Educational Theory*, 11.

[17] *Mémoires*, 111.

[18] How is the contemporary reader to harmonize the almost unstoppable desire for knowledge and reading in women such as Merlin, and the prescriptive views espoused by Rousseau? For a fascinating in-depth look at the influence of Rousseau on French women, see Mary Siedman Trouille's *Sexual Politics*.

[19] Seidman Trouille, *Sexual Politics*, 33-34.

[20] On the other hand, the education that Saint-Preux proposes for Julie is innovative and ambitious. He eliminates all language study except for Italian. Leaves only the French dramatists, and Tasso, Petrarch and Metastasio (Seidman Trouille 37).
[21] *Mémoires*, 101
[22] Ibid.,102.
[23] Ibid., 202.
[24] Ibid., 67.
[25] Ibid., 121.
[26] Ibid., 91.
[27] Ibid., 93.

Works Cited

Primary Sources

Merlin, Mercedes. *Mes douzes premières années*. Paris: Gautier-Laguionie, 1831.
—. *Souvenirs et Mémoires de Madame la Comtesse Merlin, publié pour elle- meme*. 3 Vol. Paris: Charpentier, Libraire-Editeur, 1836.
Rousseau, Jean-Jacques. *Emile; ou de l'education*. Translated by Barbara Foxley. London, New York, 1911/1993.
—. *Julie; ou la nouvelle Heloïse. Lettres de deux amants habitants d'une petite des Alpes recueillies et publiés par jean-Jacques Rousseau*. Intruduction, notes et variantes par René Bouneau. Paris: Garnier Frères, 1960.

Secondary Sources

Boyd, William. Selection and Translation. *The Educational Theory of Jean-Jacques Rousseau*. New York: Russel & Russell. 1963.
Hardt, Ulrich H. *A Critical Edition of Mary Wollestonecraft's A Vindication of Women's Rights: with Strictures on Political and Moral Subjects*. Troy, New York: Whitston Publishing Company, 1982.
Méndez Rodenas, Adriana. *Gender and Nationalism in Colonial Cuba. The Travels of Santa Cruz y Montalvo, Condesa de Merlin*. Nashville and London: Vanderbilt University Press, 1998.
Misenheimer, Helen Evans. *Rousseau on the Education of Women*. Washington, D.C.: University Press of America, 1981.
Molloy, Sylvia. *At Face Value. Autobiographical Writing in Spanish America*. Cambridge: Cambridge University Press, 1991.

Rosenblatt, Helena. "On the "Misogyny" of Jean-Jacques Rousseau: *The Letter to D'Alembert* in Historical Context." *The Society for French Historical Studies* 25:1 (2002) 91-114.

Sahakian, Mabel Lewis and William. *Rousseau as an Educator.* New York: Twayne Publishers, 1974.

Seidman Trouille, Mary. *Sexual Politics in the Enlightenment: Women Writers Read Rousseau.* Albany: State University of New York Press, c1997.

Wollstonecraft, Mary. *Maria or the Wrongs of Woman: A Posthumous Fragment.* Gary Kelly, Ed. London; New York: Oxford University Press, 1976.

Chapter Nine

The First Generation of German Female Students: Autobiographical Perspectives on the Contested Space of Gender and Knowledge

Magdalena Tarnawska

In this essay, I explore German middle-class women's intervention in the politics of gender and higher education at the end of the nineteenth and the beginning of the twentieth century. Specifically, I analyze memoirs of three of the first German female students: Franziska Tiburtius, Cläre Schubert-Feder, and Rahel Straus. These texts provide us with autobiographical accounts of the intervention in the contested space of gender and knowledge. I investigate how these women represented and creatively transformed their encounter with the academic world and focus on the strategies used by them in their struggle for acceptance and recognition as well as on questions pertaining to their self-understanding and identity in a time when some of the universities in Europe had only just begun to admit women, when female students still had a marginal presence in the academic world, and when women attempting to pursue higher education were generally considered to be less "feminine," to have doubtful character, and to demonstrate no adequate intellectual abilities.[1] The three autobiographical accounts that constitute the foundation of this essay reflect on the experiences of outsiders–female students who entered a domain that was unavailable to women for centuries and had to find their own way through the maze of this "masculine" world.[2] These women were crossing boundaries established for middle-class women by society and had to learn to face hostility, interact in the new environment, and develop strategies for dealing with the unknown. In this regard, these texts share many similarities. They all address such topics as relations among female and male students, interactions with faculty, academic accomplishments, and gendered norms of behavior at the university. Being aware of their unique position, the authors presented their own performance in a very positive way: as a challenge that they would meet through their intellect, diligence, thoroughness, and superior moral conduct. Because these women were successful in their pursuit of academic education, their autobiographical writings take on a gesture of having proven wrong the opponents of opening universities to women. In the introduction to her book *Dis/Closures. Women's Autobiography in Germany Between 1790 and 1914*, Katherine Goodmann argues that trying to understand women's autobiographies and memoirs from the past "is to observe them in the act of defining their lives in and for the culture in which they lived."[3] In the case of the texts discussed in this essay, their authors define their lives against the mainstream culture with its contempt for women attending universities. At the same time, they make their experiences accessible to the wider audience and demonstrate that female students should have their place in society.

Being written and published at different times as well as serving diverse goals, these three autobiographical accounts differ in modes of presentation, audience-awareness, and the amount of information revealed about the author and her life. Tiburtius[4] and Schubert-Feder[5] studied at the university in Zurich, the first European university to admit women on a regular basis in the late 1860s. Both women enrolled at the university during the very beginning of academic education for women, Tiburtius in 1871 and Schubert-Feder in 1878. Schubert-Feder published *The Life of Female Students in Zurich*[6] in the 1890s in order to introduce the reader to everyday lives of the first female students and to correct the general negative image of women who pursued higher education. Her intent determined, without a doubt, the content and style of her depictions, and of course, the details she decided to reveal or not to disclose. Although both the title of the pamphlet and her introduction indicate that the reader will gain a general insight into the lives of female students at the time of its publication in 1892 and 1893, the text is based on the author's personal experiences from 1878-1885, which she had generalized and presented as more or less universal. The pamphlet is not an autobiography per se, but contains a large number of autobiographical elements, which Schubert-Feder admits at the beginning of her text. Tiburtius wrote her autobiography, *Memoirs of an Eighty-Year-Old Woman*,[7] from a greater time perspective than Schubert-Feder, with the intent to portray the era in which she lived. She offered a much broader view of the political, social, and intellectual climate of the academic environment surrounding female students in the 1870s. Born into a Jewish family in Germany in 1880,

Straus[8] enrolled as the first woman at the university in Heidelberg in 1899.[9] She wrote her autobiography, *We lived in Germany. Memoirs of a German Jewish Woman 1880-1933*,[10] in Jerusalem in 1940 after successfully escaping the Nazi terror, because she decided to commemorate her family and to pass on her experiences to her children. It is clear that these women pursued various objectives while writing their accounts and must have emphasized or downplayed different elements of their lives as a result. Tiburtius and Straus, for example, could write much more openly and honestly than Schubert-Feder, whose primary goal was to counter the popular belief that higher education had negative effects on women's health and moral conduct and to persuade her audience that the opposite was true.

Without a doubt, Tiburtius, Schubert-Feder, and Straus were pioneers in higher education for women. As such, they faced similar challenges, with which they dealt by developing individual strategies[11] and, as such, they were aware of breaking new ground. Because both knowledge and its site of production–the university–were perceived as entirely male domains, the first female students disrupted the academic space by their presence and participation. They were perceived by men involved in the academic and professional life (fellow students, professors, and colleagues) as an unnecessarily disturbing element and were met in many cases with hostility and/or rejection, but also often with curiosity.[12] According to the accounts analyzed in this essay, hostility and curiosity that were initially sparked off usually turned into acceptance and recognition when female students could prove that they were capable of studying successfully and of interacting with male students and professors in a professional manner. Most of the initial encounters between female students and male students and professors took on an aura of a test or experiment, in which these women had to demonstrate that they could fit into the academic world.[13] After standing the test, female students were usually embraced by the predominantly male community. The awareness that admitting women was a kind of an unofficial educational experiment and the desire to prove oneself at all costs dominate all three accounts of female students' lives. Despite the difficulties they faced as pioneers of higher education for women, the first female students recognized that they had gained a substantial amount of autonomy and freedom that was unavailable to other women, and they described their study time as a very liberating experience.[14]

Schubert-Feder and Tiburtius seemed to recognize from the very beginning that Zurich's admission of women was a kind of experiment, and if they proved themselves it could become a regular practice, also at other universities. Straus, who enrolled as the first woman at the university in Heidelberg[15] more than twenty years later, was granted permission to study "only tentatively and on a trial basis."[16] She recalls:

> For three semesters, I was the only female among my colleagues, and looking back I now know that I was the subject of an experiment, the scope of which neither my mother, nor even less I myself realized.[17]

All three women were aware that they were constantly being "tested" by their fellow students and professors, not only in regard to their knowledge and intellectual abilities. In addition to demonstrating that they were as capable of pursuing higher education as men, female students had to prove by appropriate social skills and behavior that they were able to be part of the academic community.[18] Such "tests' included jokes, conversations, and ability to participate in courses. In addition, "feminine" attire and behavior were expected.[19] Besides acquiring knowledge, female students were not supposed to differ from other women known to students and professors. If the male world of higher education was inclined to accept women successfully participating in the academic world, it was definitely not ready to tolerate women crossing established gender boundaries in other ways. In their accounts, Tiburtius and Straus relate various anecdotes from their study time that demonstrate their awareness of constantly having to prove themselves. While looking back at her histology course, Tiburtius recalls, for example, that it was difficult for her "to grasp the cold wet fidgeting frog and to cut off its head without flinching." She continues: "[B]ut it worked nevertheless!–What a delight it would be for the male students, if one of us failed!"[20] On a different occasion, she was quite surprised when a professor paired her up with a male student during dissection lab practice. She recalls that she could work with this student very well and they told each other stories and jokes during their work. She admits proudly that she was able to analyze tissues much better than her partner. He recognized that Tiburtius was better prepared than he, but played it down by responding: "Yes, the ladies simply have a big advantage–they need not go to the bar, they can always study."[21] When the course ended, he mentioned that is was a pleasure to meet her and expressed a wish to be able to work with her in the future. This case demonstrates that Tiburtius was able to fit into the academic community. She knew the subject matter even better than her partner and had also proven to be able to carry on a conversation. In addition, he identified her as a women who did not cross gender boundaries by engaging in activities reserved only for male students such as going out and drinking.[22] By validating her knowledge and by expressing the desire to work with her in the future, the student demonstrated that he perceived Tiburtius as worthy of being part of the student body. Straus recalls an incident in which she was initially rejected by a professor but accepted as a member of the academic community by him later due to her persistence, good academic performance, and wit. Having started studies of philology, Straus decided to change her major to medicine during the first year. When she went to the dean of the medical school to ask for permission to change her field of study he tried to discourage her by arguing that she, as a woman, would not be able to study medicine successfully because of "immense demands [...] on body and soul, on head and heart"[23] He ended the conversation by wishing that she should never see him again. Straus met the same professor in her third year of studies while attending his lectures. He reminded her of the conversation they had before and announced in front of the whole group: "I know women, they won't last!" Straus, aware that "[a]ll students listened to the conversation smirking," replied humorously: "Yes, you know women, but mostly when they are ill." The professor found her response funny and they become "good friends."[24] Straus proved herself in two ways; she successfully completed several semesters of the medical school and demonstrated her wit and courage by generating an appropriate response on the spot.

All three women pursued higher education among an overwhelming majority of men and had to find ways of dealing with intimidation and getting used to this new situation.[25] The common feature in Schubert-Feder's and Tiburtius' accounts is their "feeling of merely-being-tolerated"[26] among male students. Schubert-Feder remembers her time at the university in Vienna in 1882 where, being the only female student, she "strode with constantly palpitating heart through [...] narrow hallways."[27] In these situations, she used to repeat Napoleon's saying "sans haine et sans amour," which she changed to be "sans gêne et sans amour."[28] Her strategy of dealing with her fear was to repeat this sentence "like a fearful child his prayers"[29] However, frequently she felt intimidated while attending courses and, as she recalls, "often something like helplessness and awkwardness came over me."[30] While being among so many men caused Schubert-Feder to feel shy, embarrassed, and intimidated, Tiburtius emphasized the feeling of gratitude for being able to pursue higher education:

> [W]e were guests, who had to be grateful and glad to be tolerated and could be rightly expected to understand their position and to avoid everything that could have caused a stir and a disturbing effect.[31]

The feeling of "merely-being-tolerated" combined with her appreciation for her unique opportunity caused Tiburtius to accept her marginal position and take on a rather passive and compliant role without compromising her learning. She even tried to monitor other female students who did not want to behave submissively. She recalls an incident when one of the female students brought a preserved embryo from the pathological department, wrote her name on the glass, and put it on her desk in the classroom. Not surprisingly, many sarcastic remarks appeared written next to the glass on the next day. Tiburtius recognized that the most appropriate response would have been to laugh at it. When the affected student, however, became infuriated and wanted to complain to higher authorities, Tiburtius and two other female students decided to take on a guard duty to prevent her from doing this. Tiburtius was convinced that this woman had already drawn too much attention to herself and any further action could have negative effects for all female students. Tiburtius herself reacted to jokes about female students by laughing because she perceived them as "not intended as mean"[32] In her autobiography, she patronized male students by concluding that they were behaving "like children."[33] Unlike Schubert-Feder and Tiburtius, Straus felt quite comfortable among her male classmates and never mentioned the feeling of "merely-being-tolerated." However, she admits that she often felt "small and stupid [...] as compared to all others,"[34] but adds that with time she realized that "[t]he male colleagues demonstrated great confidence, also when they did not know anything."[35] In spite of her initial lack of self-confidence, Straus seems to have made several friends and recalls being "very spoiled" as "a single girl among all the boys."[36] She remembers, for example, that her colleagues often volunteered to bring her study materials or complete less pleasant work for her. Her strategy to feel accepted by her colleagues was to be on good terms with everyone: "I was probably the only person among the students who got along with everyone. [...] this was [...] uncommon."[37]

Not only the most fervent adversaries of higher education for women but also the general public believed that academic pursuit would have devastating consequences for these women's femininity and moral conduct, not to mention that many were convinced of women's inability to study at an academic level.[38] Straus relates that during one meeting of a male students' organization, one of the participants

> explained to us in a scientific way that every female student would inevitably waste away, not only intellectually and emotionally, but that also her appearance would soon show signs of this and it would cause her to look ugly and repugnant to men.[39]

However, Straus continues that "[t]wo years later [...] he gave again a speech about the female student, and then it was a pure laud about the female student."[40] By providing a positive conclusion to the anecdote, Straus demonstrated that after a trial period the academic community indeed embraced female students. It is not surprising that over twenty years earlier, Tiburtius and Schubert-Feder had to battle similar stereotypes. For these two women, the situation was complicated by a large group of Russian female students, whose presence at the university in Zurich peaked between 1871-1873.[41] Both women considered Russian female students to be a potential threat to the rights granted to women in Zurich because most of them used the study as a pretext to engage in revolutionary activities directed against the Russian state.[42] Many of these women smoked cigarettes and wore "short hair, enormous blue glasses, [...] short, completely unadorned dress[es] that looked like umbrella case[s], round sailor's hat[s] made of shiny black oilcloth."[43] Their political activities, proclamations of anarchist philosophy, and lack of adherence to middle-class codes of dress and behavior were automatically projected onto all female students.[44] Schubert-Feder claims that only after the decree issued by the Russian government in 1873 requiring all students to return to Russia that "healthy development of women's study started in Zurich."[45] Although most of these women returned to Russia, the negative impression left by them remained and it took significant effort on the part of the remaining female students to change it.[46] Tiburtius recalls that she was often invited to visit some of the well-established people in Zurich. She accepted the invitations in spite of feeling tired because she wanted to demonstrate that not all women pursuing higher education could be associated with Russian students. She wanted people to see "a female student without blue glasses and sailor's oilcloth hat [...], who looked approximately like other people."[47] During these meetings, she had to answer many questions about her student life and was amused to hear that she was "actually like [...] any other person."[48]

Schubert-Feder, pleading for opening universities to women, had to address the issue of woman's alleged unsuitability for academic education.[49] Even Tiburtius and Straus, although not under pressure to persuade their readers, contradicted this general perception in their accounts. Tiburtius and Schubert-Feder acknowledged that many women had to study much more than their male colleagues because they had significant gaps in their knowledge due to the inadequate secondary education. However, both indicated that they were able to catch up with the material. When Tiburtius realized that she needed extra help with Latin and mathematics, she asked a professor teaching at a technical university in Zurich for help. Treating Tiburtius as an experimental case, he agreed to tutor her but expressed his lack of belief in a successful outcome because "he did not believe that women could understand mathematics."[50] Later, she found out that her teacher "was telling in a circle of professors as curiosity" that she was good in mathematics.[51] According to Schubert-Feder, professors who opposed admission of women to the university gave female students especially difficult questions during examinations. Therefore, women were exceptionally well prepared for their exams because otherwise they would not "dare" to appear in front of the examination committee. As a result, "the female student [...] comes out [...] from the fight, usually, as the winner and takes her opponent's respect as a trophy."[52] Straus, who had to obtain a special permission form the *Bundestag* to take the final examination, was also aware that she had to pass the exam with an excellent score because, among other reasons, as she claims: "everyone [expected] [that] from me, the first female student in Heidelberg."[53] Both Tiburtius and Straus emphasized their high intellectual capabilities and their educational successes. Tiburtius was very proud of her accomplishments and became quite confident about her skills and knowledge towards the end of her studies. Due to her diligence and intellect she was able to pass her final exam with excellent results. Similarly, Straus stressed her enthusiasm for learning. Upon her admission to the university, she "dived into [her] study with great intensity"[54] and proved her excellence by outstanding accomplishments.

In addition to the general perception that women lacked cognitive abilities to pursue higher education, the issue of morality was of great concern to the German middle-class.[55] Especially, the constant exposure of young women to the opposite sex was quite troubling.[56] To reassure her readers in this matter, Schubert-Feder depicted female students as morally superior to their male colleagues. Also Tiburtius and Straus described their experiences in such a way that the readers were not inclined to doubt their high moral standards, although Straus admitted to spending her free time with several male friends. Describing students' free time activities, Schubert-Feder distinguished between morally faultless conduct of female students and not so honorable behavior of male students who went out not only to attend cultural events, but also "enjoyed life in the well-known way."[57] She assured her readers that female students spent their free time at home because they did not want to raise a suspicion of any inappropriate behavior. In addition, according to Schubert-Feder, the female student was much more mature and serious about her academic pursuit because she had attained the opportunity to study often after long inner and outer battles, therefore, she was goal-conscious and goal-oriented, and it would have taken a lot to lead her astray.[58]

She characterizes the interactions between male and female students as friendly, but claims that these relations were different from those one expected to see "in society."[59] As a situation representative of the interactions between male and female students in general, she describes her first lecture experience. She felt intimidated and paralyzed when, upon entering, all students stared at her. She recalls:

> I did not have enough courage to hang my hat on the heavily loaded coat hanger. After the end of the lecture I was doing even worse; the embarrassment made me clumsy, and the unfortunate hat fell to the floor. Instead of bending down and retrieving it for me, all the students stepped back so that I should have enough room to retrieve it myself. That is the position of the female student in relation to the male student: equal rights, equal obligations, but no gallantry.[60]

Straus, attending the university more than twenty years later than Schubert-Feder, depicts a very different image of the relationships between male and female students. While portraying her own behavior as morally faultless, she does not try to hide the romantic flavor that some of these relationships had. She admits, for instance: "[f]or a whole winter month, there was a bouquet of violets lying in my closet"[61] and that one of the colleagues "brought me chocolate every day at ten o'clock."[62] Straus had several male friends, with whom she went for car rides, learned to ride bicycle, swam and rowed on the river Necker. However, she admits that although she felt relatively free, she also had to adhere to certain rules. When one of her friends wanted to teach her how to ski, she decided not to do it "because it would have caused a sensation."[63] On a different occasion, she went with one of her friends to sled, but upon her return was reprimanded by another friend not to go out with only one man. Tiburtius generally avoided the topic of relationships between male and female students, but admitted to having several friends. After the departure of the Russian students, she relates that she had "a quite productive relationship" with male students:

> [S]ince the female element was the minority and in no way aggressive, they no longer resented us, even though sometimes we knew a little more in regard to theoretical questions.[64]

She characterizes these relations as purely professional and does not miss the opportunity to point out again that female students knew more about the material than their male classmates. Although socially not as active as Straus, Tiburtius tried to engage in social life nonetheless. She enjoyed hiking with her friend Emilie Lehmus and spent a considerable amount of time with two Swiss families she befriended. Looking at the descriptions of the interactions among students and the ways they spent their free time, it is not surprising that, unlike Tiburtius and Straus, Schubert-Feder felt lonely during her studies. She maintains that female students of medicine and chemistry had more opportunities to interact with their colleagues due to the nature of the laboratory courses. According to her, students of humanities did not have such opportunities, which must have contributed to her "sense of isolation and abandonment among so many men."[65] She also contends that even among female students close friendships were not very common, not only due to the lack of time, but primarily due to pronounced cultural, social, financial, and age differences among them. Schubert-Feder mentions feeing lonely several times in her pamphlet and one actually gets an impression that it was one of the dominant feelings to which a female student was subjected. The fact that Tiburtius' and Straus' accounts contradict this assumption might be explained by different fields of study, diverse goals they pursued in their writings, or individual differences among these women, such as various personality traits.

All three women were initially confronted with the fact that they were entering a male domain and were either unwelcome or unexpected participants in the academic community. Often, they had to battle prejudices of their families and acquaintances who perceived a woman's "wish to study […] as […] condemnable" or "a sign of extreme eccentricity."[66] Like Tiburtius, they often had to face a professor who "knew very well how to scare women out of the classroom through the style of his lecture"[67] and had to deal with fellow students who greeted women with "wild noise, screaming, yelling, and howling."[68] Beyond the classroom, they had to display considerable persistence while inquiring about a room for rent when repeatedly receiving the same answer, "Gentlemen only."[69] Like Straus, they were told that a woman pursuing medical education would never find a husband and that such a quest was "unfeminine, even immoral."[70] However, these women fought to convince as many people as possible that female students had the right to enroll at the university and could succeed while pursuing academic education. Indeed, as I have argued in this essay, they proved themselves in their own eyes and in the eyes of their professors and colleagues through their dedication and persistence. All three women tried to fit into the academic world and developed their own strategies for doing so according to their personalities and individual situations. Tiburtius took any opportunity to demonstrate her knowledge and tried to respond to challenges in a positive way by reacting with humor. Schubert-Feder avoided drawing attention to herself and spent most of the time alone. She did not have many opportunities to socialize with other students but gave this situation a positive spin and asserted (indirectly) her adherence to moral norms established for middle-class women. Straus tried to get along with all her colleagues[71] and also used humor to mitigate unpleasant situations. All these women succeeded in their pursuit of higher education, graduated with good results, and gained respect and recognition of their professors and colleagues. They depicted the study time as fulfilling and happy. Even Schubert-Feder who felt quite lonely during this time, asserted: "The female student is happy [...] anticipating the achievement of her goal."[72] More enthusiastic than Schubert-Feder, Tiburtius described the time she spent at the university as "especially joyful and friendly."[73] Straus presented her study time as an idyllic space of "benevolence, friendship and love"[74] that made it possible for her "to have had a whole, entirely fulfilled life, in a way rarely bestowed on women."[75] These accounts demonstrate that, to use Gudrun Wedel's formulation, "despite the restrictions imposed on them by society, women again and again succeeded in finding and pursuing their own paths."[76]

Notes

[1] This essay is a continuation of my book *...und Medea war eine Ärztin*, in which I argued that "[i]n the context of the public discussion[s] about admission of women [...] [to the university], three different notions of femininity emerge[d] [...]: passive body without voice (corresponding to the traditional concept of womanhood as confined to the private sphere), active voice without body (relating to the symbolic transgression of the public space by female writers), and active body with voice (being physically present at a university and demonstrating that leaving the private sphere itself is a statement about women's role in society)" (Tarnawska, 11-12). While in my book I documented the "active voice without body" by focusing on essays and articles by middle-class women activists, this essay concentrates on the "active body with voice," that is, female students' perspective on the struggle for education.
[2] For analysis of other accounts of some of the first German female students see Drechsel, "Über Fascination und Ausgrenzung" 283-292; Mazón, *Gender and the Modern Research University*, 176-212.
[3] Goodmann, *Dis/Closures*, i.

⁴ Franziska Tiburtius was born in the small village Bisdamitz on the island of Rügen in 1843 as the ninth child of a Prussian landowner. She attended a private high school for girls in Stralsund between 1852 and 1859. After her graduation, she worked as a governess for six years. In 1866 she decided to leave the family for whom she had been working, passed a state examination for teachers, and traveled to England, where she collected new experiences as a private teacher for one year. Convinced by her brother Carl, Tiburtius decided to study medicine. Because none of the German universities accepted women as students, she decided to study in Zurich and enrolled at the university in 1871. She graduated successfully in 1876 and took on an internship in the gynecological and obstetrical hospital in Dresden. Together with her close friend, Emilie Lehmus, Tiburtius attempted to obtain permission to be admitted to the medical state examination in Germany but the state authorities refused. After several failed attempts to take the examination, Tiburtius und Lehmus gave up the attempt to obtain German license to practice medicine and opened their own medical practice in Berlin in 1878, nevertheless. Their private practice became very popular among women from different social classes. Tiburtius was professionally active until 1907. Following her retirement, she traveled extensively in Europe, Africa, and the United States. She died in 1927. See also Bleker and Schleiermacher, *Ärztinnen aus dem Kaiserreich*, 22-24, 297-298; Lange-Mehnert, "Ein Sprung ins absolute Dunkle," 291-294, 303-306; Sichelschmidt, *Große Berlinerinnen*, 107-114; Lange, "Nur ein unzeitgemäßer Scherz?," 226-243.

⁵ There is relatively little known about Cläre Schubert-Feder. She enrolled as an art history student in Zurich in 1878 and continued her studies later in Vienna. According to the information provided by James Albisetti, she graduated in Switzerland in 1885 (Albisetti, *Schooling German Girls and Women*, 137). In her pamphlet, she indicated that she left Zurich in 1886.

⁶ *Das Leben der Studentinnen in Zürich* (Translations of titles and quotations are mine). The pamphlet was published in two editions, 1892 and 1893.

⁷ *Erinnerungen einer Achtzigjährigen*. The first edition of the memoirs appeared in 1923 and the second in 1925 (Lange, 226). Tiburtius' memoir was also analyzed by Lange-Mehnert, "'Ein Sprung ins absolute Dunkle," 286-310; Lange, "Nur ein unzeitgemäßer Scherz?," 226-243.

⁸ Rahel Straus, née Goitein, was born in Karlsruhe in 1880 as a daughter of a rabbi. Her father died when she was 3 years old. Rahel and her three siblings were raised by their mother, who made sure all her children received the best possible education. Rahel attended the first high school for girls opened in Karlsruhe and passed the final examination, *Abitur*, in 1899. Following the exam she went with her brother to study in Heidelberg. Although she wanted to study medicine, initially she was forced to choose a different subject because medicine was too expensive. Due to the generosity of her uncle, after one year, she was able to enroll as a medical student. She graduated from the university in Heidelberg in 1905 and then moved to Munich where she wrote her doctoral thesis and completed her internship. She got married to her childhood friend Eili Straus in 1905 and then worked as a physician in Munich. After the death of her husband in 1933, she

immigrated to Palestine and worked as a physician in Jerusalem until her death in 1963. See also Krauss, "Ein voll erfülltes Frauenleben," 236-241; Asche, "Fürsorge, Partizipation und Gleichberechtigung," 203-204; Mazón, 207-209.

[9] Straus started studying philology in 1899 but then switched to medicine in the Summer Semester 1900, as she claims "as the first academic citizen" (Straus, 90). According to the information provided by the university in Heidelberg, four women enrolled at the university in 1900 for the first time ("Ausstellung 'Hundert Jahre Frauen an der Universität Heidelberg,'" 8 August, 2007. http://www.uni-heidelberg.de/ presse/ news/2010frauen.html).

[10] *Wir lebten in Deutschland. Erinnerungen einer deutschen Jüdin 1880-1933.*

[11] Mazón claims that "the first female students experimented with a variety of strategies" to fit into the academic community (Mazón, 177). In her discussion of autobiographies of three female students, Maria von Linden, Alice Salomon, and Hildegard Wegscheider, she focuses on "the strategy that each woman used to gain access to the university and make a place for herself there" (Mazón, 180). See Mazón, 180-208; 210-212.

[12] Mazón mentions that some of the first women who audited courses at various German universities "were the objects of much curiosity but were often treated with a generous chivalry." Other women, however, faced "spontaneous protests by the male students ranging from the traditional student practice of foot trampling [...] during lecture to petition to the dean" (Mazón, 124).

[13] Mazón observes that first women were allowed to audit courses at German universities "at first on an experimental basis" (Mazón, 119). While Mazón looks at the first students as "test cases" (Mazón, 128) in the broader terms of "universities' first experiments with women students" (Mazón, 151), I argue that the individual interactions between female students and the rest of the academic community became experiments on a smaller, more private scale, where women had to prove to their colleagues and professors that they were worthy and able to be students.

[14] Mazón also argues that "[w]hile women's entrance into the university did not go flawlessly, women emphasized their studies as a fulfilling and exciting time in their lives" (Mazón, 179).

[15] See note 9 above.

[16] "nur versuchs- und probeweise" (Straus, 87).

[17] "Drei Semester war ich unter den Kollegen das einzige weibliche Wesen, und rückschauend weiß ich erst, daß da ein Experiment mit mir gemacht wurde, über dessen Tragweite sich weder meine Mutter und noch viel weniger ich selbst uns klar waren" (Straus, 91).

[18] See also Mazón, 62-63.

[19] See also Krauss, 237; Mazón, 62-63.

[20] "den feuchtkalten zappelnden Frosch zu ergreifen und ihm mit fester Hand den Kopf abzuschneiden", "[A]ber es ging doch! – Welch ein Vergnügen wäre es für die Studenten gewesen, wenn man versagt hätte!" (Tiburtius, 134).

[21] "Ja, die Damen haben halt einen großen Vorzug, sie brauchen nicht in die Kneipe zu gehen, können immer studieren" (Tiburtius, 134).

[22] Mazón argues throughout her book that "academic citizenship served to inculcate a particular kind of middle-class masculine identity" (Mazón, 17). Therefore (male) "academic citizenship" involved various rituals, e.g. "drinking ceremonies" (Mazón, 20). See Mazón, 19-49.

[23] "Riesenanforderungen [...] an Körper und Seele, an Kopf und Herz" (Straus, 88).

[24] "[I]ch kenne die Frauen, das hält keine durch!", "[a]lle Studenten hörten grinsend dem Gespräch zu", "Ja, Sie kennen die Frauen, aber meist, wenn sie krank sind!", "gute Freunde" (Straus, 89).

[25] For descriptions of relations among female and male students see also Burchardt, *Blaustrumpf – Modestudentin – Anarchistin?*, 185-197.

[26] "das Gefühl des nur Geduldetseins" (Schubert-Feder, 14).

[27] "mit stets klopfendem Herzen durch die [...] engen Korridore hindurchschritt" (Schubert-Feder, 15).

[28] Ibid., 15 ("without hatred and without love" and "without embarrassment and without love").

[29] "wie ein furchtsames Kind seine Gebete" (Schubert-Feder, 15).

[30] "überkam es mich oft wie Hilf- und Ratlosigkeit" (Schubert-Feder, 10).

[31] "[W]ir waren nur Gäste, die dankbar und froh sein mußten, geduldet zu sein, und von denen man mit Recht erwarten durfte, daß sie ihre Stellung begriffen und alles vermieden, was Aufsehen erregen und ruhestörend wirken konnte" (Tiburtius, 127).

[32] "nicht bös gemeint" (Tiburtius, 133).

[33] "wie die Kinder" (Tiburtius, 135).

[34] "klein und dumm [...] gegenüber all den anderen" (Straus, 87).

[35] "[d]ie männlichen Kollegen trugen eine große Sicherheit zur Schau, auch wenn sie nichts wußten" (Straus, 87).

[36] "sehr verwöhnt", "einziges Mädchen unter all den Jungen" (Straus, 92). Krauss argues that Straus had such a privileged position among male students and professors for two reasons. First, she belonged to the second generation of female physicians in Germany and it was not so difficult for her to be accepted by her colleagues as it was for women who studied earlier. Second, she dressed and behaved in a way a woman was expected to behave at the beginning of the twentieth century (Krauss, 236-237). I agree with Krauss only partly. Although Straus studied several years later than many other women, she was one the first women studying at the university in Heidelberg and for this reason, can be regarded as a pioneer in higher education for women. Her colleagues and professors did not have any encounters with female students before and therefore could not have known how to behave around them based on their experiences. Although, without a doubt, it was much easier for Straus to pursue higher education than it was for Schubert-Feder and Tiburtius, she also had to face stereotypes about women studying at the university and deal with negative altitudes towards herself. The fact that she adhered to the rules of dress and conduct of the time and that she considered herself attractive (Straus, 111) played most likely a role in her being accepted by the fellow students.

[37] "Ich war aber auch vielleicht unter den Studenten der einzige Mensch, der mit allen gut stand. [...] das war [...] ungewohnt" (Straus, 92).
[38] See Tarnawska, 38-51.
[39] "erklärte uns da ganz wissenschaftlich, daß jede studierende Frau nicht nur geistig und seelisch als Frau verkümmern müsse, sondern daß auch ihn Äußeres sehr bald die Spuren davon zeige und sie häßlich und für Männer abstoßend erscheinen lasse" (Straus, 96).
[40] "[n]ach zwei Jahren [...] hielt er wieder eine Rede über die Studentin, und da war es der reine Lobgesang auf die studierende Frau" (Straus, 96).
[41] Tiburtius, 120. Tiburtius also relates that in the summer of 1873, there were 145 Russian students at the university, including 100 women, out of whom 75 studied medicine (Tiburtius, 154). For the relationships between Russian and German female students see Burchardt, "Schwestern reicht die Hand zum Bunde?," 293-301; Burchardt, *Blaustrumpf – Modestudentin – Anarchistin?*, 50-73, 79-92. See also Weiershausen, *Wissenschaft und Weiblichkeit*, 55-57; Lange, 234-235; Mazón, 60-62; Tarnawska, 49.
[42] Schubert-Feder, 4-5. See also Tarnawska, 49.
[43] "das kurzgeschnittene Haar, die gewaltige blaue Brille, [...] das kurze, gänzlich schmucklose, regenschirmfutterähnliche Kleidchen, der runde Matrosenhut von schwarzglänzendem Wachstuch" (Tiburtius, 130).
[44] See also Tarnawska, 49.
[45] "hob die gesunde Entwicklung des Frauenstudiums in Zürich an" (Schubert-Feder, 7).
[46] According to Albisetti several German women launched a campaign to erase this negative attitude towards female students and "[t]he most important aspect of this campaign to change popular perceptions [...] was a continuing effort to establish a more positive picture of women at the University of Zurich" (Albisetti, 197). Schubert-Feder's pamphlet written in the 1890s seems to be a part of this campaign, as also indicated by Albisetti (198-199). See also Albisetti, 197-199; Burchardt, 'Schwestern reicht die Hand zum Bunde?,' 296-298; Burchardt, *Blaustrumpf – Modestudentin – Anarchistin?*, 79-92, Mazón, 60-63.
[47] "eine Studentin ohne blaue Brille und Matrosenlackhut [...], die ungefähr so aussah, wie andere Leute auch" (Tiburtius, 147).
[48] "doch eigentlich [...] wie ein anderer Mensch" (Tiburtius, 147).
[49] See Tarnawska, 38-51.
[50] "er glaube nicht, daß Frauen Verständnis für Mathematik hätten" (Tiburtius, 142).
[51] "erzählte in einer Professorengesellschaft als Kuriosum" (Tiburtius, 142).
[52] "die Studentin [...] geht [...] aus dem Kampf, der Regel nach, als Siegerin hervor und nimmt als Trophäe die Achtung ihres Gegners mit hinweg" (Schubert-Feder, 9).
[53] "jeder [erwartete] [das] von mir, der ersten Studentin in Heidelberg" (Straus, 117).
[54] "stürzte [...] mit großer Intensität auf das Studium" (Straus, 86-7).
[55] See Tarnawska, 39-43.

[56] See also Albisetti, 199-200.
[57] "in ihrer berühmten Weise des Lebens sich freuen" (Schubert-Feder, 22).
[58] "weil sie oft nach langen, inneren und äußeren Kämpfen erst zur Möglichkeit des Studiums gelangt, sie ist daher zweck- und zielbewußt, und es würde viel dazu gehören, sie vom rechten Wege abzubringen" (Schubert-Feder, 16).
[59] "im Salon" (Schubert-Feder, 14).
[60] "[E]s langte mir kaum der Muth, meinen Hut an die schon reichbeladenen Kleiderriegel aufzuhängen. Nach Schluß des Collegs ging es mir noch schlimmer: Die Verlegenheit machte mich ungeschickt, der unglückliche Hut fiel zur Erde. Anstatt nun, daß einer der Herren Studenten sich gebückt und mir ihn aufgehoben hätte, wichen sie alle einen Schritt zurück, damit ich Raum genug behalten sollte, ihn mir selber aufzuheben. – Das ist die Stellung der Studentin gegenüber dem Studenten: gleiche rechte, gleiche Pflichten, aber keine Galanterie" (Schubert-Feder, 13-14).
[61] "[e]inen ganzen Wintermonat lag täglich ein Veilchenstrauß in meinem Schrank" (Straus, 92).
[62] "mir jeden Tag um zehn Uhr Schokolade brachte" (Straus, 97).
[63] "weil es zuviel Aufsehen erregt hätte" (Straus, 98).
[64] "ganz erschprießliche[s] Verhältnis," "[S]eitdem das weibliche Element in der Minderzahl und in keiner Weise aggressiv war, nahm man es uns auch nicht mehr übel, wenn wir in theoretischen Fragen manchmal ein wenig besser Bescheid wußten" (Tiburtius, 164).
[65] "Bewußtsein der Isolirung und Verlassenheit unter so vielen Herren" (Schubert-Feder, 14-15).
[66] "der Wunsch zu studieren […] für […] verwerflich," "ein Zeichen hochgradiger Ueberspanntheit" (Schubert-Feder, 7).
[67] "verstand es vortrefflich durch die Art seines Vortrages, die Frauen 'hinauszugrauelen'" (Tiburtius, 140).
[68] "ein wüster Lärm, Schreien, Johlen, Pfeifen" (Tiburtius, 133).
[69] "Nur an Herren" (Tiburtius, 117).
[70] "unweiblich, ja sogar unmoralisch" (Straus, 87).
[71] See also Mazón, 208.
[72] "Die Studierende sei glücklich […] in der Vorfreude des erreichten Ziels" (Schubert-Feder, 22).
[73] "besonders lichtvoll und freundlich" (Tiburtius, 113).
[74] "Wohlwollen, Freundschaft und Liebe" (Straus, 97).
[75] "voll erfülltes Leben gehabt zu haben, wie es Frauen kaum je vergönnt ist" (Straus, 108).
[76] Wedel, "Nothing more than a German Woman," 306.

Works Cited

Primary Sources

Schubert-Feder, Cläre. *Das Leben der Studentinnen in Zürich.* Berlin: R. Boll, 1893.
Straus, Rahel. *Wir lebten in Deutschland. Erinnerungen einer deutschen Jüdin 1880-1933.* Stuttgart: Deutsche Verlags-Anstalt, 1961.
Tiburtius, Franziska. *Erinnerungen einer Achtzigjährigen.* Berlin: C.A.Schwetschke & Sohn Verlagsbuchhandlung, 1925.

Scondary Sources

"Ausstellung 'Hundert Jahre Frauen an der Universität Heidelberg,'" 8 August, 2007. http://www.uni-heidelberg.de/presse/news/2010frauen.html.
Albisetti, James C. *Schooling of German Girls and Women. Secondary and Higher Education in the Nineteenth Century.* Princeton: Princeton University Press, 1988.
Asche, Susanne. "Fürsorge, Partizipation und Gleichberechtigung – die Leistungen der Karlsruherinnen für die Entwicklung zur Großstadt (1859-1914)." In *Karlsruher Frauen 1715-1945. Eine Stadtgeschichte*, by Susanne Asche, Barbara Guttmann, Olivia Hochstrasser, Sigrid Schambach, and Lisa Sterr, 171-256. Karlsruhe: Badenia Verlag, 1992.
Bleker, Johanna and Sabine Schleiermacher. *Ärztinnen aus dem Kaiserreich. Lebensläufe einer Generation.* Weinheim: Deutscher Studien Verlag, 2000.
Burchardt, Anja. Blaustrumpf – Modestudentin – Anarchistin? Deutsche und russische Medizinstudentinnen in Berlin 1896-1918. Stuttgart: Verlag J. B. Metzler, 1997.
—. "'Schwestern reicht die Hand zum Bunde?' – Zum Verhältnis zwischen russischen und deutschen Medizinstudentinnen in den Anfängen des Frauenstudiums (1865-1814)." In *Barrieren und Karrieren. Die Anfänge des Frauenstudiums in Deutschland*, edited by Elisabeth Dickmann und Eva Schöck-Quinteros, 293-301. Berlin: trafo verlag dr. wolfgang weist, 2000.
Drechsel, Wiltrud Ulrike. "Über Faszination und Ausgrenzung der Universität in den Anfängen des Frauenstudiums." In *Barrieren und Karrieren. Die Anfänge des Frauenstudiums in Deutschland*, edited by

Elisabeth Dickmann and Eva Schöck-Quinteros, 283-292. Berlin: trafo verlag dr. wolfgang weist, 2000.

Goodman, Katharine. *Dis/Closures. Women's Autobiography in Germany Between 1790 and 1914*. New York: Peter Lang, 1986.

Krauss, Marita. "'Ein voll erfülltes Frauenleben'. Die Ärztin, Mutter und Zionistin Rahel Straus (1880-1963)." In *Bedrohlich gescheit. Ein Jahrhundert Frauen und Wissenschaft in Bayern*, edited by Hiltrud Häntzschel und Hadumod Bußmann, 236-241. München: Verlag C. H. Beck, 1997.

Lange, Christine. "Nur ein unzeitgemäßer Scherz? Akademikerinnen im Deutschland des späten 19. Jahrhunderts: Franziska Tiburtius u.a." In *Geschriebenes Leben. Autobiographik von Frauen*, edited by Michaela Holdenried, 226-243. Berlin: Erich Schmidt Verlag, 1995.

Lange-Mehnert, Christa. "'Ein Sprung ins absolute Dunkle' Zum Selbstverständnis der ersten Ärztinnen: Marie Heim-Vögtlin und Franziska Tiburtius." In *Frauenkörper. Medizin. Sexualität. Auf dem Wege zu einer neuen Sexualmoral*, edited by Johanna Geyer-Kordesch and Annette Kuhn, 286-310. Düsseldorf: Schwann, 1986.

Mazón, Patricia M. *Gender and the Modern Research University. The Admission of Women to German Higher Education, 1865-1914*. Stanford: Stanford University Press, 2003.

Sichelschmidt, Gustav. *Große Berlinerinnen. Sechzehn biographische Porträts*. Berlin: Rembrandt Verlag, 1972.

Tarnawska, Magdalena. *...und Medea war eine Ärztin: Constructions of Femininity in Public Debates about Medical Education for Women in Germany and Austria between 1870 and 1910*, edited by Irmala von der Lühe and Gail K. Hart. Frankfurt a. M: Peter Lang, 2007.

Wedel, Gudrun. "'... Nothing more than a German Woman.' Remarks on the Biographical and Autobiographical Tradition of the Women of one Family." In *German Women in the Eighteenth and Nineteenth Centuries. A Social and Literary History*, edited by Ruth-Ellen B. Joeres and Mary Jo Maynes, 305-320. Bloomington: Indiana University Press, 1986.

Weiershausen, Romana. *Wissenschaft und Weiblichkeit. Die Studentin in der Literatur der Jahrhundertwende*. Göttingen: Wallstein Verlag, 2004.

CHAPTER TEN

IN THEIR OWN WAYS: EMILIA PARDO BAZÁN
AND MARÍA MARTÍNEZ SIERRA'S STRUGGLE
FOR WOMEN'S EDUCATION
IN TURN-OF-THE-CENTURY SPAIN

MAR SORIA LÓPEZ

> The lowest rank [of female classification] is that of the grotesque, and I would constitute it in this way: 1st. The radical tomboy (anarchist female writers, antimilitarist women, supporters of women's vote and equal rights); 2nd. That [female] who does not give herself to anyone for she loves herself; 3rd. That [female] who does not give herself to anyone because nobody takes her.[1]
> —Pascual Santacruz[2]

It is a given that Spain's multicultural and diverse history has had a tremendous effect on the representation of women in the Spanish collective imaginary and, therefore, on the lives of women themselves. The foundations of peninsular culture in Greek and Roman philosophical and scientific patriarchal thought led to a conception of females as being inferior to men, which consequently meant that women were excluded from public and educational realms. Philosophers such as Aristotle reinforced the idea of woman as a misbegotten man, a belief that "held sway in science, philosophy, and theology at least until the nineteenth century."[3] Later on, the presence of Islam and Judaism in Iberia for several centuries reinforced the idea "of the cloistered, sheltered woman, the woman protected in the home."[4] Likewise, a strong Catholic tradition crystallized the idea of perfect womanhood through the myth of the Virgin Mary, who embodied asexuality, maternity, and sacrifice. Texts like *The Perfect Married Woman* (1583) by Brother Luis de León and *The Instruction of the Christian Woman* (1529) by Spanish philosopher Luis Vives were the primary "learning material" for females well into the twentieth century. In these readings, women were encouraged to keep themselves far away from intellectual "perversions" that would destroy their virtue and "natural" innocence.

Besides these factors, economics also played a major role in the development of women's education and feminism, especially at the conclusion of the nineteenth century. As Mary Nash mentions, Spanish women were disadvantaged in comparison to their Western counterparts due to the slow process of industrialization in Spain.[5] This prevented them from entering the labor force in great numbers until the first two decades of the twentieth century, which delayed the acquisition of a strong feminist consciousness as opposed to countries such as Great Britain and the US where the suffragist movement was mainly originated by middle-class female workers. As a result of the construction of women as lacking men's intellectual capacities in Spanish history and the absence of a powerful feminist movement, it comes as no surprise that in 1887, 81.2 % of the female population in Spain was illiterate and by 1920, a 58.2 %.[6]

It is against these obstacles that both Emilia Pardo Bazán (1851-1921) and María Lejárraga[7] (1880-1974) had to struggle in order to achieve one of their main goals at the turn of the nineteenth century: women's empowerment through education. From their position as writers, both women occupied "the position of authority in what was a masculine genre",[8] the essay. While only males were welcome as critics in the intellectual arena of the time, Pardo Bazán and Lejárraga crossed gender boundaries in different ways and made use of the essay to criticize the society of their times. They went a step further in breaking gender boundaries physically and intellectually when they made their ideas heard in public talks at a moment when public speeches were a symbol of (male) authority and possession of knowledge.

Pardo Bazán was a strong, independent woman who separated from her husband and supported herself and her children with her literary work. She was able to create a space for herself in the clearly male intellectual arena of the time in spite of the rejection and insults that she experienced when she trespassed on territory reserved for the opposite gender. As a feminist activist, Pardo published articles and gave talks on intellectual matters to female audiences at a time when women were not welcome to either intervene or attend such events. In 1892, she gave a talk at the Pedagogical Congress and titled it "The Education of Man and Woman"[9] where the audience mostly consisted of male and female teachers. In her speech, Pardo employed a direct and assertive style, as someone who did not fear being rejected or criticized. For instance, when preparing her talk, Bazán must have been fully aware of the important role assigned to philosophers such as Kant and Rousseau in the formation of teachers at that time. Thus, she took the chance to criticize, sometimes humorously, the misogynist perspectives embraced by these two widely respected intellectuals. In general, her ideas about women's education are clear and definite: women have to be educated in order to be self-sufficient and agents of their own life. But interestingly, in order to convince her audience of the need to educate the modern woman, Pardo Bazán, just as Lejárraga would later do, appropriated the discourse that male intellectuals were using for the hot topic of the time in Spanish politics: the genesis and establishment of the modern nation. In this sense, the author makes a series of connections between women's education and modernity and, at the same time, between the need to educate women to make possible the existence of the modern nation.

Pardo Bazán divides women's education into different categories. She starts with physical education and its benefits to women's bodies. It is almost astonishing that in nineteenth-century Spain, a woman writer promoted physical activity among women as a way of being healthy. The fact is that the Spanish collective imaginary had a negative view of women, their bodies, and what they could do with their bodies regarding any type of physical exercise, either jumping a fence or experiencing sexual pleasure. This idea was encapsulated in one Spanish saying well in use until the 1970's that Pardo Bazán herself mentions in her talk: "La mujer honrada, en casa con la pierna quebrada."[10] This popular proverb not only talks about how women's bodies were subjected to immobility and enclosure in the domestic space to preserve their purity, but also how violence was socially accepted as a way of keeping them under control. In an ironical twist though, Pardo Bazán criticizes how intellectuals had used this saying since the fifteenth century. In particular, she mentions how one of these male authors, whose name she does not give, applauded in his text the practice of a certain tribe of Indians who dislocated their females' ankles to assure their stay at home. Like him, in Pardo Bazán's opinion, many others promoted and encouraged the idea of the cloistered woman, questioning the morality of those females who risked entering the streets. Turning the argument upside-down from a feminist perspective, Pardo Bazán defines Spanish male intellectuals as backward and savage as this tribe of Indians for their perception of women's roles. Unfortunately, to prove her own point, she resorts, as those who she criticizes, to a colonial perspective about the other. Drawing from the Spanish colonial past and stereotypes, Pardo Bazán accepts the dichotomy between savage/civilized, Indian/Spanish as natural when she underlines the inferiority of the Native Americans in comparison to the advancement and modernization of the

Western world. In fact, her strong colonial perspective built upon Spain's glorious imperial past is one of the major drawbacks of her talk.

Another type of education that Pardo deals with is moral education. She criticizes the double standard society applied to women and their sexuality. Women have to remain faithful and pure, while males are allowed to exercise their sexuality outside the confines of marriage. In her opinion, and relying on the precepts of naturalism, she understands that the lack of morals leads to the physical deterioration of the individual, and therefore, of the organism of society and the nation. It is men's and women's responsibility to remain "clean" since it is "the only guarantee on the health, strength and beauty of future generations."[11] Even though Pardo Bazán sees the importance of transmitting a proper moral education to the younger generations for the good of the nation, she relieves females of this duty by employing two traditional beliefs regarding women's role: the "pessimistic postulate"[12] and the notion of "relative destiny."[13] In her opinion, Spanish society has relied on a pessimistic perception of women's education producing a clash between intellectual and moral education. She disapproves of the idea that "the more ignorant and stationary a woman is, the more apt she is for her providential destiny," and the desire and possession of a highly refined intellectual capacity "constitute honor and glory for the man, but for the female, dishonor and almost a monstrosity."[14] Society envisioned maternity as woman's providential destiny and charged her with producing the raw material that would form the nation. But since a highly cultivated intellectual education—which could produce "female monsters"—was against their moral education, it was thought then that women's moral instruction should prevail over the intellectual so that they could transmit those values to their progeny. For Pardo Bazán this is part of women's "relative destiny" that forces them to subordinate their lives to the existence of their husband, children, father or "when they are missing, to the abstract entity of the masculine gender."[15]

The author, however, deconstructs the essentialist notion of motherhood as the only aim in women's lives and of moral education as their primary instruction. Maternity is not only a temporal function in women's existence but it is also "adventitious" since "all women conceive ideas, but not all conceive children."[16] It is interesting to notice the presence of Pardo Bazán's subversive stance towards the widely-used principles of phrenology in this instance as in others in her talk. At a moment when this science was classifying the social world in terms of race, gender, and class, privileging the white male bourgeois on the grounds of physical and intellectual superiority, she contested its biological deterministic notions in relation to women's inferiority, claiming their equal capacity to men to acquire knowledge. At the same time, nonetheless, she herself recurs to another essentialist perspective of motherhood to discredit the idea that women's education should be focused on the formation of good mothers: "A mother cannot be educated; the mother is the master work of natural instinct."[17] Mothers cannot be taught to be mothers and therefore their education should be not wasted on perfecting motherhood but on improving their own "understanding and . . . heart."[18]

Pardo Bazán also resorts to notions of nation building and civilization when studying in depth the intellectual education of women. For her, modern and, therefore, civilized nations are those which lean on the commonalities and equal position of men and women and the translation of these facts into equal education and same access to the job market: "today we could judge the culture of a State by the amplitude given to the intellectual education of women, not only [reflected] in written law, but also in society."[19] In this fashion, she accuses Spain of not adhering to notions of modern civilization since women are still considered intellectually inferior to men and, therefore, are given a more simplistic education. This, in turn, frustrates any attempt to achieve a modern and civilized nation.

The nation-building project plays an essential role in the civic and aesthetic education of women as well. For the author, the classic models of Rome and Greece epitomize this type of education. In her opinion, these societies nourished the notion of the ideal nation through the indoctrination of their citizens with a sense of patriotic duty and attachment to the imaginary community, "promoting the vigorous development of the national spirit."[20] But according to her, only men acquired full rights without distinction after the French Revolution, whereas women were excluded from the nation's political and civic life, remaining indifferent to political corruption and ignoring the idea of the nation as a fraternal community. Thus, females acquired a selfish understanding of the family not as a healthy cell constituting modern society but as corrupt organism—"nibbling moth"[21]— that degenerates the nation, something that supposedly did not happen in Greece and Rome. Although Bazán is right when admitting that the French Revolution did not bring the expected equality among men and women,[22] it is also true that when turning Rome and Greece into model roles of perfect citizenship and nationhood, she ignores the fact that women in Roman and Greek societies were second-class citizens and rarely received their counterparts' education.

In the conclusion of her presentation, Pardo Bazán, sharing a regenerationist discourse with other intellectuals of the time, laments the decaying state of Spain as a nation and empire.[23] Six years after she gave her talk, Spain lost its last two colonies: the Philippines and Cuba. It was a strong blow to the nation's self-assurance as a powerful entity. Pardo Bazán wanted Spain to remain a dominant country as a colonizing power in the international arena and for that reason she invokes the imperial times of the reign of the Catholic king and queen of Spain four hundred years before. For her, as for many, this was "the greatest period of prosperity and burgeoning for Spain"[24] as an international power because a woman was in command, Isabella, the Catholic Queen. Pardo Bazán adopts then the motto of the Catholic queen to support her own cause: "Tanto monta."[25] In this sense, she compares her own support of women's education to Isabel's support of Colon's idea that the Earth was round at a time when nobody believed in this. Against the scientist's prospectus of the time, Isabella's "very glorious intervention"[26] allowed the "discovery" of America. Hence Pardo Bazán perceived that if her ideas on women's education took place, Spain would turn into a powerful and modern civilized nation again. Obviously, Pardo Bazán appropriated history to her own benefit as she did throughout her talk to fit her own nation building project in which women's education played a major role. Immersed in her fight for the defense of women's education, Pardo Bazán remained oblivious to all the social, economic and political drawbacks, and injustices that the "discovery" of America entailed.[27]

Almost thirty years after Emilia Pardo Bazán gave her talk, María Lejárraga wrote a paper, "Of feminism"[28] for the Madrid art festivals in 1917 organized in pro of the protection of women's work. Interestingly enough, it was not Lejárraga herself who gave the talk as part of these charity events, but her husband, Gregorio Martínez Sierra, who also appeared as the author of the paper. In fact, this is the case of most of her literary production. Thanks to the research work carried out by different critics such as Alda Blanco, Antonia Rodrigo, and Patricia W. O'Connor, we know now that Lejárraga authored many of the writings previously assigned to her husband.[29] The reasons for this desire to remain in silence while her husband took on the public role of a successful male writer are still under scrutiny. In particular, and as Blanco suggests, it could be thought that "the 'feminist' essays of María Martínez Sierra are, in fact, not feminist at all, because their author chose not only to veil her identity behind the name of a man, but also to write in a voice inscribed in the texts as masculine."[30] Nonetheless, Blanco also argues that Lejárraga's gesture to remain anonymous is not "a sign of confusion, weakness, or even neurosis"[31] but a possible strategy to articulate her problematic position as a female writer in the strictly male literary world of the early twentieth century. Hiding behind her husband's identity and authorship—and the use of a clear paternalistic narrative voice usually employed by male authors with a female audience/reader—Lejárraga was able to manifest her feminist ideas without the boundaries imposed to the female literary writers of the time. As Blanco states, "feminist reasoning from the mouth of a man would have more weight than that which came from a woman."[32] Whereas she decided to hide most of her literary authorship behind her husband's name, she became a public political figure when she joined the International Woman Suffrage Alliance (IWSA) as its secretary in 1916, the Feminine Association for Civic Education (AFEC) in 1930, and the National Committee of Women Against Fascism in 1934. Lejárraga's visible role as a political and feminist activist allowed her to start publishing a series of articles on feminist issues in various Spanish magazines and sign them as "María Martínez Lejárraga". However, it would not be until the year 1952 when she used this name again to sign her literary work.

In the paper her husband presented at the festivals in 1917,[33] "De feminismo," the narrative voice continuously adulates and patronizes the audience to make it sympathize with the speaker. Whereas Pardo Bazán was addressing an audience comprised of professionals of the education, mostly male, Lejárraga wrote her paper for a public made up of aristocratic and upper middle-class women who belonged to a charity group. Given the gender and class of the audience, Lejárraga conferred a more conservative overtone to her talk and her rhetoric. In addition to the fact that aristocracy usually held traditional values of the Old Regime, Spanish women were also thought to be more reactionary than their male counterparts. Seen as the bulwark of traditional values,[34] females carried much of the weight of representing the moral foundations of the nation. Since Lejárraga's main goal was to persuade the audience of the benefits of feminism, she needed to inscribe new meanings to this term.

Indeed, the late and weak consolidation of feminism in Spain after World War I attests for the little popularity and understanding of the movement in Spanish society in comparison to other Western countries. Lejárraga knew well enough the negative ideas that feminism brought about, especially in regards to the social mental construction of the female feminists as "pitiful ugly spinsters"[35] who were against the family and femininity. So, the narrative voice dares to refer to the audience as "Christian, ultramodern, and feminist,"[36] putting together terms generally considered as opposite. Anticipating the audience's negative reaction to her statement, the narrative voice exclaims "Don't be alarmed, my ladies!"[37] to then proceed to explain why she has made such unthinkable connection. In doing so, Lejárraga allows the audience to see feminism as a familiar term and reconstruct the image of a feminist not as an ugly masculine violent woman but, in a totally different guise, as a Christian, modern, respectable, feminine, and married lady. In this sense, Lejárraga is playing with the ambiguous position many middle and upper-middle class women were occupying in society. Although respectability and decency were supposedly to be found in women who remained in the private space, these well-off females were already contributing to and appearing in many public spaces such as salons, conferences, and charity associations. From the audience's own experience then, Lejárraga makes the connection between leaving "the enchanted boundaries of their own home" to "approach life[,] understand it, [and] realize that there is a beyond, or a lower stratum, made out of injustices."[38] Therefore, she claims that it is necessary for women—she is mostly referring here to middle and upper class women—to enter the public space in order to become more knowledgeable and interested in the surrounding world, which does not imply the loss of femininity since "culture . . . cannot bring anything else than an improvement of [woman's] natural qualities, but never a change in [her] nature."[39]

Moreover, when a woman is successful in obtaining a superior education and performs what are traditionally considered male jobs— "expanding the field of her activities"—[40]it does not imply that she becomes emasculated. On the contrary, for Lejárraga womanhood is achieved by the cultivation of women's intellectual capacities. An ignorant woman is a person in her infancy that remains in a barbaric state. In fact, the more cultivated a woman is, the more woman and modern she is. Also, an educated woman will be more responsible for her own acts and will be able to defend herself against the *don Juans* that take advantage of female's ignorance about sexuality. A good education does not imply moral corruption for women as many intellectuals and religious men feared, but the preservation and improvement of female virtue since "innocence is not synonymous with ignorance."[41] Besides this, education will provide women with the same rights and duties as men. Lejárraga clarifies, though, that women will not have the same "immoral" freedom as the males, but that males should have the same moral standards as women. In all, for the author, to become an educated woman means that the nation will enjoy a higher moral state.

According to Lejárraga, economy should be a very important part in women's education too. She realizes the power of capital in the modern world where traditional values have been substituted by capitalism. But instead of regretting this change and trying to bring back old traditions in a melancholic gesture, Lejárraga claims that women need to adjust to modern times through their control over capital, which would grant them power in modern society: "The ability to buy is the only royal crown for the modern man."[42] This cannot be done, however, unless women change the laws, since it is not until the establishment of the Second Republic in the year 1931 that gender equality was legally granted. Up to that moment, and as shown in the 1889 Spanish Civil Code, the husband was the only administrator of the marital property.[43] Women, thus, needed to know the legal system and transform it after acquiring the right to vote. In this respect, Lejárraga is also interested in deconstructing the meaning of the female suffragist as she did with the term feminist: a suffragist is not a childless unmarried woman, but a mother and wife who wants to change the laws in order to make a better nation for her children. Moreover, she claimes that "because [they] are Spanish"[44] and mothers, it is expected that they worry about the political situation of the country. Therefore, if women as mothers had access to politics and the government too, a cleaner and better nation could be created:

> Do you believe that if in the city council there were as many women as men the streets would be as dirty and badly cobbled as they are? . . . Would there be hired and exploited children begging in the streets in the freezing nights of January?[45]

Besides, if feminists—mothers and wives—could change the legal system, the foundations of the nation, marriage, and family would be strengthened because they would be institutions in which women and men would have the same power without feeling trapped. As it can be noticed, to support her modern argument, Lejárraga makes use of more essentialist and traditional ideas of femininity in order not to alienate her audience. In her own words "woman is born for the family, for the home, for maternity, and this cannot be denied by anyone, either feminist or antifeminist. The greatest happiness of a woman is at home."[46] Thus, it is women's responsibility, together with men, to create "a nest of perfect safety for the children, a guarantee for a superior future humanity."[47]

To finish her paper, Lejárraga calls for these modern feminist maternal women not only to create a better nation, but to save Spain from the precarious situation in which men have left it. Hence, women as mothers must feel that the nation is their child in need and that they must fight to save it. Interestingly, the author, starting from a conventional definition of womanhood as motherhood, adds new transgressive meanings to it.

Women are not imagined then as passive individuals wasting their lives in the private space but as active agents in the salvation and betterment of the nation. Lejárraga inscribes them as romantic fighters on whom the future of the nation depends:

> To the fight, countrywomen, with all your courage! "Oh, my fair warrior!" Othello tells Desdemona. To the conquest of Spain, Spanish women![48]

During the thirty years that separate Lejárraga's paper and Bazán's, women's social position of disadvantage had not experienced any significant change in Spain as it had in other Western societies. In fact, it was not until 1918 that the first Spanish feminist movement—the "National Association of Spanish Women" (ANME)—which had certain political and social repercussions was formed. Thus, by 1917, when Lejárraga wrote her paper, Spanish society was still anchored in backward perceptions of both femininity and the role that women should play in the private sphere. In this fashion, what really set the difference between Bazán's assertive paper and Lejárraga's more conservative one was that whereas Pardo Bazán did not even mention the word "feminism" in her talk but happened to be more confronting with the audience, María Lejárraga, in trying to convince her conservative upper-class audience of the positive aspects of feminism, had to use a less assertive and liberal discourse continuously appealing to notions of motherhood and tradition.

In their own ways and going against dominant ideologies about females, both writers strove to improve women's education in Spain and, as an extension, women's lives in general as shown in these two talks and in their prolific literary production. Pardo Bazán's work on women's education had a mixed reception. Whereas literary figures such as Benito Pérez Galdos and Juan Valera supported Bazán's ideas, other conservative critics harshly criticized her. For instance, Bieder mentions that Pardo Bazán's translation of Stuart Mill's *The Subjection of Women* (1869) was received in Spain with "ridicule and reproof".[49] However, as Kirkpatrick points out, Pardo Bazán proved to be an alternative and prestigious model for younger generations of women,[50] who would later implement her notion of education into their own lives and work. Lejárraga also made an impact on Spanish society when it came to understand the importance of women's education in the society of her times. Under her husband's name and her own, she produced her "applauded and highly respected"[51] literary work focusing on feminist issues and paying particular attention to women's education. As a member of diverse political and feminist associations, Lejárraga aimed to give a practical use to her feminist theoretical thinking, establishing a direct dialogue with women. By means of public talks, conversations, and the correspondence she held with her readers, she exchanged ideas about women's education and other feminist topics.[52]

It is sad to say that the few advances that the feminist movement made in Spain in the hands of women like Pardo Bazán and María Lejárraga suffered from a sudden halt in the year 1939 when dictator Francisco Franco took power. Under the control of his autocratic Catholic government, women's education was reduced to a mere rehearsal of their role as angels of the home. During this time, Pardo Bazán was recognized as an aristocratic writer and her work was mostly studied in relation to aesthetic issues, obliterating her feminist contribution. On the other hand, María Lejárraga was silenced not only for her secondary role as her husband's literary collaborator—when in fact she was "the" author,—but also for "the outstanding position that she had occupied in the political work of the Republic."[53]

The year 1975, when Franco died, was the turning point for a country that had remained in the obscurity of isolation and oppression for fourty long years. Since then, scholarly research in Spain and the US has recuperated much of the work done by these female writers and has recognized their contributions to the definition of Spanish feminism of the late twentieth century to the present. However, and in spite of all the research carried out by these scholars, there is still much inquiry and investigation left to do to fully understand the importance and implications of the legacy left by Emilia Pardo Bazán and María Lejárraga toward the improvement of women's education in Spain.

Notes

[1] "La última jerarquía es la de lo grotesco, y la formaría de este modo: 1.ª, el marimacho radical (escritoras anarquistas, antimilitaristas, partidarias del voto y de la igualdad de derechos; 2.ª, la que no se da a nadie por amor a sí misma; y 3.ª, la que no se da a nadie porque nadie la toma." Santacruz, "El siglo de los marimachos," 86. Unless otherwise noted, all translations are my own.

[2] Pascual Santacrúz was a prolific critic, philosopher, and journalist who regularly published in 19th and 20th-Century popular Spanish newspapers and magazines such as "La España moderna" and "Heraldo granadino". His perception of women and their role in society was typical at this time.

[3] Tuana, *The Less Noble Sex*, ix. Looking at Freud's theories and their influence in Spanish psychology, it can be stated that this vision endured until the 20th Century as Mary Nash claims: "even on the eve of the [Spanish Civil] War, . . . the ideological assumptions of the division of spheres is still accepted by both men and

women. The entry of women into the public sphere is slow, motivated by neccesity rather than by the belief in their rights" (aún en vísperas de la guerra civil, . . . sigue vigente tanto por parte de hombres como de mujeres una aceptación de los presupuestos ideológicos de la división de esferas. La penetración femenina en la esfera pública es lenta, impulsada más por la necesidad que por la convicción de un derecho). Nash, *Mujer, familia y trabajo*. 59-60.

[4] Socolow, *The Women of Colonial Latin America*, 6.
[5] Nash, *Mujer*, 43.
[6] Scanlon, *La polémica feminista*, 50.
[7] María was born as María de la O. Lejárraga. I prefer to use "María Lejárraga" because, in my opinion, it contains her two other identities: "Gregorio Martínez Sierra," as the female writer hidden behind a male pen, and "María Martínez Sierra," as the female writer who claimed her authorship. I would also like to thank her nephew Ricardo Lejárraga for being the first one to reveal her real name to me.
[8] Bieder, "Women, Literature, and Society," 29.
[9] "La educación del hombre y de la mujer."
[10] "In order to be a respectable woman, you need to be at home with a broken leg."
[11] Pardo Bazan, "La educacion del hombre y de la mujer," 80.
[12] "postulado pesimista." Ibid., 75.
[13] "destino relativo." Ibid., 88.
[14] "La mujer es tanto más apta para su providencial destino cuanto más ignorante y estacionaria."
"constituye para el varón honra y gloria, para la hembra es deshonor y casi *monstruosidad*." Ibid., 74.
[15] "cuando estos faltaren, [a] la de la entidad abstracta género masculino." Ibid., 75.
[16] "Adventicia" "todas las mujeres conciben ideas, pero no todas conciben hijos." Ibid., 89.
[17] "No se puede formar a la madre; la madre es la obra maestra del instinto natural." Ibid., 81.
[18] "entendimiento y . . . corazón." Ibid., 94.
[19] "podríamos hoy juzgar de la cultura de un Estado, por la amplitud concedida a la enseñanza intellectual de la mujer, no solo en la ley escrita, sino en la sociedad." Ibid., 86.
[20] "fomentando el vigoroso desarrollo del espíritu nacional." Ibid., 90.
[21] "Polilla roedora." Ibid., 91.
[22] See Jean B. Landes' *Women and the Public Sphere in the Age of the French Revolution* to explore this idea.
[23] See Harrison and Hoyle's book *Spain's 1898 Crisis* for a more detailed discussion on Regenerationism.
[24] La mayor época de prosperidad y florecimiento para España. Ibid., 97.
[25] "Tanto monta, monta tanto, Isabel como Fernando" (They amount to the same, Isabel and Ferdinand). It is interesting to notice Pardo Bazán's gesture when only

mentioning Isabella's part of the motto and leaving out Ferdinand's. In this sense, Bazán plays with the audience's expectations since most people would know how the motto goes. Singling out Isabella's part of the motto would create a sense of surprise in the audience, drawing their attention to the queen's importance.

[26] "intervención gloriosísima." Ibid., 97.

[27] The author does not mention either the position of female Indians after Colon arrived in America. Taking into consideration the general Western perception of European countries seen as superior civilizations, Pardo Bazán's colonial ideas are a product of her time.

[28] "De feminismo."

[29] See also Lejárraga's own account of both her personal and professional relationship with Gregorio in *Gregorio y yo. Medio siglo de colaboración*.

[30] Blanco, "Feminist Essays," 76.

[31] Ibid., 76.

[32] Ibid., 87.

[33] Ibid., 84. For Alda Blanco, Lejárraga made a conscious decision about what talks she would deliver personally depending on what type of public attended the event. Apparently in this case, the presence of the aristocracy in the audience did not awake Lejárraga's desire to give the talk herself in spite of her effort to transmit her ideas about feminism.

[34] Scanlon, *La polémica feminista*, 159.

[35] "Pobres solteronas viejas." Lejárraga, "De feminismo," 16.

[36] "Cristiana, ultramoderna y feminista." Ibid., 12.

[37] "¡No se alarmen ustedes, señoras mías!" Ibid., 12.

[38] "los lindes encantados de su propio hogar, acercarse a la vida[,] comprenderla, [y] de darse cuenta de que hay un más allá, o un más abajo, hecho de injusticias." Ibid., 13.

[39] Ibid., 14.

[40] "dilatando el campo de sus actividades." Ibid., 15.

[41] Ibid., 19.

[42] "La posibilidad de comprar es la única corona de realeza del hombre moderno." Ibid., 20.

[43] Nash, *Mujer*, 160.

[44] "porque son . . . españolas." Lejárraga, "De feminismo," 22.

[45] Ibid., 27.

[46] Ibid., 29.

[47] Ibid., 29.

[48] Ibid., 34.

[49] Bieder, "Women, Literature, and Society," 54. It is clear that Spain was not ready for the idea of women performing intellectual tasks. Pardo Bazán's extensive and good-quality literary work was belittled when she was denied a position in the Spanish Royal Academy of the Spanish Language on three occasions. Likewise, her intellectual value as educator was underestimated when only one student

attended her lecture during the first day as a professor at Madrid's Central University.
[50] Kirkpatrick. *Mujer, modernismo y vanguardia*, 24.
[51] Blanco, "Feminist Essays," 79.
[52] See, for instance, her book *Cartas a las mujeres de España* where she presents and answers some of her readers' questions and concerns about women's education.
[53] "el significante lugar que había ocupado en los quehaceres políticos de la Republica." Blanco, Foreword to *Gregorio y yo*, 14.

Works Cited

Primary Sources

Martínez Sierra, Gregorio. "De feminismo." *Feminismo, feminidad y españolismo*. Madrid: Saturnino
Calleja, 1920: 11-34.
Pardo Bazán, Emilia. "La Educación del hombre y la de la mujer." *Nuevo teatro crítico* 22 (1892): 14-82.

Secondary Sources

Bieder, Maryellen. "Women, Literature, and Society: The Essays of Emilia Pardo Bazán." In *Spanish
Women Writers and the Essay*, edited by Kathleen M. Glenn and Mercedes Mazquiarán de Rodríguez, 25-54. Columbia; London: University of Missouri Press, 1998.
Blanco, Alda. "*A las mujeres de España*: The Feminist Essays of María Martínez Sierra." In *Spanish Women Writers and the Essay*, edited by Kathleen M. Glenn and Mercedes Mazquiarán de Rodríguez, 75-99. Columbia; London: University of Missouri Press, 1998.
—. ed. Foreword to *Gregorio y yo. Medio siglo de colaboración* by María Martínez Sierra, 9-42. Mexico:
Candesa, 1953.
Harrison, Joseph and Alan Hoyle, eds. *Spain's 1898 Crisis*. Manchester: Manchester University Press, 2000.
Kirkpatrick, Susan. *Mujer, modernismo y vanguardia en España (1898-1931)*. Madrid: Cátedra, 2003.
Landes, Jean B. *Women and the Public Sphere in the Age of the French Revolution*. Ithaca: Cornell

University Press, 1988.
León, Luis de. *La perfecta casada*. Barcelona: Casa Miquel-Rius, 1930.
Martínez Sierra, María. *Cartas a las mujeres de España*. Madrid: Saturnino Calleja, 1923.
—. *Gregorio y yo. Medio siglo de colaboración*. México: Candesa, 1953.
Mill, John Stuart. *The Subjection of Women*. London: Longmans, Green and Co., 1869.
Nash, Mary. *Mujer, familia y trabajo en España, 1875-1936*. Barcelona: Anthropos, 1983.
Santacruz, Pascual. "El siglo de los marimachos." *La España moderna* 4, no.19 (1907): 74-94.
Scanlon, Geraldine. *La polémica feminista en la España contemporánea, 1868-1974*. Translated by Rafael
Mazarrasa. Madrid: Siglo XXI, 1976.
Socolow, Migden Susan. *The Women of Colonial Latin America*. Cambridge: Cambridge UP, 2000.
Tuana, Nancy. *The Less Noble Sex: Scientific, Religious, and Philosophical Conceptions of Woman's
Nature*. Bloomington; Indianapolis: Indiana University Press, 1993.
Vives, Juan Luis. *La instrucción de la mujer cristiana*. Buenos Aires: Espasa-Calpe, 1940.

CHAPTER ELEVEN

"KNOWLEDGEABLE OTTOMAN GIRLS": OTTOMAN WOMEN'S EDUCATION IN THE NINETEENTH CENTURY

HÜLYA YILDIZ

In Fatma Aliye Hanım's[1] second novel, *Re'fet* (1897),[2] Binnaz, the mother of Re'fet says the following to her daughter just before dying: "I leave you with your diploma that will look after you much better than your mother and father."[3] This strong and moving statement from a woman who worked as a laundress to support her daughter and finally died because her body could not take the hard work marks a significant change in the perception of what education can do to women's lives. The fact that Binnaz codes the diploma her daughter will earn from the Teacher Training School for Women as a critical instrument that enables Re'fet to survive on her own is unique in Ottoman women's history.

This understanding of education and what it can do for underprivileged women refers to the initial steps of modernization efforts in the Ottoman Empire in the second half of the nineteenth century. The changes in the political culture that allowed the improvement of women's status were the results of debates that lasted generations and constituted a major factor in many works of nineteenth century fiction. *Re'fet* is a forerunner of such novels. It is a celebration and the story of the first generation of Ottoman Muslim women who had a chance to study beyond the secondary schools to become teachers. *Re'fet* is the first novel in which a new type of woman is introduced and valorized as an ideal for female readers. Fiction like *Re'fet* provides an extremely rich and complex set of sources for understanding the cultural and political changes that led women to participate more fully in the public sphere. Faced with contemporary conflicts, nineteenth century Ottoman writers wrote on the intersections of public issues and women's roles in the private sphere. The novels did not just reflect public attitudes toward these issues they also challenged existing values and actively participated in the struggle over women's wider access to rights, including education rights. In this chapter, before I move to my discussion of *Re'fet*, which narrates the story of the "malumatlı Osmanlı Kızları" (Knowledgeable Ottoman Girls),[4] I discuss how the discourse around women's education was framed in elite Ottoman men's writings. I also explain how women's magazines and journals contributed to the advancement of women's rights not only by providing women a public space to take part in discussions on education but also by creating an active agenda around more educational rights for women.

The nineteenth century in Ottoman historiography was a period of change and reformation. Threatened by the imperial and financial challenges of the Great Powers, the Sublime Porte saw the solution in making some changes not only in its administrative structure but also in its social structure. New systems of administration and education were instituted during the *Tanzimat* (Reorganization) period, which is customarily accepted as starting with the Imperial Decree of Gülhane of 1839, and elaborated during the reign of Abdülhamid (1876-1909), who strengthened them further through the introduction of telegraphs and railways—the rudiments, that is, of a modern system of communication.[5] Perhaps the most influential reforms initiated by the *Tanzimat* were in the field of education. The Woman's Question in the Ottoman Empire was also put on the agenda especially after the *Tanzimat* period. The Woman's Question, as it was put, was mainly discussed within the framework of what the role of women should be in the society, whether women needed to be educated, and if so, what should be the limits and content of this education.

During the nineteenth century, as a result of domestic and foreign influences, the Ottoman political and bureaucratic elite faced and understood the significance of political and cultural challenges in the field of education. The activities of European and American missionaries, the educational awakening of the Ottoman non-Muslim groups, and the neighboring states exerting influence in the Ottoman lands led to this awareness. The Ottoman state tried its best to expand and reform public education within its borders as a means both to control its population and to rise up to challenges from outside and inside. Schools were established in provinces such as Bosnia, Crete, and Damascus as political tools for building loyalty to the state and preventing the influence of other political entities. In the Hamidian period (named for Sultan Abdülhamid II, who ruled from 1876 to 1908/1909), the Ottoman state established approximately 10,000 public schools.[6]

Two important developments in Ottoman educational reform were the establishment of the Ministry of Public Education (*Maârif-i Umûmiyye Nezâreti*) in 1857 and the Regulation of Public Education (*Maârif-i Umûmiyye Nizâmnâmesi*) in 1869, both of which aimed to centralize and standardize the school system throughout the Empire. As historian Selçuk Akşin Somel explains, the education policy of the Hamidian period was "to use public schools as an institutional tool of social disciplining and modernization."[7] An important part of this modernizing mission was the education of girls.

Although upper-class girls had long been educated in elite homes, public institutions for the education of girls from lower classes were established only in the nineteenth century. First, *Tıbbıye,* or the Medical School in İstanbul, launched the extension of educational opportunities to girls by training them under the supervision of midwives brought from Europe in 1842. As a result of these courses, in 1845 midwife diplomas were given to ten Muslim and twenty-six Christian women. This was followed by the opening of the *Kız Rüşdiyeleri* (Secondary Schools for Girls) in 1858. *Kız Sanayi Mektebi,* or the Girls' Vocational School, was opened in 1864. In 1869, the *Maarif-i Umumiye Nizamnâmesi* (the Regulation for Public Education) was issued. The attendance to the *Sıbyan Mektepleri* (Primary Schools) was made compulsory for girls between the ages of six and eleven. Finally, *Darü'l-Muallimat* (Teacher Training School for Women) was established in 1869 and opened its doors to students on April 26, 1870.[8] In 1873, seventeen girls graduated from this school.[9] Until the *İnas-ı Darülfünûn* (University for Women) was opened in İstanbul in 1914, the Teacher Training School for Women was the only higher education institution for women.

The opening of the Teacher Training School for Women was a major development in Ottoman women's struggle for more educational rights in many ways. First of all, it enabled poor and middle-class Ottoman women to enter into the profession of teaching, which was previously monopolized by male teachers or European governesses and teachers. Therefore, the initial entry of Muslim women into professional life took place in the field of education before their entry into industry, which occurred during the Balkan Wars (1912-13).[10] Furthermore, for the first time in Ottoman history, some of the opportunities that had been exclusively available to elite women previously were also available to women from lower classes. The Teacher Training School for Women in the Ottoman Empire led to the emergence of a new class of intellectual women. These young female graduates wrote and published articles in the women's magazines next to those written by women from upper classes and expressed their own views and perspectives. Perhaps the best example of this is the group of women who wrote in the *Hanımlara Mahsus Gazete* (Ladies' Own Gazette). Fatma Aliye Hanım's novel *Re'fet* is the first novel in which we see a detailed account of not only these schools but also the girls who attend them.

Expanding educational opportunities for women increased their ability to participate in public life. An interesting feature that we see in some of the readers' letters sent to be published in women's journals is the way some women define themselves. Increasingly during this period the letters were signed with words describing attributes that specify the writers' education. The following examples are from a women's periodical called the *İnsaniyet* (Humanity): "İki Okumuş Hanım" (Two Educated Women), "Mektepli bir Kız" (A school girl), and "Lisana-aşina bir Hanım" (A lady who knows languages). The letter from the "school girl" had a threatening tone, demanding that the letter be published and that she should be assigned as a correspondent of the journal. Interestingly, the editor of the periodical welcomed this proposal.[11]

The Issue of Women in Public Discourse

During the second half of the nineteenth century, discussions around the issue of women's education were intermingled with the idea that women needed to be educated so that they could better help their husbands in a rapidly changing world. For instance, to inform and encourage the public to send their daughters to school, the government published a brief in the newspapers in 1861, which read in part as follows:

> Literacy is essential for both men and women, and the only way for men who do heavy work to provide for the home to be comfortable at home is that women should also know about their world and religion and that they obey their husbands.[12]

So, the education of women was presented as part of the ideology of patriarchy and Islam: women could help their husbands better if they knew more about their world and religion. This understanding of women's education was also advocated by the male elite of the time.

For instance, Namık Kemal, a famous intellectual and writer of the time, explained in his essay "Terbiye-i Nisvan Hakkında Bir Layiha" (A Treatise on the Education of Women), published in the newspaper *Tasvir-i Efkâr* (Description of Opinion), how the education of women was necessary and that it wasn't against Islam as some claimed. In this essay, he complained about how women were kept away from all aspects of work life and seen as objects of desire. He stated that the only contribution women made to the society was bearing children. Although they could contribute to humanity like men do, they were not making efforts to do so. According to him, the only reason for this was that women were ignorant. He explained the vital role of women in the education of children and that the education of women wasn't forbidden in Islam; on the contrary, women needed to be educated for the betterment of the whole of the society.[13]

Another intellectual who contributed to the discussions on women's place in society and why they needed to be educated is Şemseddin Sami. In his book called *Kadınlar* (Women), published in 1882, Şemseddin Sami put forth his thoughts on the status of women and advocated their education and participation in work life. In this book, Sami gave three main reasons that women should be educated. First, men could live happily only with educated women. Second, because half of the human beings living in the world were women, educating them would mean that a large portion of the people in the world would be educated. Third, because women educate their children, the education of women would also influence their children, which meant that future generations would become educated, too. According to Sami, "Family means woman."[14] Şemseddin Sami even published and edited a women's magazine titled *Aile* (Family) in 1880.

Women's Journals

One of the most effective mediums women used to fight for their rights, including their right to education, were women's magazines and journals. In fact, these publications were educational tools in their own right as they not only informed women about their sisters in other places but also created an agenda for women's demands. Between 1868, which was the year of the first women's magazine, *Terakki-i Muhaddarat* (Progress of Women), and 1923, the year when the Turkish Republic was established, there were more than forty women's magazines, which published the essays and short stories of about 265 women.[15] While most of these magazines were published by men but included women writers, some of them were published by women exclusively.

These Ottoman women's journals present us with a unique historical and cultural source and give us an opportunity to recover the voices of women. Collectively, the journals are one of the earliest sources of material of this sort because this was the first generation of Ottoman women to write in numbers and to produce and publish their works as printed texts. In fact, they may even be the first Muslim women to publish their ideas in printed form publicly. Women, through these journals, had an opportunity to voice their views about many issues publicly. The journals also gave women an opportunity to make their way into Ottoman literature, which was dominated by men. Many women, though not well-known, engaged in literary activity and got a chance by means of these journals both to publish their pieces and to publicize their recently published books, thus enabling them to reach the general public more effectively. For example, the poetess Makbule Leman (1865-98) became famous for her essays, short stories, and poems published in *Hanımlara Mahsus Gazete*.[16] The dawn of the women's press led to the rise of a new female literary culture in Turkey. Women's journals also contributed significantly to Ottoman women's education. They not only informed women about new educational opportunities but also created an agenda for more educational rights for women.

Among the several, mostly short-lived Ottoman women's newspapers and magazines, the two most significant and longest-running ones are the *Hanımlara Mahsus Gazete* and *Kadınlar Dünyası* (Women's World). *Hanımlara Mahsus Gazete* was the longest-running women's periodical, published between 1895 and 1908.[17] The *Hanımlara Mahsus Gazete* was the only magazine to have an editorial board that consisted exclusively of women until the publication of the *Kadınlar Dünyası* on 17 April 1913. It functioned as a forum for women to practice writing publicly and voicing their opinions publicly. *Kadınlar Dünyası* was the most overtly political and a self-declared feminist magazine. *Kadınlar Dünyası* was the first women's magazine that used the word "feminism" to describe Ottoman women's struggles for their rights. Its editorial staff was composed of women only.

Women's journals advocated educational opportunities for the masses, not just a small group of elite women. The fact that there were some elite educated women such as Fatma Aliye, Halide Edib, and Nigar Hanım was not a solution to the problem of women's education. Lasting solutions for the education of women needed to be found. Education needed to become more widespread in the society.[18]

In addition to calling the government to open more schools for girls, the journal also advocated the opening of private schools. It stated that women might come together and open a school and then get help from the *Maarif Nezâreti* (Ministry of Education). The first example of this was the first private kindergarten for girls founded by Aziz Haydar, who was a member of the *Osmanlı Müdafaa-i Hukuk-ı Nisvan Cemiyeti* (Ottoman Association for the Defense of Women's Rights).The journal also advocated the opening of a *Darüşşafaka* for the education of orphan girls.[19]

Another important issue that *Kadınlar Dünyası* fought for was women's right to higher education. For instance, in one of the essays published in this magazine, Mükerrem Belkıs used a strong rhetorical strategy in appealing to the religious feelings of fellow Ottomans and asked why even Muslim women in Russia living under the rule of another nation had the rights of higher education and what kind of thoughtlessness would deny this right to Ottoman women. As a result of a long battle for higher education for women, the doors of the *Darülfünûn* in İstanbul were opened for women in 12 September 1914.[20] The journal also supported the idea that women should be sent to Europe for further education.

In activism around voicing women's demands about education rights, two women's names come to the foreground: Azize Haydar Hanım and Mükerrem Belkıs Hanım. In addition to her several essays on the importance of women's education in magazines, Azize Haydar also opened the first private school for girls in İstanbul. In Mükerrem Belkıs's essays, she described in detail what kind of an education she wanted, covering issues such as the qualifications of teachers and how they should be prepared. In many of her essays, she pushed for further rights for women that were promised by the new cadres of the Second Constitutional Period. She called for activist women teachers to work for the emancipation of their sisters in one of her essays. Addressing the female teachers directly, she stated:

> We do not want lazy, timid female teachers. We want active female teachers who are in love with freedom, and intellectual female teachers. If the educated women do not raise women who will save women from slavery as the womankind wants, then the biggest responsibility will be on the female teachers.

She then added:

> Female teachers, know that you are holding in your hands the greatest power of the future. The lever of humanity is in your hands. Do not neglect this power. You will make the future generations live the desired life style.[21]

It is noteworthy that around this time, women authors writing at the women's journals started to advocate a new role for women, especially female teachers. They were asked not only to be selfless in their efforts to reach their fellow sisters but also to act with the knowledge that they could shape future generations. In this sense, perhaps, this new ideology of womanhood, crystallized around the identity and the role of the female teacher, was an extension of women's traditional domestic roles. The new ideology of the female teacher is nowhere clearer than it is in *Re'fet*, the second novel by Fatma Aliye Hanım.

Re'fet

Re'fet is the first novel in Turkish that represents an Ottoman Muslim professional woman. Re'fet is a fatherless girl who is struggling to graduate from the Teacher Training School for Women in İstanbul in order to earn a living for her mother and herself. The novel can be read as a manifesto that promotes education for upward mobility. It advocates the cultural production of a "new woman" who is rational and educated, who can make important decisions for her life, and who is equipped to carry the responsibilities of living in public without sacrificing her reputation, honor, and decency in society. Furthermore, teaching is presented as one of the very few options for earning a decent life for women like Re'fet who are poor and orphaned. This is a new concept for the Muslim Ottomans of the period. The following dialogue between Ref'et and her mother is an interesting example that illustrates how education is viewed by women like them. The conversation takes place after Re'fet tells her mother that she wants to go to the *Darü'l-Muallimat*:

> Binnaz: Darülmuallimat? What is that?
> Re'fet: You know our teachers, right? It is the school that they graduated from.
> Binnaz: What is it to you then?
> Re'fet: What do you mean? Can one become a teacher without graduating from there?
> Binnaz: Teaching? Do you think that they would let poor people like us do that?
> Re'fet: Mom, they would give it to whoever studies hard.
> Binnaz was surprised by these words.
> Re'fet, half smiling: And only the poor like us become female teachers. The rich do not go to school to become teachers. They go there to get knowledge.[22]

It is also important to note that several times in the novel, Re'fet's lack of physical beauty is underscored. Therefore, a new type of woman is portrayed and promoted. This is a woman who is not physically attractive or beautiful, but a woman who can prove that she can be liked and respected not because of her looks, but because she works and earns her own living with honor. She is presented as the new ideal for young women, and her difference among her peers is emphasized:

> Her dream wasn't like that of other young girls of her age. She was going to earn a living, manage her household, make her mother comfortable, educate many children and train them as the children of the homeland. Those children would all respect and love her, as saying 'our teacher.' That was Re'fet's dream.[23]

The Teacher Training School for Women functioned as a place where girls from different social classes and backgrounds could intermingle as there were girls coming from affluent households such as Şihab Hanım, who was sent to school not only to learn but also to have firsthand experience with less fortunate girls such as Re'fet and Şule, who are both orphaned and poor. The solidarity between Re'fet and Şule is exemplary in that they are able to finish the school only by helping each other materially and emotionally. For instance, when Şule's mother dies, Re'fet offers to let her stay with Re'fet and her mother in the single room they occupy until the girls graduate, and the limited monthly allowance that Şule gets from her uncle sometimes becomes the only money Re'fet and her mother have to pay their rent. In fact, the whole novel takes place in a community of women and as a result of the solidarity found there. Şihab's elder sister Cazibe Hanım comes to the aid of Re'fet and her mother during their most difficult times when Binnaz is sick. Cazibe Hanım not only sends a family doctor to take care of Binnaz but also gives them some money to buy food.

The novel also describes the intellectual interaction between women, which is not exclusive to the school environment. During a summer that Re'fet and Şule stay at Cazibe Hanım's summer house, we see a strong emotional and intellectual bond developing between them, especially between Cazibe and Re'fet, who talk for hours on a wide range of topics including painting and ancient Greek philosophy. So, this depiction of the importance of informal education is another aspect of the novel. Overall, the fictional space *Re'fet* represents is constructed on female solidarity where women support each other emotionally, financially, and intellectually.

Wider access to public education not only ensured educational opportunities for more women from diverse backgrounds but also reinforced the freedom women gain when they lack a father figure at their homes. However, this doesn't necessarily mean that they were liberated from any form of control. For most of these young orphan women, the state became the Father figure to whom they felt responsible. For instance, in the conversation between Şule and Re'fet after Re'fet's mother's death, Şule reminds Re'fet that, from now on, "Re'fet belongs to the state" because it provided her education.[24] So, at this critical moment that Ottoman women are free of one form of control—familial patriarchy—, they fall into the more intricate control mechanisms of the modern state.

Previously, it was mostly elite women who had the educational facilities at their mansions provided by their enlightened fathers who believed that their daughters should be educated. Fatma Aliye is a good example of this pattern common to elite women of the time. She was the daughter of a well-known historian, statesman, and jurist of the time, Ahmet Cevdet Paşa.[25] Her father was a liberal-minded man in that he also allowed his daughter to join the private lessons provided for her elder brother, Ali Sedat Bey. She took lessons on various subjects including linguistics, cosmology, astronomy, French, mathematics, history, philosophy, and literature. However, the Teachers' Colleges for Women broke this pattern and gave women from lower social classes an opportunity to have education and a profession, which ensured them not only a tool to earn their living but also more active participation in public life. Re'fet is the first example of a strong female figure who can stand on her own feet due to the education she received at the Teacher Training School for Women, and she is also the first example of a self-transforming heroine in Turkish literature. Although it was the dire living conditions that made women like Re'fet abandon domestic space, this act also emancipated them from patriarchy to a certain extent.

Notes

[1] Fatma Aliye Hanım (1862-1936), one of the first Ottoman woman novelists, started her publishing career as a translator in 1889-90 and continued to write well after the establishment of the Turkish Republic in 1923. Her writing career included not only translations and novels but also treatises and newspaper and magazine essays and articles on matters related to philosophy, religion, history, women, and other social issues. She was an influential intellectual, especially during 1889-1922.

[2] First published as a serial in Ahmet Mithat's *Tercüman-ı Hakikat* (the Interpreter of Truth) newspaper between 22 Şaban-3 Şevval (26 January-7 March 1897). Then, it was published as a book, *Re'fet*. İstanbul: Kırk Ambar Matbaası, 1314. The page numbers I cite are from the text transcribed by Abdülkadir Dağlı, "Fatma Aliye Hanım'ın 'Ref'et' Romanı (Tahlil ve Yeni Harflere Aktarılması." (Unpublished Master's Thesis. Harran Üniversitesi, Şanlıurfa, 1999). It is the only available source I could find in the Latin alphabet. I have also consulted the

original manuscript at the Fatma Aliye Hanım Evrak-ı Kataloğu, Atatürk Library in Taksim, İstanbul. Unless otherwise noted, all translations are my own.
[3] "Seni validenden iyi idare edecek pederinden ziyade himaye eyleyecek olan diploman ile bırakıyorum." *Re'fet*, 114.
[4] *Re'fet*, 81.
[5] Mardin, *The Genesis of Young Ottoman Thought*, 212-219.
[6] For a detailed discussion of modernization efforts in the Ottoman education system in the nineteenth century, see Fortna. *Imperial Classroom*, and Somel, *The Modernization of Public Education of the Ottoman Empire 1839-1908*.
[7] Somel, *The Modernization of Public Education of the Ottoman Empire 1839-1908*, 12.
[8] Arıkan, "Osmanlılar'da Tanzimat Dönemi'nde Kadınlarla İlgili Gelişmeler," 324.
[9] Taşkıran, *Cumhuriyetin 50. Yılında Türk Kadın Hakları*, 25-29.
[10] On the women workers during the Balkan Wars and World War I, see Karakışla, *Women, War and Work in the Ottoman Empire*.
[11] Çakır, *Osmanlı Kadın Hareketi*, 25-6.
[12] "Okuyup yazmanın erkek ve kadınlar için elzem olup geçinmek için ağır işler gören erkeklerin ev işlerinde rahat etmeleri ancak kadınların dahi dini ve dünyalarını bilerek kocalarının emirlerine itaat etmeleriyle ve istemediklerini yapmakdan sakınmalarıyla ve iffetlerini koruyup kanaat ehli olmalarıyla mümkündür." Cited in Aşa, "1928'e Kadar Kadın Mecmuaları," 16.
[13] Namık Kemal, "Terbiye-i Nisvan," 1.
[14] "Aile demek kadın demektir." Şemseddin Sami, *Kadınlar*. 24.
[15] Demirdirek, *Osmanlı Kadınlarının*, 8.
[16] Aydın, *Ne Yazıyor Bu Kadınlar*.
[17] All of its issues are available in the Beyazıd Devlet Kütüphanesi in İstanbul, where I examined this magazine along with others. I would like to use this opportunity to thank Dr. Serpil Çakır from the Department of Political Science at the University of İstanbul for her help in guiding me during my library search in İstanbul in 2006, especially at the Beyazıd Devlet Kütüphanesi. The Associate Director of the library, Ms. Süheyla Şentürk has also been extremely helpful in providing me the copies of all of the Ottoman women's journals the Beyazıd Library owned. I thank her very much for her help during my research there.
[18] Nimet Cemil, "Kadınlar Hakkında Nikbinlik," 2-3. Cited in Çakır, *Osmanlı Kadın Hareketi*, 242.
[19] Mükerrem Belkıs, "Kız darüşşafakası," 1.
[20] Mükerrem Belkıs, "Millete ve Hükümete Bir Hitabe: Hak İsteriz," 1. Cited in Çakır, *Osmanlı Kadın Hareketi*, 253; Ulviye Mevlan, "Kadınlık Maarif Nazırı," 2; Cited in Çakır, *Osmanlı Kadın Hareketi*, 260.
[21] "Miskin, korkak muallimeler istemeyiz. Cevval, hürriyete aşık, mütefekkir muallimeler istiyoruz. Eğer mektepliler alem-i nisvanın istediği gibi, alem-i nisvanı esaretten kurtaracak bir halde yetişmezlerse en büyük mesuliyet muallimelerde olacakdır." "Muallimeler biliniz, şunu pek iyi biliniz ki istikbalin en

büyük kuvvetini elinizde tutuyorsunuz. Beşeriyetin manivelesi elinizdedir. Bu kuvveti, bu maniveleyi hüsn-i istimal ediniz. Nesl-i âtiye istenilen sekl-i hayatı siz yaşatacaksınız." Cited in Toska, "Tanzimat'tan Cumhuriyet'e Osmanlı Kadın Tarihinde İstanbul ve Önde Gelen Kadın Simaları," 10.
[22] Binnaz: Darülmuallimat mı? O da ne demek? Re'fet: Haniya bizim hoca hanımlar yok mu? İşte onların çıkdığı mektep. Binnaz: Ay, onlar çıkmış ise sana ne? Re'fet: Nasıl bana ne? Oradan çıkmayınca hoca olunur mu? Binnaz: Tamam Hocalık sana kalmış!...Hiç bizim gibi fıkaralara öyle şey verilir mi? Re'fet: Nineciğim kim çalışıyorsa ona verirler. Binnaz bu sözlerden şaşırdı. Re'fet, Nim tebessümle: Hem de ancak bizim gibi fakirler muallime olurlar. Zenginler muallime olmak için okumazlar. Malumat öğrenmek için oraya gelirler...*Re'fet*, 32-33.
[23] "Onun tahayyulatı o yaşdaki sair genç kızların tahayyulatına benzemiyordu. Kazanacak, evini idare edecek, validesini rahat ettirecek, bir çok çocuklar okutup evlad-ı vatanın talim ve terbiyesinde bulunacak o çocukların hepsi buna hürmet edecekler 'hacemiz' diye sevecekler! İşte Re'fetin tahayyulatı hep bundan ibaret idi." *Re'fet*, 63-4.
[24] *Re'fet*, 119.
[25] He was among the reformist group of the *Tanzimat* period. As the person who knows the Ottoman legal system best, he was given the duty of writing the new legal system in the Ottoman Empire, called the *Mecelle* system. He is also known as a historian of his time. His most famous work is a twelve-volume Ottoman history book.

Works Cited

Primary Sources

Atatürk Kitaplığı Fatma Aliye Hanım Evrakı Kataloğu-I. Hazırlayanlar Yard. Doç. Dr. Mübeccel Kızıltan and Tülay Gençtürk. İstanbul: İstanbul Büyükşehir Belediyesi Kültür İşleri Daire Başkanlığı Kütüphane ve Müzeler Müdürlüğü, 1993.

Dağlı, Abdülkadir. "Fatma Aliye Hanım'ın 'Ref'et' Romanı (Tahlil ve Yeni Harflere Aktarılması." Unpublished Master's Thesis. Harran Üniversitesi, Şanlıurfa, 1999.

Fatma Aliye. *Re'fet*. İstanbul: Kırk Ambar Matbaası, 1314.

Mükerrem Belkıs. "Kız darüşşafakası." *Kadınlar Dünyası*, no. 95 (7 Temmuz 1329).

—. "Millete ve Hükümete Bir Hitabe: Hak İsteriz." *Kadınlar Dünyası*, no.86 (28 Haziran 1329).

Namık Kemal. "Terbiye-i Nisvan." *Tasvir-i Efkâr*, no. 457 (29 Kanunisani 1283).
Nimet Cemil. "Kadınlar Hakkında Nikbinlik." *Kadınlar Dünyası*, no.162 (24 Kanunisani 1330).
Şemseddin Sami. *Kadınlar*. (1311). Hazırlayan İsmail Doğan. Ankara: Gündoğan, 1996.
Ulviye Mevlan. "Kadınlık Maarif Nazırı." *Kadınlar Dünyası*, no.131 (15 Şubat 1329).

Secondary Sources

Arıkan, Gülay. "Osmanlılar'da Tanzimat Dönemi'nde Kadınlarla İlgili Gelişmeler." In *Tanzimat'ın 150. Yıldönümü Uluslararası Sempozyumu*. Ankara: Türk Tarih Kurumu Yayınları, 1994.
Aşa, Emel. "1928'e Kadar Kadın Mecmuaları." Unpublished Master's Thesis. İstanbul Üniversitesi, İstanbul, 1989.
Aydın, Mehmet. *Ne Yazıyor Bu Kadınlar. Osmanlıdan Günümüze Örnekleriyle Kadın Yazar ve Şairler*. Ankara: İlke Yayınevi, 1995.
Çakır, Serpil. *Osmanlı Kadın Hareketi*. İstanbul: Metis Yayınları, 1996.
Demirdirek, Aynur. *Osmanlı Kadınlarının Hayat Hakkı Arayışının Bir Hikayesi*. Ankara: İmge Kitabevi, 1993.
Fortna, Benjamin C. *Imperial Classroom: Islam, the State and Education in the Late Ottoman Empire*. Oxford: Oxford University Press, 2002.
Karakışla, Yavuz Selim. *Women, War and Work in the Ottoman Empire: Society for the Employment of Ottoman Muslim Women (1916-1923)*. İstanbul: Tarih Vakfı and Ottoman Bank Archive and Research Centre, 2005.
Mardin, Şerif. *The Genesis of Young Ottoman Thought. A Study in the Modernization of Turkish Political Ideas*. Princeton: Princeton University Press, 1962.
Somel, Selçuk Akşin. *The Modernization of Public Education of the Ottoman Empire 1839-1908. Islamization, Autocracy, and Discipline*. Leiden: Brill, 2001.
Taşkıran, Tezer. *Cumhuriyetin 50. Yılında Türk Kadın Hakları*. Ankara: Başbakanlık Basımevi, 1973.
Toska, Zehra. "Tanzimat'tan Cumhuriyet'e Osmanlı Kadın Tarihinde İstanbul ve Önde Gelen Kadın Simaları," Kadın Eserleri Kütüphanesi, İstanbul. n.d.

Chapter Twelve

Contradictory Designs: Mary Lyon's Mount Holyoke Female Seminary

Beatrice Jacobson

On September 30, 1847, at the age of 17, Emily Dickinson began her studies at Mount Holyoke Female Seminary. Located in South Hadley, Massachusetts, the seminary might have been selected by her family for its proximity, merely 13 miles from Dickinson's home in Amherst. Or, perhaps her father, Edward Dickinson, had been impressed by the school's connection to Amherst College's president, Edward Hitchcock: Mount Holyoke's founder and current director, Mary Lyon, had been Hitchcock's student and protégée. Or, perhaps it was the opportunity to share a dormitory room with one of her cousins that drew Dickinson to the gates of Mount Holyoke. Despite such advantages, the school also presented challenges to Emily Dickinson and her family. At a time when women's educational institutions were considered with suspicion, Mount Holyoke was developing a reputation for academic ambition unusual and perhaps unsettling in a women's institution, offering a course of study that would eventually equal the curricula of men's colleges. Further, unlike students at other women's boarding schools, Mount Holyoke students—all white and mostly from the middle class—were required to perform domestic chores, responsibilities for which Dickinson's upbringing, which included the services of domestic servants, had not prepared her. Suspicious of this plan for manual labor, Dickinson writes in a letter to her friend, Abiah Root, that she had expected things to be coarse, but finds that the opposite is true: "I expected to find rough & uncultivated manners . . . but on the whole, there is an ease & grace a desire to make one another happy, which delights & at the same time, surprises me very much."[1]

Dickinson also found Mount Holyoke to be academically challenging. Responding to the initial series of placement examinations, she comments, again writing Abiah Root: "I am sure that I never would endure the suspense which I endured during those three days again for all the treasure of the world."[2] Though some biographers conclude that, once evaluated, Dickinson might have found Mary Lyon's curriculum repetitive after her academic foundation at Amherst Academy, her comments in letters suggest a high level of satisfaction.[3] She enjoys her studies; she resists (unsuccessfully) when her family insists she leave Mount Holyoke to return home to nurse an illness. Moreover, despite her inability to experience spiritual conversion—a main focus at the Seminary—she finds the climate of the school agreeable. After two months at Mount Holyoke, she can report: "One thing is certain & that is, that Miss. Lyon & all the teachers, seem to consult our comfort & happiness in everything they do & you know that is pleasant."[4] Exploring the creative tensions experienced by Dickinson and her classmates during the early years of Mount Holyoke Female Seminary, and especially the role played by its founder, uncovers two somewhat contradictory elements in the design of Mount Holyoke: an ambitious plan to raise the academic level of Mount Holyoke to that of men's colleges is coupled with a novel domestic program requiring all students to perform the household chores necessary to maintain a large residential educational institution.

Such a tension—between genuinely progressive developments in women's education and programs that underscore women's domestic sphere—is only one example of the complex and at times contradictory experiments in women's schools during the first half of the nineteenth century in the United States. During this time, a number of institutions dedicated to the education of young women appear, including several founded by key advocates of women's education: Troy Female Seminary (Troy, New York) was founded by Emma Willard in 1821; Hartford Female Seminary (Hartford Connecticut) was opened by Catharine Beecher in 1823; and in 1837, after several years of research, fundraising, and planning, Mary Lyon opened Mount Holyoke. This same period of time saw the publication of numerous arguments, proposals, and plans in support of women's education. As they envisioned and developed their institutions, Willard, Beecher, and Lyon advanced arguments for women's education, outlined their indictments of present educational efforts, and invited the public to join in their efforts to improve women's schooling.

All three women addressed questions of pedagogy and textbooks, institutional administration, and, overall, they sought to justify improvements in women's education. Certainly their own academic accomplishments supported the argument made several decades earlier by Mary Wollstonecraft in *A Vindication of the Rights of Woman* (1792) that the failure to develop women's intellects was due to social factors, not biological deficiency. While the question of woman's intellectual ability continued to stalk their projects, the reformers won over supporters by advancing the popular understanding of women as servants of religion whose sacred domestic work complemented men's public tasks and by arguing that women's responsibilities in the home, and, by extension in the classroom, called for careful and thoughtful attention to their education. Yet this socially acceptable rationale complicated their projects, even while it advanced their cause, especially in the case of Mary Lyon.

The reformers adopted a compensatory stance regarding female education, whereby, as Jill Ker Conway explains, women's roles are understood as supplementing men's. Specifically, women are clearly identified as the nurturers, providing socialization, basic education, and moral guidance for the young; hence their sphere of activity extends from the home to the schoolroom or the mission; men, on the other hand, are responsible for politics, commerce, and other areas such as philosophy and theology, domains that lie beyond woman's nurturing sphere. Calculating to avoid the impression of competing with men over the same academic or political ground, female reformers capitalized on the excellence of women's divine call to serve the family, endorsing women's patriotic and religious function within the home and the school, and praising her domestic mission. By doing so, they were insuring a hearing for themselves by the American public on whom they depended for financial and moral support; further, they were fusing their projects with the strongest of nineteenth-century social mainstays, the middle-class social concept of True Womanhood.[5]

These sometimes competing arguments complicate the reformers' proposals. Although Emma Willard's 1819 treatise, *A Plan for Improving Female Education*, written to secure state support for girls' education, claimed to promote the advancement of women, her proposals actually reinforced established opinions about the role of women. She carefully anchored women's social foundation in motherhood, women's primary end, and except perhaps for teaching, their sole role. As mothers, she asserts, women "have the charge of the whole mass of individuals . . . .during that period of youth when the pliant mind . . . is steadily guided by a forming hand."[6] Developing that "forming hand" serves as the basis of Willard's rationale for women's education. Further, Willard linked this compensatory concept of women's education to the young republic's need for new standards of education:

> . . . such improvement of one half of society, and that half, which barbarous and despotic nations have ever degraded, would of itself be an object, worthy of the most liberal government on earth; but if the female character be raised, it must inevitably raise that of the other sex . . ."[7]

Notwithstanding the limitations of her reformist perspective, Willard attacked the prevailing attitudes towards female education and clearly indicted society's lackadaisical efforts to educate its young women. She criticized the tendency of males to consider women as "the pampered babies of society, who must have some rattle put into our hands, to keep us from doing mischief to ourselves or others,"[8] and she demonstrated the educational inequities that such attitudes produced:

> How often have we seen a student, who, returning from his literary pursuits, finds a sister, who was his equal in acquirements . . . While his youth was devoted to study, and he was furnished with the means, she, without any object of improvement, drudged at home, to assist in the support of the father's family, and perhaps contribute to her brother's subsistence abroad . . . [9]

To such a brother, Willard attributed embarrassment and shame at the condition of his sister who has become "a being of a lower order."[10] She further attributes to the brother a sense of remorse as he "weeps at his neglect,"[11] a strategic use of pathos in a primarily financial proposal.

A decade later, Catharine Beecher likewise located the objectives of the Hartford Female Seminary, which she and her sister Mary Beecher had opened in 1823, in the domestic sphere. However, their priorities differ somewhat from Willard's. Female education, according to Beecher, is necessitated primarily if not solely by the religious mission of women, a mission she defines as a profession in her 1829 treatise, *Suggestions Respecting Improvements in Education*:

> What is *the profession* of a *woman*? Is it not to form immortal minds, and to watch, to nurse, and to rear the bodily system, so fearfully and wonderfully made, and upon the order and regulation of which, the health and well-being of the mind so greatly depends?[12]

Beecher's choice of the term "profession," a word with both religious and worldly connotations, suggests the systematic training that women need to fulfill their responsibilities. Yet, as with Willard, Beecher accepted the division of human endeavors into two spheres. Later, in 1851, she publishes *True Remedy for the Wrongs of Women* in which she claims for her educational projects a compensatory objective:

> But where are we to arise such an army of teachers as are required for this great work? Not from the sex which finds it so much more honorable, easy, and lucrative, to enter the many roads to wealth and honor open in this land. It is WOMAN who is to come at this emergency, and meet the

demand—woman, whom experience and testimony have shown to be the best, as well as the cheapest guardian and teacher of childhood, in the school as well as the nursery.[13]

As the "cheapest" teachers available, women would surely appeal to state and religious institutions as a practical means of staffing schools and missions; further, they would be practicing the self-abnegation characteristic of True Womanhood; yet cheapness seems to run against the sanctity of woman's mission, implying an exploitation rather than an employment of female talents. Beecher's assertion demonstrates the confusion of the ideal and the practical which marks so many of the writings produced by reformers of female education during this period. Like Willard's use of pathos in the midst of a fiscal argument, Beecher's use of the term "profession" with all its complex associations with affairs both spiritual and mundane, confuses divergent agendas.

The contradiction in their rhetoric reflects the space between the reformers' positions on female education and their own positions as leaders in the community. While they taught that women were subservient to God and men, and needed to be trained as "professionals" in their self-effacing yet powerful roles, the reformers themselves, as individuals, had become self-assertive, confident public figures who spoke out on behalf of their cause, wrote extensively, organized and directed elaborate institutions, and attended to the finances of their operations. In short, they had assumed many male-identified responsibilities and proven themselves successes. Yet their traditionally pious rhetoric and objectives were essential if their works were to gain public support. Thus by endorsing the code of separate spheres, they guaranteed themselves the opportunity to exercise many male skills and privileges.

In none of the reformers of women's education is the discrepancy between the stated objectives of her project and the realities of her life and her experiment more clearly marked than in the example offered by Mary Lyon. Contemporary accounts of Lyon as well as her own writings describe a woman deeply motivated by religion, a characteristic which would in itself seem to limit her efforts to challenge traditional values. Modern-day readers, however, must take into account the historical context within which Lyon lived and wrote. Writing in 1928, M. A. DeWolfe Howe begins a review of Lyon's life with an emphasis on the contemporary social climate:

> . . . a century ago it was possible to be at the same time an earnestly evangelical Christian, more "fundamentalist" than all but a few still living,

and yet of a spirit essentially so modern as to fall under contemporary suspicion as a dangerously innovating radical.[14]

As founder and director of Mount Holyoke Female Seminary, Mary Lyon demonstrated great piety but also great power, one of the many paradoxes she was able to negotiate in her career. At Mount Holyoke she not only took women's intellectual development seriously and challenged her institution to advance its curriculum to a level equal to men's colleges, but, in what might seem a contradictory move, she also created a home where both students and faculty lived, where domestic tasks were shared, and where the sick and the dying--eventually including Lyon herself— were cared for. While attempting to enrich women's traditional sphere by facilitating their intellectual advancement, Lyon made a more radical move: her system of student domestic work, coupled with a challenging curriculum, allowed Mount Holyoke to bring domestic and academic spheres, the public and private spheres, to bear on each other.

With the opening of Mount Holyoke, Mary Lyon brought a long preparation in education to fulfillment. Born in 1797 in Buckland, Massachusetts, in a family of limited means, Lyon had worked her way through an education unusual for even upper middle class women. Her ambition to teach was nurtured by Joseph Emerson's Female Seminary at Byfield. Her education was furthered through instruction and encouragement given her by Edward Hitchcock who quickly recognized her potential. Her work with Zilpah P. Grant Banister at her school in Ipswich and her collaboration with Catharine Beecher enabled her to think through her goals for her own institution and to witness the workings of a variety of schools, all of which influenced her design for Mount Holyoke Female Seminary.[15]

Her institutional purposes and goals are spelled out her 1837 circular, "General View of the Principles and Design of the Mount Holyoke Female Seminary":

> The design is to give a solid, extensive, and well balanced English education, connected with that general improvement, that moral culture, and those enlarged views of duty, which will prepare ladies to be *educators* of children and youth, rather than to fit them to be mere teachers, as the term has been technically applied.[16]

The curriculum would prepare a young woman to teach and administer schools, "and when she has done with the business of teaching in a regular school, she will not give up her profession but will still need the same well balanced education at the head of her own family, and in guiding her own household."[17] Yet this traditional grounding of women's education in their domestic mission was to be achieved using many of the elements of men's schools. For instance, understanding the vulnerability of women's schools, Lyon founded Mount Holyoke "on the high principle of enlarged Christian benevolence. . . . for the public good."[18] As a not-for-profit organization, the school would not operate for the gain of its founder. Lyon determined that the institution "would be permanent"[19]—lasting through successive generations, as men's schools were, in contrast to many female schools that went out of business when the headmistress retired or moved on. Although Lyon describes a curriculum modeled on that of Ipswich Female Seminary, where the "intellectual discipline and moral culture are of no inferior order,"[20] the early years of Mount Holyoke demonstrate a constant upgrading of the initial curriculum.

Further, Lyon specified that students should be at least sixteen years old, an age requirement higher than most women's schools. In "Female Education," she explained the importance of the period following sixteen:

> It is then that all the precepts, example, and salutary influence of early years may be embodied into general rules of duty—when principles are to be adopted for life, and when character is to receive almost its last and final impression.[21]

Her decision to devote the Academy's efforts to this age group was based on her own experience and observations in a wide range of teaching positions. However, David Allmendinger suggests that there were other factors: an increase of the years between grade schooling and marriage in the first half of the nineteenth century had placed women in their late teenage years in a social vacuum, one which schools like Mount Holyoke served to fill.[22] Further, although religious conversion of every student was an institutional goal, Lyon stipulated that all students were to be treated equally regardless of their financial or their spiritual conditions.[23]

Lastly, Mount Holyoke would offer the best facilities "at a very moderate expense,"[24] in order to provide education for women of average means. Allmendinger notes that Lyon considered all aspects of the school—from geographical location to institutional economy—with an eye toward keeping expenses for students within the reach of average families—to such effect that Seminary tuition was only one-third the cost of Troy of Ipswich, and less than a third of the cost of Amherst College.[25]

Lyon further determined that Mount Holyoke would be a residential school where not only all students but teachers as well would live together, to "constitute one family."[26] Perhaps the most radical dimension of her proposal was the domestic plan: all residents would be responsible for the school's cooking, cleaning, laundry, and other household tasks.[27] There were, of course, multiple reasons for the domestic program: there were practical considerations (avoiding the expense of hired servants), and formative goals (preparing students for any life situation they might encounter), and moral objectives (gratuitous service), as well as goals related to health—and physical exercise was taken seriously at Mount Holyoke. Yet, the elaborate nature of this domestic experiment, requiring an organizational system with considerable oversight, suggests deeper motivations and goals.

Further, Mary Lyon's early life may offer some explanation. Having lost her father when she was five, she was later separated from her mother who moved away when she remarried. Lyon then lived with her brother who paid her a small wage for housekeeping. Later, she lived with relatives, exchanging household chores for her board while she attended school. Her teaching career and her efforts to establish a school demanded frequent moves and travel, a program that denied her any sense of a home of her own. Thus, creating an academic institution that would also serve as a home for her teachers, students, and also for herself responded to a personal need.

Yet communal living at Mount Holyoke was also an impressive experiment in women's organization and self-sufficiency. Arthur C. Cole describes the division of students into departments and circles assigned regular tasks:

> . . . a circle of fourteen was summoned by the bell at five o'clock to prepare breakfast—one to make the fires, eight to set the tables, and five to peel the potatoes and prepare the simple meal; another group cleaned up after breakfast—washing tumblers . . . scouring knives . . . sweeping the dining hall, the "space ways," and the stairways; other circles were allotted to dinner duties and to supper . . . [28]

An individual student, however, might not have realized the elaborate system in which she worked. Helping to maintain a residence with 235 students, and faculty and staff as well, Emily Dickinson takes her domestic assignment in stride—perhaps a tribute to Lyon's smooth organization: "My domestic work is not difficult," reported Dickinson "and consists in carrying the knives from the first tier of tables at morning and noon, and at night washing and wiping the same quantity of knives."[29]

To maintain a residence for a sizeable number required a system and order that could overwhelm the academic and spiritual emphases of the Seminary. Instead, however, the domestic organization encouraged a sense of community and family. Though she became asocial later in her life, Emily Dickinson seemed to have thrived as a member of this community:

> Everything is pleasant & happy here & I think I could be no happier at any other school away from home. Things seem much more like home than I anticipated & the teachers are all very kind & affectionate. They call on us frequently & urge us to return their calls & when we do, we always receive a cordial welcome from them.[30]

The domestic plan provided the material basis for Mount Holyoke's primary objective, the academic program, which, even initially was impressive. Yet Mary Lyon set about upgrading the course of studies over the institution's first decade, as demonstrated by comparisons of the courses of study announced in two catalogues, one from 1837-8, the school's first year, and another—the school's eleventh—published in 1847-8, the year Dickinson was a student.[31] Both catalogues indicate three years of study—junior, middle, and senior, but the curricula for these three years, as well as entrance requirements vary. For instance, a list of subjects and texts listed in the 1837-38 catalogue as "Preparatory Studies" is identified in the later catalogue as "Studies Required for Admission to the Seminary." This list includes English grammar, both mental and written arithmetic (with recommended texts and testing methods), but also adds both Stoddard's *Latin Grammar* and Andrews' *Latin Reader*. Applicants are also advised that Latin and Ancient Geography may be deferred but they are warned that by doing so, they will need two years to complete the junior year. The junior year requirements for 1847-8 exchange "English Grammar" for "review of English grammar" and add more Latin (Cornelius Nepos). The Middle year drops English grammar in the later version and adds Latin, physiology, chemistry, astronomy, and rhetoric, along with Alexander's *Evidences of Christianity*. These last five were earlier listed for Senior year. The Senior year of 1847-8 adds mental philosophy and Milton's *Paradise Lost* to subjects that have been retained from the earlier catalogue listing: geology, logic, moral philosophy, natural theology and Butler's *Analogies*. Thus, during its first decade, the Seminary's original curriculum was transformed into a challenging course of studies which, in addition to creating the foundation for the transformation of the Seminary into a College in 1888, also challenged traditional norms of what should constitute education for women. The addition of more challenging subjects and texts, and especially the gradual inclusion of Latin in the curriculum announced academic ambitions that went beyond women's traditional sphere. As Walter Ong has noted, teaching Latin to women students had become politicized,[32] thus Lyon was wise to insinuate Latin into the curriculum gradually—first as a requirement for admission and only later as a subject at the Seminary.

While either the domestic plan or the upgraded curriculum would suffice to make Mount Holyoke a powerful experience in a young woman's life, students during the institution's first twelve years also learned from the example of Mary Lyon and her emphasis on living a life deliberately. Richard Sewall reflects on the impact made on Emily Dickinson by "the example of a brilliant and loving woman who had found her work and had given her life to it."[33] Whether or not they pursued the careers that Mary Lyon envisioned for them, the young women under her care enjoyed a climate that encouraged self-evaluation and reflection, that combined mundane duties with intellectual rigor, and that challenged each to set and pursue goals. Allmendinger quotes one student, Eliza Peabody, who wrote in 1840: "Her intent seems to be to improve all the time, & she plans admirably, & executes with rapidity."[34] In 1845, another student, Lucinda Guilford reflected on Lyon's determination: "I do mean to improve all I possibly can. I mean to be as wise, as consistent, as energetic, as 'planning,' as sedate, as thinking, as thorough as Miss Mary Lyon's beau ideal of a lady can be."[35] Determining that "beau ideal" must have required considering more of Lyon's attributes: a successful, unmarried woman who had achieved her dream of a women's educational institution, who lived in a family-like setting surrounded by like-minded teachers and students, who understood the intricacies of spiritual growth, institutional finances, Butler's *Analogies,* and bread baking. She had both designed and realized the institution in which they found themselves intellectually and spiritually challenged, a space dedicated to the development of specifically female potential. Not surprising, then is this observation, again by Lucinda Guilford, this time recorded in Edward Hitchcock's tribute to Mary Lyon: "We have great power over ourselves. We may become almost what we will."[36] And while Lyon had specific goals in mind for her students, she also encouraged them to think for themselves. Beth Gilchrist's biography of Lyon reports this comment of hers, found in minutes of her lectures to students: "[Do] not attempt anything because I think it is best,—not unless you believe it is desirable, practical, and expedient. Feel the force of it."[37] Despite the conformity suggested by the religious orientation of the Seminary, Lyon insisted that "Each is to try to make the most of her own powers and not to try to become somebody else."[38] Surely Dickinson, one of the religious "no-hopers" during her time at Mount Holyoke, found in this last principle a source of comfort.

Gilchrist and Howe also trace an emphasis on energy in Lyon's thinking, a quality seldom identified with sedate and submissive nineteenth-century women. Lyon is reported to have remarked that "Happiness is in activity. . . . the remembrance of energy makes us happy."[39] And, paradoxically, "Learn to sit with energy"[40] sums up one of Lyon's goals for her students in a challenging formulation that transforms sedentary female behavior from passivity into a vital, invigorating experience. This phrase also echoes the design of Mount Holyoke where traditional female-identified traits of domesticity were coupled with a program of intellectual energy. Perhaps more than any other of her students, Emily Dickinson responded to this climate in radical ways. Returning to her family home after just one year at Mount Holyoke, Dickinson would spend the rest of her life there, baking bread, tending her ailing mother, all the while generating close to two thousand poems charged with a beauty born of the complexities of polarized phenomena—reason and emotion, life and death, time and eternity.

Notes

[1] Dickinson, *Letters*, I. 55.
[2] Ibid., I. 54.
[3] For a helpful assessment of Dickinson's response to the academic challenges of Mount Holyoke, see Richard Sewall's *The Life of Emily Dickinson*, pp. 362-367.
[4] Dickinson, *Letters*, I. 55.
[5] See Barbara Welter's study of True Womanhood in *Dimity Convictions*.
[6] Willard, 6.
[7] Ibid.
[8] Ibid., 14.
[9] Ibid.
[10] Ibid.
[11] Ibid.
[12] Beecher, *Suggestions*, 7.
[13] Beecher, *True Remedy*, 240-241
[14] Howe, 45-46.
[15] The most recent substantial biography of Mary Lyon is Mary Alden Green's *Mary Lyon and Mount Holyoke: Opening the Gates*. Green documents the facts of Lyon's life used here and below.
[16] Lyon, "General View," 4. I wish to acknowledge the Mount Holyoke College Archives and Special Collections (< http://clio.fivecolleges.edu/>), which provide online access to an extensive collection of Mary Lyon materials.
[17] Ibid., 3.
[18] Ibid.

[19] Ibid.
[20] Ibid., 5.
[21] Lyon, "Female Education," 6.
[22] Allmendinger, "Mount Holyoke Students," 28.
[23] Lyon, "Female Education," 7.
[24] Ibid.
[25] Allmendinger, "Mount Holyoke Students," 33.
[26] Lyon, "Female Education," 6.
[27] Ibid., 7.
[28] Cole, (40).
[29] Dickinson, *Letters*, I.55.
[30] Ibid., I.54.
[31] Both of these catalogues are available online through Mount Holyoke Catalogues (see Works Cited for full information). The sections that provide the information for the analysis that follows begin on page 8 of the 1837-8 Catalogue and on page 11 of the 1847-8 Catalogue.
[32] Ong, *Orality and Literacy*, 249-253.
[33] Sewall, *Life of Emily Dickinson*, 367.
[34] Allmendinger, 27.
[35] Ibid.
[36] Hitchcock, *The Power of Christian Benevolence*, 372.
[37] Gilchrist, *The Life of Mary Lyon*, 131.
[38] Ibid., 132.
[39] Ibid., 131.
[40] Howe, *Classic Shades*, 44.

Works Cited

Primary Sources

Beecher, Catharine E. *Suggestions Respecting Improvements in Education*. Hartford: Packard & Butler, 1829.

——. *True Remedy for the Wrongs of Women*. Boston: Phillips, Sampson, & Co., 1851.

Dickinson, Emily. *The Letters of Emily Dickinson*. Edited by Thomas H. Johnson. 3 vols. Cambridge: Harvard University Press, 1958.

Lyon, Mary. "General View of the Principles and Design of the Mount Holyoke Female Seminary." Circular 7 (1837). Mount Holyoke College Archives and Special Collections. <http://clio.fivecolleges.edu/mhc/lyon/b/1published/> (12 October 2007).

——. "Female Education." Circular 8 (1839). Mount Holyoke College Archives and Special Collections.

<http://clio.fivecolleges.edu/mhc/lyon/b/1published/> (12 October 2007).
Mount Holyoke Female Seminary. *First Annual Catalogue, 1837-1838*. Available at Mount Holyoke College: Annual Catalogues, 1837-1900. <http://clio.fivecolleges.edu/mhc/catalogs/> (12 October 2007).
—. *Eleventh Annual Catalogue, 1847-1848*. Mount Holyoke College: Annual Catalogues, 1837-1900. <http://clio.fivecolleges.edu/mhc/catalogs/> (12 October 2007).
Willard, Emma. *A Plan for Improving Female Education*. 2nd edition. Middlebury: J. W. Copeland, 1819.
Wollstonecraft, Mary. *A Vindication of the Rights of Woman* in *A Vindication of the Rights of Woman: An Authoritative Text, Backgrounds, the Wollstonecraft Debate, Criticism*. Ed. Carol H. Poston. 2nd ed. New York: W. W. Norton, 1988. Originally published in 1792.

Secondary Sources

Allmendinger, David F. "Mount Holyoke Students Encounter the Need for Life-Planning, 1837-1850." *History of Education Quarterly* 19 (1979): 27-46.
Cole, Arthur C. *A Hundred Years at Mount Holyoke College: The Evolution of an Educational Ideal*. New Haven: Yale University Press, 1940.
Conway, Jill Ker. "Perspectives on the History of Women's Education in the United States," in *History, Education,and Public Policy*, edited by Donald R. Warren, 273-285. Berkeley: McCutchan, 1978.
Gilchrist, Beth. *The Life of Mary Lyon*. Boston: Houghton Mifflin, 1910.
Green, Mary Alden. *Mary Lyon and Mount Holyoke: Opening the Gates*. Hanover: University Press of New England, 1979.
Hitchcock, Edward, ed. *The Power of Christian Benevolence in the Life and Labors of Mary Lyon*. New York: American Tract Society, 1858.
Howe, M.A. DeWolfe. *Classic Shades: Five Leaders of Learning and their Colleges*. Boston: Little, 1928.
Ong, Walter. *Orality and Literacy*. London: Methuen, 1982.
Sewall, Richard. *The Life of Emily Dickinson*. New York: Farrar, Straus, Giroux, 1974.
Welter, Barbara. *Dimity Convictions: American Women in the Nineteenth Century*. Athens: Ohio University Press, 1976.

CHAPTER THIRTEEN

TEACHING, PREACHING AND PRACTICE: NÍSIA FLORESTA'S SHIFTING VISION OF WOMEN'S EDUCATION IN NINETEENTH-CENTURY BRAZIL

CHARLOTTE LIDDELL

The subject of women's education not only pervades the extensive work of the Brazilian writer Nísia Floresta (1810-1885), it also plays a central role in her life, since she supported herself and her family through teaching for some twenty years.[1] This dual participation as writer and educator offers a valuable opportunity to compare the theoretical vision of education for women as expounded in her texts with the reality of that which she provided in her school. The striking differences that emerge between what she "practiced" and what she "preached" tell us much about the development of her ideas and the social and ideological influences at work upon them. An analysis of her many writings on education also reveals an evolution in her approach from a focus on education as a route to feminine virtue to the importance of motherhood and the social value of the mother-educator.[2] Furthermore, Floresta begins to make use of discourses of nation-building, directly linking female education to the spiritual and material prosperity of the nation and drawing attention to Brazil's educational failures as a source of national shame. Whilst this patriotic rhetoric lends greater power and appeal to her arguments, she also harnesses it to justify her own participation as a woman within an essentially male social discourse.

Although I shall refer to other texts in order to chart the progression of Floresta's ideas regarding women's education, this essay will focus primarily on her 1853 work *Opúsculo Humanitário*.[3] This work is a sustained, detailed and informed critique of Brazil's education system. It is also the text which offers the clearest and most complete expression of the education she advocated for women in her writing and the ways in which she sought to sell that vision to a conservative and patriarchal society. However, I shall begin by looking at Floresta's school and the curriculum she favored for her own pupils, since she in fact began to teach several years before publishing a work of her own, and her pedagogic practices must inevitably contextualize her writing on education. Unhampered by the conventions and restrictions of the published word, her teaching arguably provides a more honest insight into the level of instruction Floresta considered appropriate and advantageous to her sex.

Floresta's teaching career appears to have begun in Porto Alegre in 1833, following the premature death of her husband, suggesting that she sought paid teaching work in order to support her young family.[4] In 1837, Floresta moved to Rio and almost immediately established the Colegio Augusto. It is interesting to compare the advertisement she placed with similar ones for other girls' schools at the time. For example, an establishment operating in 1846 is advertised as teaching "reading, writing, arithmetic, Portuguese grammar, French, dance, sewing, embroidery, needlepoint, and everything that is fitting to a girl's education."[5] The reader is led to understand that what is appropriate for a girl's education is a continuation of the list of domestic skills which the advertisement begins. In contrast, Floresta advertises her school as:

> A school for girls in which, as well as reading, writing, arithmetic, sewing, embroidery, needlepoint, and everything else relating to a girl's domestic education, we also teach Portuguese grammar by a simple method, French, Italian, and the most general principals of Geography.[6]

Whilst Floresta still highlights the teaching of domestic skills, a necessary focus in order to attract most parents at that time, the use of the expression "as well as" reveals her desire to emphasize the ways in which her curriculum extended beyond this domestic focus. More significantly, in the first advert domestic skills constitute a large part of what is seen as a girl's education per se. Floresta, on the other hand, sees such skills only as part of "domestic education." What is also interesting about Floresta's choice of wording is that she includes the basic skills of literacy and numeracy in her definition of domestic education, apparently equating them with needlework. It is clear that whilst Floresta saw these as being fundamental to even the most basic female instruction, she saw *education* for women as being something distinct from the mere acquisition of domestic skills.

The curriculum taught at the Colegio Augusto was in fact considerably broader even than that advertised above. In 1846 Floresta published the results of the school's examinations in the press and the subjects examined included literature, poetry, translation and grammar in French and Italian, geography and cosmography, ancient and modern history and Latin.[7] At the time Floresta's own daughter, who won one of the prizes, was just short of her seventeenth birthday, indicating that the Colegio Augusto taught girls well beyond the usual age of twelve or thirteen. The school appears to have received support from some elevated sources. Ten gentlemen of standing, including the papal nuncio, whose names were published in the above article, assessed the examinations and awarded the prizes, indicating that they were happy to be associated with such a forward-thinking establishment, whilst an accompanying article was full of praise for Floresta and her pupils.[8] However, the school was also criticized in the Carioca press.[9] An example can be seen in this cutting observation on the curriculum: "Studies of language were plentiful, those of needlework completely overlooked. Men need wives who work more and talk less."[10] This kind of condemnation exemplifies the patriarchal prejudices Floresta and like-minded educators of girls would have encountered, reflecting the continuing, widespread belief that the instruction of girls should prepare them only for the practicalities of marriage.

It is certainly apparent that Floresta was convinced of the benefits of a broad, enlightened and intellectually-focused curriculum for her students and was prepared to face public criticism and personal insults to provide it. A comparison with her published writing, however, reveals that she was not willing to risk, or was not interested in risking a similar attack on her published work by defending such a challenging position for the wider female population. On the contrary, the education she appears to advocate in her written work becomes increasingly conservative and limiting as her vision of women's role in society becomes more tightly bound to the domestic sphere. I shall first look briefly at Floresta's position on women's education in her earliest writing, before charting the development of her arguments through to her later writing in Europe.

Floresta's first publication *Direitos das Mulheres e Injustiça dos Homens* (Rights of Women and Injustice of Men) appeared in 1832, before she embarked on her teaching career.[11] The text is a translation of a little-known English work entitled *Woman not Inferior to Man*, published under the pseudonym Sophia in 1739,[12] a Cartesian, humanist tract which claims women's absolute equality with men and thus their ability and right to participate in the most elevated aspects of public life. Although the revolutionary conclusions drawn by the English text appear, and indeed are contradictory to Floresta's position as expressed in her own writing (in which women's access to the public sphere is increasingly denied), some of the core arguments Floresta consistently uses in her defense of women's education can first be found here. In *Direitos* we see the assertion that women are rational creatures, intellectually equal to men, and that they therefore have a natural right to equal education.[13] We also see the establishment of a direct link between education and virtue and the identification of poor education as the root cause of women's condition and their repression, an idea which is accompanied by the repeated suggestion that men have deliberately deprived women of education in order to keep them in a state of inferiority.[14] These potentially radical ideas can still be glimpsed in Floresta's subsequent writing but are disabled by more conservative and limiting discourses of female virtue, maternalism and nation-building.

After the publication of the first edition of *Direitos* in Recife in 1832, Floresta's life was to be dominated by motherhood and her teaching career, and it would be ten years before she published a work of her own. When she did return to writing, her early publications continue to indicate an overwhelming concern for female education. Between 1842 and 1847 Floresta published four short works, three didactic texts, which she probably also used as teaching aids in the Colegio Augusto, and the text of a speech given to her pupils, which appears to have been published primarily as an advertisement for the school. These pieces must be read in the context of Floresta's teaching career, since their publication was undoubtedly influenced in large part by a concern for the success of her school, which was her most important project at this time and, as far as is known, her primary source of income. As such, Floresta could not afford to attract polemic by putting her name to ideas that might have damaged her reputation.

The first of these texts, entitled *Conselhos a minha filha* (Advice to my Daughter) (1842), takes the form of an extended moral lesson in which Floresta outlines the behavior appropriate to a young woman.[15] In 1847 she published two short pieces of didactic fiction, one of which has sadly been lost. The surviving text, with the self-explanatory title *Fany, ou o modelo das donzelas* (Fany, or the Model Young Lady), presents a fictitious model of the saintly virtues expounded in *Conselhos a minha filha* and it seems likely that the similarly-titled lost piece served the same purpose. Some notion of the content of this text, *Daciz, ou a jovem perfeita* (Daciz, or the Perfect Girl), can be gleaned from a reference to it in the medical thesis of Floresta's brother-in-law, which suggests that it may outline a woman's maternal duties.[16] The speech addressed to her pupils, which was published the same year, reiterates the message found in the previous texts, emphasizing the importance of virtue and religious faith.[17] Despite their different genres, all three surviving texts from this period are extremely similar in content and tone, firmly establishing the relationship between education and virtue, which can be interpreted as Catholic obedience, sexual purity and thus marriageability, in Floresta's thinking. Although the texts address the issue of female education and are all written within a didactic framework, the dominant focus in each is the virtue which education fosters and the happiness, security and social regard which women can only earn by showing themselves to be virtuous. At this point the value of motherhood is only hinted at and the employment of a nation-building discourse is absent.

In 1849, Floresta travelled to Europe with her children, spending more than two years there, primarily in Paris. Immediately upon her return in 1852, she published what is undoubtedly her most ambitious Brazilian text, *Opúsculo*. Despite touching on a range of social issues, the essential focus and purpose of this lengthy work is a discussion and defense of female education and the text offers clear evidence of the progression of Floresta's ideas since the publication of her early didactic pieces referred to above, suggesting that she was greatly influenced by her experiences in Europe. Most notably, Floresta's time abroad appears to have given her a new consciousness of her own nation on the world stage, which results in an overtly patriotic tone and justification of her ideas.

Alongside the by now familiar argument that a sound religious and moral education provides the best and only route to virtue, in *Opúsculo* we find the first clear expression of Floresta's support for education within the home and her belief that a properly educated and virtuous mother is the best educator of her own daughters. Most importantly, though, Floresta now goes to considerable lengths to show how an improvement in women's education is vital to Brazil's future well-being and progress. *Opúsculo* is structured as a comparative history of women's education, in which a depiction of the situation in Germany, Great Britain, France and the United States, is juxtaposed with a detailed consideration of the development and current state of the education system in Brazil, a comparison which Floresta clearly employs in order to provoke a sense of national shame in her reader.

In her discussion of education in Brazil, Floresta criticizes the limited curriculum taught to most girls; condemns the lack of secondary education available to them; and is extremely critical of the lack of regulation of private schools, which she suggests are set up by anyone who can read.[18] By allowing individuals to run schools without ensuring that they are fit to do so, she accuses her government of actively jeopardizing national well-being.[19] Floresta is also critical of her fellow teachers, questioning the motivations and morals of those involved in education, observing that whilst public primary schools have become totally discredited, many private schools are little better. In the end, despite passing harsh judgments on both, Floresta settles in favor of private schooling, believing that a need to remain solvent provides at least some motivation to maintain standards.[20] However, this preference clearly establishes women's education as an elite prerogative and she makes no suggestion as to how the poor might afford the private education she favors. Her failure to defend, or even discuss the right to free education is clear evidence of her overwhelming concern for and identification with the privileged, elite social classes.

Having condemned the efforts of the government and the vast majority of teachers, Floresta then turns her attention to the parents. She stresses parents' responsibility to find good schools,[21] but parental support within the formal education system is not her primary concern. Instead she is interested in the education, in the widest sense, which parents themselves offer their children and since it is mothers who have most contact with their children, in particular their daughters, it is they who have the most important role to play in Floresta's vision of education in the home. Thus it is for their future role as mother-educators that girls must themselves be educated. This idea, all but absent from her earlier texts, in fact constitutes a core defense of women's education in *Opúsculo*, as the following passage makes clear: "we would like to provide all girls with the knowledge, skill and interest necessary for them to properly fulfill the honorable and sublime mission of teachers of their own daughters."[22] This vision of the mother-educator in fact echoes growing maternalist discourses, employed by men and women alike, during the nineteenth century,[23] and can be found in Brazilian writing on women's education published during the 1850s and later.[24] In fact, the significance of maternal influence can be found considerably earlier, for example in an 1827 law on public education, which stated that women were in greater need of schooling [*instrução*], "because it is they who provide their son's initial education [*educação*]."[25] However, the rhetoric of the educated mother contributing to national progress through her children only finds a popular voice after mid-century, suggesting that Floresta was at the forefront of this movement and a possible source of inspiration and influence to later writers.

Although Floresta's thinking has clearly evolved since her early publications, in *Opúsculo* we still find a constant reiteration of the essential arguments with which she defends her claims for improved female education. The core argument identified in her early texts, that education leads to virtue, which in turn leads to happiness and social regard for women, continues to form the foundation of Floresta's positioning, but it no longer constitutes her primary defense. Instead it serves as a starting point for a more tangible and targeted appeal, which identifies the real, practical benefits of women's education for men, society and the nation. By specifically pointing out the advantages which men can gain from better educating women, Floresta makes a calculated play for the self-interest of her male readers, in whose hands any hope of change inevitably lay. She not only suggests that no Brazilian woman wants the kind of existence encouraged by superficial instruction, but also directly challenges Brazilian men, asking: "what honest and reasonable man would be content with a wife ... caught up in the futilities of a life of dissipation and indolence, rather than in the constant task ... of improving herself through the practice of virtue."[26]

Yet Floresta's interest does not really lie in the small-scale effects of female education on individual lives. She is concerned instead with the progress of the nation and, perhaps most importantly, with Brazil's reputation and standing within the supposed civilized world. This concern with international judgments of her country is the obvious and inevitable result of her two year visit to Europe where she gained her first real insight into the abundance of prejudices and perceptions, accurate or otherwise, regarding the New World.[27] Central to this concern for her nation's status is Floresta's employment of the notion of women's education as an index of civilization and her identification of Brazil's unhappy position within this scale (a concept subsequently used by other, male writers).[28] An improvement in female education would, of course, enable Brazil to move up this civilization index and Floresta appeals to her fellow women with this argument, emphasizing how they can contribute "to the dignity of the family and the glory of the *pátria*."[29] In fact it becomes clear that it is the question of Brazilian standing in the world which is of greatest importance to Floresta. In an extremely significant passage within *Opúsculo*, she writes:

> The ardent desire ... to see our country placed level with the most progressive nations, obliges us to frankly and impartially analyze the education of women in Brazil, hoping to inspire ... more able pens than ours to write on the subject.[30]

I would suggest that this statement represents a deliberate attempt by Floresta to protect herself against accusations of radicalism and inappropriate engagement in public, political debate. By emphasizing her own patriotism she effectively silences those who might suggest her claim for women's education is subversive and prejudicial to society (or to their own interests). Moreover, the limited hope which she claims to have for the effect of her work might be seen as an apology or justification for what is in fact a deeply political text that is highly critical of the Brazilian establishment. Elsewhere in *Opúsculo* we find a forceful disclaimer that she leaves the defense of women's rights to European writers in favor of the more useful subject of education,[31] which confirms her desire to adopt a concessionary tone in order to reassure her conservative readers. Brazilian women writing about education fifty years later still felt obliged to issue equivalent disclaimers in their work in order to "reassure readers that women wanted reform, not revolution."[32]

Although Floresta's concern with women's domestic virtue dominates her defense of education in *Opúsculo*, certain ideas can still be glimpsed regarding women's essential right to education, ideas which remind the reader of the humanist arguments found in Floresta's 1832 translation of *Woman not Inferior to Man*, as when she asserts that intelligence has no sex, and that God created Adam and Eve with "the same feelings, the same intelligence, the same prerogatives."[33] She also accuses men of deliberately maintaining women in ignorance in order to keep them in a state of humiliating subservience.[34] Despite acknowledging women's spiritual and intellectual equality with men, however, on only one occasion in the text does Floresta categorically state their right to education,[35] and even then it is by no means implicit that women have a right to an equal education with men.

The limiting nature of the education she advocates for women is most apparent when Floresta turns her attention specifically to the education of poor women. Despite expressing her support for lower class women's access to gainful employment,[36] she does not advocate a practical education teaching useful skills through which they might contribute to the family income. Instead her concern remains clearly in the realm of feminine virtue and she suggests that, because money and title can protect and hide a rich woman's fall into vice, poor women have an even greater need for education. It is "the voice of humanity, first, and then, that of the honor of our country,"[37] which therefore impels her to appeal for the education of lower class women. It is telling that in Floresta's eyes it is of greater value to the nation to ensure a virtuous female population than to equip women to contribute to the practical alleviation of poverty. This position is particularly surprising when we consider that Floresta supported herself and her family for many years through her teaching, and confirms her inability to engage with Brazil's poorer classes in her writing.

It is clear from a reading of *Opúsculo* that a fundamental shift in approach has occurred since the didactic publications of the 1840s. The text is founded almost exclusively on a nation-building discourse which allows Floresta to hide her challenge to the more conservative and reactionary attitudes still prevalent in Brazilian society behind a façade of patriotic devotion. This overt nationalist construction is precisely what is absent from her earlier writing and this difference certainly reveals the influence of Floresta's time in Europe on her perception of Brazil as a nation-state. More importantly, she is now acutely aware of the power this patriotic rhetoric can afford when harnessed to her appeal for improved education. However, it must be noted that the education she endorses is no broader than that advocated in her early writing. The focus remains absolutely on morality and Catholic virtue. In fact, the role which education is now required to facilitate is even more clearly demarcated within the confines of the family and home.

This steady move away from the humanist ideals of absolute equality, which she translated in *Direitos*, towards a social construction of women, and the increasingly rigid boundaries that imposes, is fully realized in her later works, published in France and Italy from 1857 onwards. In this final phase of Floresta's writing, her demands for women's education are sidelined in favor of more expansive claims to the value of woman as moral guardian and regenerator of society and the nature of that education becomes even more narrowly defined by the specific functions of their domestic imprisonment and sanctification. Floresta is now emphatic in her identification of the role of mother-educator for both sons and daughters,[38] and her concern now lies exclusively with the moral education of society, which has a particularly profound effect on the education she deems necessary for women in order to prepare them for this role. One of the most significant passages to be found in all Floresta's European writing on education clearly confirms her definitive abandonment of the curriculum offered in the Colegio Augusto. She states that women do not need intellectual instruction to fulfill their duty as mother-educator, which requires them only to be loving, fair, honest and modest:

> There is no need to have studied the great masters; if you have heart, you have open before you the most important, most eloquent and useful of all books, every page of which will furnish you a lesson ... far more useful than any to be found in print, or in the discourse of the ablest professors.[39]

Having embraced the full extent of women's role as moral regenerator of man, and the supreme patriotic value ascribable to this domestic definition of womanhood, it would seem that Floresta no longer saw the need for the progressive, scholarly curriculum which she had worked so hard, and faced criticism and ridicule, to teach her own pupils in Rio.

Inevitably, it is this fundamental contradiction within her own writings and between her writing and practice that makes an analysis of her position on education so challenging, but it simultaneously offers insights into the forces affecting her work. Floresta's own intellectual formation, her life spent in elevated intellectual circles, the curriculum she taught, her decision to translate Sophia's defense of women's public participation, and her continued use of that text's arguments regarding the equality of the soul and mind (at least until 1853), all combine to indicate that the writer was herself convinced of women's equal intelligence, and of their ability to receive an equal education to men. However, a gulf divides this fundamental belief, and the practice of it in her own life and her school, from the definition of education to be found in her work. An analysis of Floresta's writing on education reveals the influence of the prevailing conservative, Catholic discourses and attitudes of the day, and allows a clear development to be traced in the writer's defense of education away from the humanist ideas she translated in 1832, towards a fundamentally limiting definition of education within an explicitly patriotic discourse of national construction and progress. Whilst this rhetoric lent considerable power to her arguments, by appealing to concerns regarding national progress and status, Floresta makes female education a male issue, and a means by which to protect men's interests.

Whilst she may challenge the image of woman as an idle, foolish plaything, education is not a truly liberating or de-gendering tool in her writing. Rather, by embracing Catholic and nation-building discourses, and later Positivism (through her friendship with Auguste Comte), to shore up her defense, she can only offer an alternative construction of woman, still predicated exclusively on gendered natural and spiritual differences. At no point in her writing does Floresta suggest that education can be a source of personal fulfillment for a woman, although this was undoubtedly the primary motivation behind her own lifetime of learning and erudition. Neither, in her writing, does she discuss female education in terms of employment and women's possible need for financial independence, despite the fact that she herself depended on her teaching to maintain her family for many years.

However, despite its limitations and inconsistencies, the significance of Floresta's participation in the debate on women's education in Brazil should not be denied. She was writing at a time when arguments for limiting women's education, fuelled by popular, patriarchal prejudices, were widespread,[40] and very few women were contributing to the debate on either side. As one of the earliest and most prolific women writers on the subject, she may well have helped to shape the arguments that others were to use throughout the remainder of the century—echoes of her writing can certainly be found in texts defending an improvement in women's education published decades later.[41] It cannot be doubted that Floresta reaped considerable rewards, both financial and intellectual, from her own unusually broad knowledge and it seems that she bravely sought to share these advantages with her pupils. Given the social climate in which she was operating, it is hardly surprising that she came to depend on fundamentally andocentric discourses in order to soften and at times disguise her arguments, justify her own presence and attract a wider audience amongst a conservative, patriarchal and essentially male reading public. Her contribution must be evaluated through, but should not be devalued by her use of these discursive tactics, which prevented her from including the same advantages in the vision of women's education she set out in her writing.

Notes

[1] See Duarte, *Nísia Floresta: Vida e Obra* for a comprehensive biography of Floresta's life.

[2] It is worth noting that education [*educação*] has a broader meaning in Portuguese, encompassing an individual's general upbringing as well as their formal schooling. This is significant in the context of Floresta's writing, since much of her vision of women's "education" refers to the moral lessons best learnt at home.

[3] Henceforth abbreviated to *Opúsculo*.

[4] More than one scholar mentions a school run by Floresta there in the Rua Nova, for example Duarte, *Nísia Floresta: Vida e Obra*, 27, and Seidl, *Nísia Floresta, 1810-1885,* 18. Floresta herself states that she had already been teaching for four years when she arrived in Rio de Janeiro in 1837 (*Jornal do Commercio*, 31 January 1838).

[5] "Ler, escrever, contar, grammatica nacional, francez, dansa, coser, bordar, marcar e tudo quanto é proprio para a educação de uma menina." *Jornal do Commercio*, 18 December 1846. Unless otherwise noted, all translations are my own.

[6] "Hum collegio de educação para meninas, no qual, além de ler, escrever, contar, coser, bordar, marcar, e tudo o mais que toca à educação domestica de huma menina, ensinar-se-ha a grammatica da língua nacional por hum methodo fácil, o francez, o italiano, e os princípios mais geraes da geographia." *Jornal do Commercio*, 31 January 1838.

[7] *Jornal do Commercio*, 18 December 1846 and *O Mercantil*, 23 December 1846.

[8] *O Mercantil*, 23 December 1846.
[9] Duarte, *Nísia Floresta: Vida e Obra*, 34.
[10] "Trabalhos de língua não faltaram; os de agulha ficaram no escuro. Os maridos precisam de mulher que trabalhe mais e fale menos." *O Mercantil*, 02 January 1847.
[11] Henceforth abbreviated to *Direitos*.
[12] Floresta in fact translated the French translation of this text, dating from 1750/1751. For a long time this text was thought to be a free translation of Mary Wollstonecraft's *A Vindication of the Rights of Woman*, and is still sometimes referred to as such. See Liddell, "Brazil's First Feminist?" for a full discussion of the debate surrounding this text.
[13] Floresta, *Direitos*, 41, 64, and 71; 47; 49, 52 and 56.
[14] Ibid., 49-52; e.g. 47, 52, 56, 64, 76.
[15] A second edition was published in 1845 with the addition of forty short verses reiterating the message of the main text.
[16] Medeiros, *A Mamentação Materna é quase sempre possível* (Maternal Breast-Feeding is Almost Always Possible), 8.
[17] Floresta, *Discurso que a suas educandas dirigio N.F.B. Augusta em 18 de Dezembro de 1847* (A Speech which NFB Augusta Addressed to her Pupils on 18th December 1847).
[18] Floresta, *Opúsculo*, 110; 86; 80.
[19] Ibid., 80.
[20] Ibid., 71.
[21] Ibid., 92.
[22] "Desejaríamos proporcionar a todas conhecimentos, aptidão e gosto a fim de preencherem elas mesmas, como deviam, a honrosa e sublime missão de preceptoras de suas filhas." Floresta, *Opúsculo*, 91.
[23] See, for example, Loomba, *Colonialism/Postcolonialism*, 219, and Offen, "Contextualizing the Theory and Practice of Feminism", 351.
[24] Including Zaira Americana's lengthy 1853 text and articles written and published by Joana Paula Manso de Noronha in the *Jornal das Senhoras*, between 1852 and 1856. See also Hahner, *Emancipating the Female Sex*, 48-49 for some later examples.
[25] "Porquanto são elas que dão a primeira educação aos seus filhos." Quoted in Lopes, "A Educação da mulher", 26.
[26] "Qual é aí o homem razoável e honesto, que se contente de uma esposa ... entregue às futilidades de uma vida de dissipação e indolência, antes que no empenho constante ... de ilustrar-se pela prática das virtudes." Floresta, *Opúsculo*, 61.
[27] E.g. Floresta, *Opúsculo*, 101 and 136.
[28] See Saffioti, *Women in Class Society*, 158. This concept is by no means original to Floresta. Harriet Guest, for example, documents the same argument in English texts from the eighteenth century (Guest, *Small Change*, 155-57).
[29] "À dignidade da família e à glória da patria." Floresta, *Opúsculo*, 112.

[30] "O desejo ... de ver o nosso país colocado a par das nações progressistas, nos impõe a obrigação de franca e imparcialmente analisar a educação da mulher no Brasil, esperando excitar ... penas mais hábeis que a nossa a escreverem sobre [o] assunto." Floresta, *Opúsculo*, 45.
[31] Ibid., 29.
[32] Costa, *The Brazilian Empire*, 263.
[33] "O mesmo sentir, a mesma inteligência, as mesmas prerrogativas," Floresta, *Opúsculo*, 63; 6.
[34] Ibid., 6.
[35] Ibid., 44.
[36] Ibid., 132.
[37] "a voz da humanidade, primeiro, e, depois, a da honra do nosso país," Floresta, *Opúsculo*, 131.
[38] Floresta, "Woman", 111. This essay, first published in Florence in 1859, was translated into English by Floresta's daughter and published in London in 1865.
[39] Ibid., 112.
[40] Costa, *The Brazilian Empire*, 263-4; *Mulher Brasileira*, 220-21.
[41] See, for example, Costa, *The Brazilian Empire*, 262-4.

Works Cited

Primary Sources

Floresta, Nísia. "Woman." Translated by Livia A de Faria. Appendix to Peggy Sharpe, "Nísia Floresta: *Woman.*" *Brazil: A Journal of Brazilian Literature*, 14, (1995): 83-119.

—. "Conselhos a minha filha." In Constância Lima Duarte, "Nísia Floresta: Vida e Obra." PhD diss., vol. III appendices, 33-64. Universidade de São Paulo, 1991.

—. "Fany, ou o modelo das donzelas." In Constância Lima Duarte, "Nísia Floresta: Vida e Obra." PhD diss., vol. III appendices, 65-73. Universidade de São Paulo, 1991.

—. *Direitos das Mulheres e Injustiça dos Homens*. 4th edition? São Paulo: Cortez Editora, 1989.

—. *Opúsculo Humanitário*. 2nd edition. São Paulo: Cortez Editora, 1989.

—. *Discurso que as suas educandas dirigio N F B Augusta, em 18 de dezembro de 1847*. Rio de Janeiro: Typographia Imparcial de F. de Paula Brito, 1847.

Secondary Sources

Costa, Emilia Viotti da. *The Brazilian Empire: Myths and Histories*. London: University of North Carolina Press, 2000.
Duarte, Constância Lima. *Nísia Floresta: Vida e Obra*. Natal: EDUFRN, 1995.
Guest, Harriet. *Small Change: Women, Learning, Patriotism, 1750-1810*. Chicago; London: The University of Chicago Press, 2000.
Hahner, June. *Emancipating the Female Sex: The Struggle for Women's Rights in Brazil, 1850-1940*. Durham and London: Duke University Press, 1990.
Jornal do Commercio. Rio de Janeiro, 31 January 1838 and 18 December 1846.
Liddell, Charlotte. "Brazil's First Feminist? Gender and Patriotism in the Works of Nísia Floresta". PhD diss., University of Manchester, 2005.
Loomba, Ania. *Colonialism/Postcolonialism*. London: Routledge, 1998.
Lopes, Eliane Marta Santos Teixeira. "A Educação da mulher: A feminização do magistério." *Teoria & Educação*, 4, (1991): 22-40.
Medeiros, José Henrique de. *A mamentação materna é quase sempre possível*. Medical thesis, Rio de Janeiro: Typ. Imparcial de Francisco de Paula Brito, 1848.
Mulher Brasileira – Bibliografia Anotada. Vol. 2. São Paulo: Fundação Carlos Chagas; Brasiliense, 1981.
O Jornal das Senhoras. Rio de Janeiro, January 1852 to December 1855.
O Mercantil. Rio de Janeiro, 23 December 1846; 2 and 17 January 1847.
Offen, Karen. "Contextualizing the Theory and Practice of Feminism in Nineteenth-Century Europe (1789-1914)." In *Becoming Visible: Women in European History*, edited by Renate Bridenthal, Susan Stuard and Merry Wiesner, 327-55. Boston; New York: Houghton Mifflin Company, 1998.
Saffioti, Heleieth I B. *Women in Class Society*. Translated by Michael Vale, New York; London: Monthly Review Press, 1978.
Seidl, Roberto. *Nisia Floresta, 1810-1885*. Rio de Janeiro: [n. pub.], 1933.
Sophia, A Person of Quality. *Woman Not Inferior to Man: or, A Short and Modest Vindication of the Natural Right of the Fair-Sex to a Perfect Equality of Power, Dignity and Esteem, with the Men*. Facsimile edition, London: Brentham Press, 1975.

Zaira Americana Mostra as Imensas Vantagens que a Sociedade inteira obtém da Ilustração, Virtudes e Perfeita Educação da Mulher, como Mãe e Esposa do Homem. Rio de Janeiro: Tip. Dois de Dezembro de Paula Brito, 1853.

Chapter Fourteen

Beyond the American Home: The Contributions of Catharine Beecher and Clorinda Matto de Turner to Women's Education

Julia C. Paulk

In her groundbreaking text, *Sexual Politics*, Kate Millet describes the Victorian attitude towards female education: "[A] decorative and slender instruction is not only feminine and aesthetic, it also complements masculine higher learning. Serious education for women is perceived, consciously or unconsciously, as a threat to patriarchal marriage, domestic sentiment, and ultimately to male supremacy- economic, social, and psychological."[1] Perhaps not surprisingly, this attitude prevailed throughout the Americas in the nineteenth-century. At the time, few schools were available for women, and the ones that did exist rarely offered instruction beyond what Millet calls the "decorative," that is, the finishing school curriculum intended to "polish" young ladies for their entrance into society and marriage. Needless to say, such programs were typically for middle and upper class, white women only. However, a number of men and women in the Americas did spend their careers trying to improve female education in the nineteenth century. A study of the educational texts prepared by two such women helps to clarify the ideological underpinnings of education for women in the nineteenth-century and also serves to open a new area of investigation for inter-American literary and cultural studies.

The subjects of this essay are educational textbooks written by Catharine Beecher, born in East Hampton, New York, United States, in 1800, and Clorinda Matto de Turner, born in Cusco, Peru, in 1852. At first glance, considerable distance appears to lie between the two women, not only in geographic terms but also in their approaches to women's rights and issues of race and class. When compared on these topics, Matto de Turner was the more radical of the two, although Beecher did make some surprising assertions regarding career and family options for women later in life. An analysis of the two women's approaches to female education reveals how closely aligned their ideological positions actually were and helps to demonstrate the extent to which women of the Americas have a shared history despite their linguistic and cultural differences.

In their textbooks for women, both authors employed a strategy that appears to be designed to assuage the fears described by Kate Millet. Beecher's *Treatise on Domestic Economy* (US, 1841), along with the revised version, *The American Woman's Home* (1869), and Matto de Turner's little-studied *Elements of Literature According to the Rules of Public Education for the Use of the Fair Sex* (Peru, 1884)[2] rely heavily on the familiar "Cult of True Womanhood."[3] Both texts support the notion that a woman's sphere is in the home, where she will influence her husband and children to live moral and good lives. Rather than undermine patriarchal society, the ideal woman will influence the men in her family to abide by certain values in the public sphere, thereby strengthening democratic, Christian society. In a surprising turnabout, however, the very same educational textbooks that explicitly tell women that they belong in the domestic sphere also contain the means by which the traditional, patriarchal model of the family can be undone.

Catharine Beecher's activities as an educator, writer, theorist, and philosopher have been much more extensively studied than Clorinda Matto de Turner's.[4] She was the oldest daughter of Lyman Beecher, a very influential Calvinist minister. Most of Catharine Beecher's siblings were quite famous in their day. Her sister, Harriet Beecher Stowe, wrote *Uncle Tom's Cabin* (1852); Isabella Beecher Hooker was a well-known activist for women's rights; and each of the brothers became an influential clergyman. Despite the cultural expectations of her day, Catharine Beecher never married. Unwilling to live as a dependent, in the dreaded role of the "spinster aunt," Beecher had to find a way to support herself. Unable to become a minister, Beecher chose the only option available to her: a career in education. Rather than take a position in one of the few schools for girls in existence, Beecher acted in typical manner by founding her own school, the Hartford Female Seminary, in Connecticut in 1823. Beecher made a number of discoveries in her role as the head of the Harford Seminary. She deplored the serious lack of textbooks designed for women, particularly in more challenging topics, and undertook to write her own. Further, she discovered that teaching and running a school is hard work; she preferred to spend her time writing and directing others in the task of educating.

Although she went on to found two other schools for women, Beecher dedicated most of the remainder of her long career to writing on a number of topics ranging from religion to medicine, developing educational texts in such areas as mathematics, calisthenics, and philosophy, and steadfastly promoting women's education and rights. By the time of her death in 1878, Beecher had published prodigiously, had profoundly impacted the education of women in the United States, and had become one of the most well-known women in her country.

Although contemporary feminist scholars have been analyzing the nineteenth-century ideology of domesticity in earnest for more than thirty years, a final consensus has yet to be reached as to whether this ideology represents a form of empowerment for women or whether it glorifies an impossible ideal and perpetuates the isolation of women from the public sphere. Further, the extent to which Catharine Beecher propagates what are understood to be the negative aspects of this ideology continues to be the subject of some debate. Of particular concern to today's scholars are Beecher's failure to promote the idea of education for all women, and not only those from white, middle-class backgrounds, her xenophobia, and her unwillingness to support suffrage for all women. However, the case of Beecher's own life and the alteration in the model of the ideal family she describes over the course of her career are themselves radical examples of nineteenth-century womanhood.

Men dominated education at all levels when Beecher entered the profession in 1823. Almost half a century later, however, even more conservative writers like Sarah Josepha Hale fully supported the idea that women should have the charge of classrooms for both women and children.[5] Throughout her career, Beecher based her arguments in favor of female education on the tenets of the Cult of True Womanhood as she perceived them. For example, in the first chapter of *The American Woman's Home*, which is entitled, "The Christian Family," Beecher proposes that "[t]he family state [...] is the aptest earthly illustration of the heavenly kingdom, and in it woman is its chief minister. Her greatest mission is self-denial, in training its members to self-sacrificing labors for the ignorant and weak."[6] However, Beecher understood a woman's work in education as an activity to be done both within and beyond the home. She actively promoted training for women to work in the classroom and also encouraged their placement at the highest levels of administration. Moreover, Beecher tirelessly, but fruitlessly, sought the endowment of a women's college so that female students and teachers might have the same opportunities that were available for men at all-male colleges and universities. Throughout her career, Beecher supported the notion that what she considered women's work should be professionalized and compensated. As the introduction to *The American Woman's Home* states, "It is the aim of this volume to elevate both the honor and the remuneration of all the employments that sustain the many difficult and sacred duties of the family state, and thus to render each department of woman's true profession as much desired and respected as are the most honored professions of men."[7] What Millet refers to as "serious education" for women is justified and necessary because of woman's central and essential role in the family and, by extension, the nation. As Beecher repeatedly emphasized throughout her career in texts such as *Treatise on Domestic Economy*, *The American Woman's Home*, and *Educational Reminiscences and Suggestions* (1874), the work a woman does in her home requires training, relies on extensive knowledge of topics ranging from health care to plumbing, and insures the maintenance of a Christian democracy through the care and education of other family members. For example, one of the earliest chapters of the *Treatise* provides a detailed and illustrated description of the human anatomy.

By the end of her career, Beecher had extended her understanding of woman's true profession and of the family unit in ways that were both logical conclusions to and radical developments in her thinking. In the first of these surprising developments, she began to promote professions other than teaching for women. At the end of *Letters to the People on Health and Happiness* (1855), Beecher argues that women should claim the practice of medicine, particularly in the treatment of other women, as part of their domain.[8] Elsewhere, she argues that occupations women can do "in sunlight and the open air," such as growing fruit, cultivating cotton, and dairy farming, are acceptable for women.[9] Beecher's own career as a successful writer also helped pave the way for other professional, literary women.[10] Her most radical maneuver, however, was to redefine what constitutes a family. In *The American Woman's Home*, Beecher and her sister, Harriet Beecher Stowe, who helped with the revision, propose that single women may form households with other unmarried women: "Any woman who can earn a livelihood, as every woman should be trained to do, can take a properly qualified female associate, and institute a family of her own, receiving to its heavenly influences the orphan, the sick, the homeless, and the sinful."[11] Women can deliberately choose this option and thereby gain all the rights pertaining to a male head of household.[12] As Catherine Villanueva Gardner argues, men become superfluous, even "useless," in this arrangement.[13] By emphasizing women's moral power, Beecher undercuts civil, economic, and domestic power of men.[14] Indeed, when one considers the on-going controversy in the United States over same-sex adoption of children and same-sex marriage, Beecher's proposals for the kind of life a woman should have the choice to lead is striking. Perhaps even more interesting is the fact that Beecher and Stowe made this proposal in a textbook for both school and home use that was in fact widely studied in both institutional and domestic settings.

Like Catharine Beecher, Clorinda Matto de Turner was also a life-long crusader for the education and rights of women. Again similar to Beecher, she primarily earned her living through her published work, but also conceived of her writing career as placing her in the role of an educator.[15] At the age of eighteen, Matto de Turner married an English doctor, Joseph Turner, who, unusually for the era, encouraged her to publish her writings.[16] This was perhaps a fortunate turn of events for her because her husband died in 1881 and left his wife with nothing but debts to pay. Matto de Turner recovered from this personal tragedy by becoming the editor of several important newspapers in Peru and publishing a considerable body of work, including many articles, editorials, biographical and historic sketches, a play, three novels, and two textbooks for female students.[17] The publication of Matto de Turner's first novel, *Aves sin nido* (*Torn from the Nest*; 1889), which constituted an attack on the clergy, on the oppression of indigenous Peruvians, and on the treatment of women, sparked a severe outcry against the writer.[18] A number of additional scandals, including her newspaper's publication of a blasphemous story and Matto de Turner's public support of politician Andrés Cáceres, led to the author being burned in effigy and excommunicated. After her home and feminist print shop were destroyed, she fled to Argentina, where she lived the remainder of her life. In her new country, Matto de Turner continued to support women's rights, promoting suffrage, female education, and economic equality, while also teaching at several schools for women, publishing, and speaking in public. Shortly after completing a trip to Europe to study women's education, Matto de Turner died in 1909.

In her discussion of women's roles throughout her career, Matto de Turner demonstrated a belief in the power women hold in the domestic sphere. She argued that women's status needed to be reevaluated because it is they who educate the children of the nation.[19] Women should no longer to be treated as they traditionally had been, as unpaid and unappreciated laborers: "'Looking at the great painting of the past, called history […] one sees that woman was under the most shameful subjection and slavery.'"[20] For her role in the home and in society, a woman requires a solid education. This theory is illustrated in Matto de Turner's most widely read novel, *Torn from the Nest*, in which the author proposes that it is righteous, motherly influence that will unite a nation deeply divided by ethnic and class differences.[21] Not only is the education of children a duty to both God and country, but Matto de Turner also discussed both the paucity and benefits of an intellectually rigorous education for women. As the author argued, in her later years, when she is no longer considered physically attractive, and, therefore seen as unmarriageable or no longer producing children, the educated woman will still have a role to play in society.[22]

The connection between the need for education and the special role women play in society is manifest in one of the textbooks Matto de Turner wrote for female students, *Elements of Literature [...] for the Use of the Fair Sex*, which is not often included in studies of the author's work. Published in 1884, this textbook predates Matto de Turner's *Torn from the Nest* by five years and anticipates the position she takes regarding female influence and the importance of female education in her novels. In the prologue to *Elements*, the author clarifies that she has compiled this text for the use of female professors and students because of the moral duty to provide women with good models of literature and because there simply is no other good text available. The prologue reiterates the paradox of the domestic angel that necessitates her education and provides the ideological framework for the book. Woman's sphere is in the home, yet she is essential to society: "Woman [...] is not called to the pulpit, nor to the turbulence of the podium but to the education of the family, the peace of the home, and the beautification of society, because of her virtues combined with a thorough education."[23]

Matto de Turner's opening remarks become all the more striking when one takes even a brief look at another textbook that was in print at the time, José Bernardo Suárez's *El tesoro de las niñas* (*The Girls's Treasure*; Argentina, 1868). *The Girls's Treasure* is a collection of readings designed to teach girls moral and social lessons that would, as the author claims, promote "virtue and work."[24] However, as Liliana Zuccotti points out, Bernardo Suárez's text is marked by a profound fear of both female intellect and speech.[25] In this text, female knowledge is suspect ("Curiosity is the fault / that in woman most stands out")[26] and silence is the most desired quality ("A profound silence has always been / a woman's most beautiful adornment").[27] Despite their shared emphasis on female virtue, Matto de Turner's approach to female education is markedly different from Bernardo Suárez's, as an analysis of her textbook will demonstrate.

Matto de Turner's text offers an introduction to many aspects and forms of literature in an effort to provide female students with useful information and to spark intellectual curiosity. *Elements* does, nonetheless, claim that particular areas of literary study are especially suited to women's needs. Rhetoric, which she defines as "General Eloquence,"[28] is of particular use to women in their roles at home and in society: "As a teacher, and as a friend as well, a woman is called to teach, advise, and pour out comfort to those who suffer and cry. Mother, exhorts, orders, dissuades; wife supplicates, persuades, and shares; and in all these cases, eloquence offers its help, providing the triumph reserved for the virtuous and enlightened woman."[29] The author lists the heart as one of the sources of eloquence, and a woman's heart in particular has great power to move others: "The mother's feeling heart, begging a pardon for her disgraced son, is capable of making an executioner cry; the wife's great heart, exhorting the citizen to do his duty to his country, can greatly move its listeners and create a hero."[30] In this way, a woman's influence is perceived as shaping society beyond the confines of the home and even as participating in the project of building the nation. Moreover, it is her control of rhetoric, that is, her ability to speak effectively, that allows a woman to perform in these various, necessary capacities.

Although the text highlights the importance of the role of the wife and mother as educator and moral standard-bearer, glimpses of other possibilities for women nonetheless appear. The most notable of these is the work of the female writer. As many contemporary texts do, *Elements* provides examples of the aspects of literature it describes. Although there are a number of quotes from expected sources, such as the Bible, Cervantes, and even the notorious Fray Luis de León, who also advocated silence for women, many of the examples are taken from works written by women. Among others, she quotes Santa Teresa de Jesús, Gertrudis Gómez de Avellaneda, and Juana Manuela Gorriti. One of the most interesting examples is a poem by Mercedes Cabello de Carbonera, entitled, "Mujer escritora" ("Woman Writer"). The first half of the poem is a declaration by a young man who is ready to marry that he wants anything but a "woman writer" for a wife: "What use are women / who, instead of taking care of / our clothes and the table / talk to us about Byron, Dante, and Petrarch?"[31] A young woman, Cristina, listens to him and replies, "How wise is nature / that has thus separated / with blessed dislike / the rook from the skylark / [...] / Thus for the fool / there is nothing attractive about / *the woman writer*."[32] Quotations from literature by women, like the Cabello de Carbonera poem, demonstrate to the young women studying the book that the role of the intellectual is also available to them. In practical terms, this opens the fields of writing and teaching to young women. This aspect of *Elements* anticipates the argument Matto de Turner makes explicit almost twenty years later in *Boreales, miniaturas y porcelanas* (*Boreal, Miniatures, and Porcelain*, 1902). As Meléndez describes, in the later work, Matto de Turner attributes a special status to the female writer as one who fights for women's rights and thus for the good of the republic: "'The true heroines [...] fight day by day [...] to produce books, pamphlets, newspapers, that embody the ideal of female progress.'"[33] Texts such as *Elements* helped pave the way for such work by educating and inspiring young women to express themselves through both the written and spoken word.

Matto de Turner also provides glimpses in her textbook of the rhetorical needs of occupations denied to women, such as public speaking and business. She claims that these are not areas for women but nonetheless gives a sense of what they might entail. Having stated in the prologue that women are not called to the pulpit or to the podium, she nonetheless outlines the structure and purpose of an effective and convincing speech. When describing letters, she implies that the world of business is not for women: "Men style their letters in ways that are appropriate to the job, dignity and rank of the person to whom they write. For women, this is not required."[34] Although they are being reminded that these jobs are not for them, the readers of *Elements* will still learn something about the world of work beyond the home. As a professional writer, however, Matto de Turner encourages the readers of her textbook to take advice she herself does not follow in the same way that Beecher does when highlighting a woman's role as a mother and homemaker.

As time and her career advanced, Matto de Turner increasingly supported the idea of women working outside the home. Her approval of women laboring in factories provides a contrast to Beecher, who thought such work unsuitable for women. In a speech entitled, "The Woman Worker and the Woman," which she gave in Buenos Aires in 1904, Matto de Turner declared that only the economically self-sufficient person is free.[35] Although this was in fact an antistrike speech, Matto de Turner nonetheless called for better treatment and training for female workers: "'[L]et us ascertain that [woman's work] is properly remunerated since factory owners do exist who pay women less simply because they are women, even though their work is identical to that of men. [...] Let us found centers for education and recreation, and societies that protect the rights of women workers.'"[36] Matto de Turner was not able to abandon class distinctions, but she did call for education and fair treatment for women of all walks of life. Additionally, in this speech, she depicts a family in which both spouses work outside the home.

The careers and teachings of both Catharine Beecher and Clorinda Matto de Turner suggest that the Victorian fear of female education described by Kate Millet may have been well placed for those who did not advocate changes in the status quo. Ultimately, both women did threaten patriarchal institutions such as marriage and the traditional family. Ironically, each based her argument on the traditional role of a woman as a virtuous wife and mother. However, the same notion of female virtue that allowed an author such as Bernardo Suárez to argue in favor of female silence became a useful tool for Beecher and Matto de Turner as they promoted the development of the female intellect. Eventually, both writers pushed the boundaries of what was considered appropriate education and work for women and extended female reach beyond the home in a way that surpassed mere influence. This suggests that the Cult of True Womanhood is in fact a quite flexible belief system. Although Beecher and Matto de Turner may appear to be encouraging women to live according to an impossible ideal, their work is marked by an intent to elevate women's status and increase their options through the very practical notion of providing them with a thorough education.

Notes

[1] Millet, *Sexual Politics*, 127.
[2] The complete title is *Elementos de Literatura Según el Reglamento de Instruccion Pública Para Uso del Bello Sexo*. All translations are mine unless otherwise indicated. The use of diacritical marks in the original text does not correspond to contemporary usage, and they have been quoted here as they appear in the original.
[3] As Barbara Welter explains in her influential study, "The attributes of True Womanhood, by which a woman judged herself and was judged by her husband, her neighbors and society could be divided into four cardinal virtues-piety, purity, submissiveness and domesticity. Put them all together and they spelled mother, daughter, sister, wife-woman. Without them, no matter whether there was fame, achievement or wealth, all was ashes. With them she was promised happiness and power." Welter, "The Cult of True Womanhood: 1820-1860," 152.
[4] Kathryn Kish Sklar's *Catharine Beecher: A Study in American Domesticity* is still the seminal study of Beecher's life and works.
[5] Tonkovich, *Domesticity with a Difference*, 154.
[6] Beecher and Stowe, *The American Woman's Home*, 19.
[7] Ibid., 19.
[8] Boydston et al, *The Limits of Sisterhood*, 231.
[9] Quoted in Gardner, "Heaven Appointed Educators of Mind," 10.
[10] Nicole Tonkovich's *Domesticity with a Difference* chronicles the writing careers of Beecher, Sarah Josepha Hale, Fanny Fern, and Margaret Fuller, and the ways in

which these women redefined domesticity and professional writing careers for women.

[11] Beecher and Stowe, *The American Woman's Home*, 25.
[12] Tonkovich, *Domesticity with a Difference*, 183.
[13] Gardner, "Heaven Appointed Educators of Mind," 12.
[14] Ibid., 13.
[15] Meléndez, "Obreras del pensamiento," 582.
[16] Berg, "Writing for Her Life," 81. My discussion of Matto de Turner's biography is indebted to this article by Mary G. Berg.
[17] Matto de Turner wrote two textbooks, one earlier and another later in her career. *Elements* was published in 1884, while *Analogía. Segundo año de gramática castellana en las escuelas normales según el programa oficial* (*Analogy. Second Year of Spanish Grammar in Normal Schools According to the Official Program*) was published in 1897. Peluffo, *Lágrimas andinas*, 14.
[18] Catharine Beecher was also the author of an attack on clergymen. Her defense of Delia Bacon, *Truth Stranger than Fiction* (1850), was very critical of Congregationalist clergy and the double standard that prevents women from aggressively pursuing marriage. Sklar, *Catharine Beecher*, 188-190.
[19] Mariselle Meléndez includes Matto de Turner in her study of nineteenth-century essays by Spanish-American women writers, "Obreras del pensamiento y educadoras de la nación: el sujeto femenino en la ensayística femenina decimonónica de transición." See especially pages 580-582 for a discussion of Matto de Turner's approach to female education and the role of women in Peru.
[20] "'Fijando la vista al grandioso cuadro del pasado, que se llama historia [...] se ve que la mujer estaba bajo la más vergonzosa sugeción y esclavitud.'" Quoted in Meléndez, "Obreras," 581.
[21] Please refer to Peluffo's *Lágrimas andinas* and Julia C. Paulk, "Allegory and Antislavery Literature of Latin America and the United States," for more thorough discussions of this novel. Peluffo's text offers analyses of a number of Matto's works, including lesser-known ones. Susana E. Zanetti points out that Matto's interest in education is also apparent in her later novels, *Herencia* and *Índole*, as well as in the periodical she founded in Buenos Aires, *Búcaro Americano: periódico de las familias*. Zanetti, "*Búcaro Americano*," 265, 273 note 3.
[22] Meléndez, "Obreras," 580.
[23] "[L]a mujer [...] no está llamada al púlpito, ni á la turbulencia de la tribuna sino á la enseñanza de la familia, la paz del hogar y el embellecimiento de la sociedad, por sus virtudes unidas á una educación esmerada." Matto de Turner, *Elements*, 3.
[24] "VIRTUD I TRABAJO" [*sic*]. Bernardo Suárez, *El tesoro de las niñas*, v.
[25] Please see pages 100-102 of Liliana Zuccotti's article, "Gorriti, Manso: de las *Veladas literarias* a 'Las conferencias de maestra'" for a brief but potent analysis of Bernardo Suárez's textbook.
[26] "La curiosidad es la falta / Que en la mujer más resalta." Bernardo Suárez, *El tesoro de las niñas*, 14.

[27] "Un profundo silencio siempre ha sido / De las mujeres el más bello adorno." Bernardo Suárez, *El tesoro de las niñas*, 18.
[28] Matto de Turner, *Elements*, 7.
[29] "Como maestra, como amiga también, está llamada á instruir, aconsejar, y derramar los consuelos entre los que sufren y lloran. Madre, exhorta, manda, disuade; esposa, suplica, persuade, y comparte; y en todos estos casos la elocuencia le prestará su apoyo dejándole el triunfo reservado á la mujer virtuosa é ilustrada." Ibid., 7.
[30] "El corazon sensible de la madre implorando perdon para el hijo desgraciado, seria capaz de arrancar lágrimas al verdugo; el corazon grande de la esposa, exhortando al ciudadano al cumplimiento de sus deberes para con la patria, podrá entusiasmar á los oyentes y hacer á su vez un héroe" Ibid., 12.
[31] "¿Qué sirven mujeres / que en vez de cuidarnos / la ropa y la mesa, / nos hablen de Byron, / del Dante y Petrarca" Ibid., 60-61.
[32] "¡Qué sabia es natura / que así ha separado / con odio bendito, / del grajo á la alondra / […] / Así para el necio / no tiene atractivo / *mujer escritora.*" Ibid., 61-62.
[33] "'[L]as verdaderas heroínas […] luchan día a día […] para producir el libro, el folleto, el periódico, encarnados en el ideal del progreso femenino.'" Quoted in Meléndez, "Obreras," 582.
[34] "Los hombres emplean en sus cartas los tratamientos propios al empleo, dignidad y rango de la persona á quien se dirijen. Para las mujeres no es obligatorio tal uso." Matto de Turner, *Elements*, 42.
[35] Matto de Turner, "The Woman Worker," 96.
[36] Ibid., 97.

Works Cited

Primary Sources

Beecher, Catharine E., and Harriet Beecher Stowe. *The American Woman's Home*. Ed. and intro. Nicole Tonkovich. Hartford: Harriet Beecher Stowe Center; New Brunswick: Rutgers U P, 2002.

Beecher, Catharine E. *Educational Reminiscences and Suggestions*. New York: J.B. Ford, 1874.

—. *Letters to the People on Health and Happiness*. New York: Harper, 1855.

—. *A Treatise on Domestic Economy*. Boston: T.H. Webb, 1842.

—. *Truth Stranger than Fiction: a narrative of recent transactions, involving inquiries in regard to the principles of honor, truth, and *justice, which obtain in a distinguished American university.* Boston: Phillips Sampson and Company, 1850.

Bernardo Suárez, José. *El tesoro de las niñas.* Buenos Aires: Imprenta Tipográfica de Pablo E. Coni, 1868.

Matto de Turner, Clorinda. *Analogía. Segundo año de gramática Castellana en las escuelas normales, según el program oficial.* Buenos Aires: J.A. Alsina, 1897.

—. *Aves sin nido.* Ed. Luis Mario Schneider. New York: Las Americas Publishing Company, 1968.

—. *Elementos de literatura según el reglamento de instrucción pública para uso del bello sexo.* Arequipa: Imprenta de "La Bolsa", 1884.

—. *Herencia.* Ed. Mary G. Berg. Buenos Aires: Stockcero, 2006.

—. *Índole.* Ed. Mary G. Berg. Buenos Aires: Stockcero, 2006.

—. "The Woman Worker and the Woman." In *Rereading the Spanish American Essay: Translations of 19th and 20th Century Women's Essays*, ed. Doris Meyer, 90-98. Austin: U of Texas P, 1995.

Stowe, Harriet Beecher. *Uncle Tom's Cabin.* New York: Oxford University Press, 1998.

Secondary Sources

Berg, Mary G. "Writing for Her Life: The Essays of Clorinda Matto de Turner." In *Reinterpreting the Spanish American Essay: Women Writers of the 19th and 20th Centuries*, ed. Doris Meyer, 80-89. Austin: U of Texas P, 1995.

Boydston, Jeanne, Mary Kelley, and Anne Margolis. *The Limits of Sisterhood: The Beecher Sisters on Women's Rights and Woman's Sphere.* Chapel Hill: U of North Carolina P, 1988.

Gardner, Catherine Villanueva. "Heaven Appointed Educators of Mind: Catharine Beecher and the Moral Power of Women." *Hypatia* 19.2 (2004): 1-16.

Meléndez, Mariselle. "Obreras del pensamiento y educadoras de la nación: el sujeto femenino en la ensayística femenina decimonónica de transición." *Revista Iberoamericana* 64.184-185 (1998): 573-586.

Millet, Kate. *Sexual Politics.* Urbana: U of Illinois P, 2000.

Paulk, Julia C. "Allegory and Antislavery Literature of Latin America and the United States." PhD diss., Indiana University, 2003.

Peluffo, Ana. *Lágrimas andinas: Sentimentalismo, género y virtud republicana en Clorinda Matto de Turner*. Pittsburgh: Instituto Internacional de Literatura Iberoamericana, 2005.

Sklar, Kathryn Kish. *Catharine Beecher: A Study in American Domesticity*. New York: Norton, 1973.

Tonkovich, Nicole. *Domesticity with a Difference: The Nonfiction of Catharine Beecher, Sarah J. Hale, Fanny Fern, and Margaret Fuller*. Jackson: U P of Mississippi, 1997.

Welter, Barbara. "The Cult of True Womanhood: 1820-1860". *American Quarterly* 18.2 (1966): 151-174.

Zanetti, Susana E. "*Búcaro Americano*: Clorinda Matto de Turner en la escena femenina porteña." In *Mujeres y cultura en la Argentina del siglo XIX*, ed. Lea Fletcher, 264-275. Buenos Aires: Feminaria Editora, 1994.

Zuccotti, Liliana. "Gorriti, Manso: de las *Veladas literarias* a 'Las conferencias de maestra.'" In *Mujeres y cultura en la Argentina del siglo XIX*, ed. Lea Fletcher, 96-107. Buenos Aires: Feminaria Editora, 1994.

Chapter Fifteen

The Struggle for the Independence and Education of the African American Woman in the Works of Frances Ellen Watkins Harper

Terry Novak

When she was born in Maryland in 1825, Frances Ellen Watkins Harper entered a world of immediate disadvantage. Yet, at the same time, she entered a world of unique opportunity. Though born in a time when the majority of African Americans were illiterate, and though born in a slave-holding state, Harper herself was also born free to free parents. And though she lost both parents very early in her life, Harper was raised by her uncle, William Watkins, who ran the William Watkins Academy for Negro Youth. This meant that, though she was born female in an era steeped in such ideals as The Cult of True Womanhood, which strove to restrict the intellectual and economic freedoms of women in order that women would more easily be molded into society's idea of a good Christian woman, Harper was afforded a rigorous education by attending her uncle's school. This also meant that the young Frances Watkins was molded quite unlike most young women, black or white, slave or free, of the time, for William Watkins believed in teaching oratorical skills, writing and rhetoric skills, and political leadership along with other classical subjects. Still, Harper was always aware that she belonged to a race much abused and with many hardships ahead, just as she was always aware that being born female relegated her to a distinct lower class, one void of certain rights that men simply took for granted. A determined woman, Harper made it a point to react to these disadvantages by fighting for equality of race and gender. Two methods became critical to Harper's fight: the education of *all* members of her race and economic independence for all women.

Despite Harper's determination, she still found herself subject to the laws, regulations and prejudices of nineteenth century American society. She attended formal schooling only until she reached her teens, at which time she left her native Baltimore for a teaching position at Union Seminary in the free state of Ohio. What she taught was not rhetoric or the classics but sewing, as she herself had been trained to work as a seamstress, in addition to her other education. From there Harper moved on to a teaching position in York, Pennsylvania. Neither teaching position afforded Harper much satisfaction; each had its challenges and each likely reminded her of how she missed her home; in addition, she mourned the fact that Maryland was caught up first in the heat of the Fugitive Slave Act of 1850 (the year Harper left) and then in the 1853 passage of a law forbidding free blacks from the North entry into the state; those who defied this law risked being subjected to slavery. These frustrations eventually worked to help Harper's career, as she moved to Philadelphia to work with William Still and the Underground Railroad. This move helped Harper channel her passion for justice. Through the antebellum years she worked in New England as well as in Philadelphia for the cause of the abolition of slavery, writing and lecturing on behalf of a variety of anti-slavery societies.

Harper's career slowed considerably from 1860-1864, the years she was married to Fenton Harper and living with him, his children, and her and Fenton's daughter, Mary. During this time Frances Harper seemed to have fallen almost peacefully into the restrictions of True Womanhood, although it could be that, with a ready-made family, she was simply too busy to continue her own work with abandon. That changed when Fenton died early on in the marriage, making this brief period in Harper's life almost a footnote. Harper and Mary moved to New England for several years and then back to Philadelphia in 1871. With the Civil War ended and the Reconstruction era underway, Frances Harper took to her pen and pulpit with renewed energy, continuing her work for the betterment of the race through education and economic independence until her death in 1911.

Though Harper chose to take the path of writing and lecturing rather than the path of classroom teaching to fulfill her agenda, she worked nonetheless for the causes of education and independence for women. In her fiction particularly one can see Harper's dedication to this mission. Harper's first work of fiction, the short story "The Two Offers," appeared in an 1859 edition of *The Weekly Anglo-African.* This story is interesting on many levels, most notably in that Harper's characters are not assigned a race and in that the main characters are women dealing with the issues of temperance—one of Harper's key social concerns as well as one of the key social concerns of many American women leaders of the century, especially those fighting for women's suffrage—and of a woman's right to choose against marriage. If one thinks about that latter issue for a moment, putting it into the context of the mid-nineteenth century U.S., one cannot help but admire Harper's courage in laying out a story with such a theme, especially when one considers the timing of the story's publication in conjunction with Harper's own marriage. In the story, with the cousins Laura Lagrange and Janette Alston , Harper presents the reader with one woman, Laura, who makes the choice to marry and the other, Janette, who remains comfortably and happily "an old maid." Contrary to the popular nineteenth century notions of True Womanhood, Janette's choice turns out to be the wiser, the happier, and the more fulfilling, with Laura's marriage becoming a disastrous liaison with an alcoholic. Harper describes Janette as a child of poverty who, "[t]oo self reliant to depend on the charity of relations, endeavor[s] to support herself by her own exertions."[1] This she does successfully, both financially and emotionally, so much so that in her latter years of life, "…as old age descended peacefully and gently upon her, she had learned one of life's most precious lessons, that true happiness consists not so much in the fruition of our wishes as in the regulation of desires and the full development and right culture of our whole natures."[2] Janette chose the life of intelligence and self-sufficiency; hers was a life of the mind as well as of the soul. By having this character so completely chart her own course with the result of contentment and happiness, Harper begins a canon of fiction that pays tribute to women's strength and to the rewards that come from education and industry. It is important to note that Harper presents the option of a fulfilling life outside of marriage through this character. Although this is not an option that fits neatly into the scheme of True Womanhood, it is an option that may have appealed to many nineteenth century women and illustrates that these women could still be virtuous and Christian in spirit—key elements of True Womanhood—despite being unmarried and childless. Indeed, Janette is described as a loving being whose heart reaches out to many, a trait that does fit neatly within the realm of True Womanhood. Just as important to "The Two Offers" is the omission of race as a descriptor for the two characters. By leaving her characters raceless, Harper begins her canon of fiction by making the case for the importance of gender issues in the nineteenth century a critical one. Any woman reader of any race could consider her life options through a study of Harper's two characters.

Harper continues in this vein in her three novellas, *Minnie's Sacrifice* (1869), *Sowing and Reaping* (1876-77), and *Trial and Triumph* (1888-89), all of which were initially serialized in *The Christian Recorder*. In the first novella Harper brings racial issues to the forefront; the two main characters, Minnie and Louis, are biracial, physically appear white, are raised as white, and discover their true heritage in adolescence. Louis and Minnie eventually marry; both represent an educated portion of the race, raised with every advantage, that nonetheless decides to ally itself with the maternal race and work diligently in the causes of Reconstruction. Harper adamantly portrays the young couple as a modern one, with Minnie asserting both the rights and responsibilities of women while Louis at least listens to her concerns, albeit with a bit of patronization. In one memorable scene in the novella, Harper sets Louis and Minnie in a discussion about suffrage, a discussion that leads to a disagreement on whether suffrage should be granted to all members of the race or to the men alone, a topic that was in reality leading to heated debates throughout the nation. Minnie passionately asserts,

> ...I cannot recognize that the negro man is the only one who has pressing claims at this hour. To-day our government needs woman's conscience as well as man's judgment. And while I would not throw a straw in the way of the colored man, even though I know that he would vote against me as soon as he gets his vote, yet I do think that woman should have some power to Defend herself from oppression, and equal laws as if she were a man.[3]

Both Minnie and Louis toil as educators, political activists, and social workers in the South as part of the Reconstruction movement. Harper makes it clear that working for the race takes precedence over all else and that those who have been given advantages owe it to the others to help them to rise toward equality as well. Harper seems especially aware in this novella of the propensity for nineteenth century African Americans of advantage and especially of mixed race to attempt to quietly blend into the majority rather than to embrace their own minority and wholeheartedly work for its uplifting. In her sermonizing conclusion to *Minnie's Sacrifice,* Harper chides,

> We have wealth among us, but how much of it is ever spent in building up the future of the race? in encouraging talent, and developing genius? We have intelligence, but how much do we add to the reservoir of the world's thought? We have genius among us, but how much can it rely upon the colored race for support?[4]

Harper's *Sowing and Reaping,* though primarily concerned with the temperance issue and the evils even one glass of alcohol can have on a man, also contains a fair amount of discussion on women's issues and woman's need to take control of her life, especially through education and suffrage, which the author clearly views as the only path to true equality, to "power as well as influence."[5] Harper returns full force to an admiration of women who take their education seriously and who are prepared to make their own way in the world—whether they ultimately need to or not—through the character Annette in *Trial and Triumph*. Harper also makes it clear that Annette is an anomaly in her day and place. As Harper describes the reaction of Annette's neighbors from the Tennis Court neighborhood to her graduation from normal school, the neighbors

> were, generally speaking, too unaspiring to feel envious toward any one of their race who excelled them intellectually...[S]ome of her neighbors felt a kind of pride in the thought that Tennis Court would turn out a girl who could stand on the same platform and graduate alongside of some of their employers' daughters.[6]

Harper's deep belief in the power of education and in the responsibility all have to being their best shines through in parts of this novella.

Without question, Harper's masterpiece of thematic passion—a work that blends all of her favorite social themes into one work--comes with her only full-length novel, *Iola Leroy,* which was published in 1892 after many years of toil. Harper's protagonist in this novel, Iola Leroy, seems to be the type of woman Harper herself strove to be. She is certainly the type of woman who espouses the ideals about which Harper wrote and lectured. Iola is born into a wealthy family in the South and raised white, although she is indeed biracial. She does not discover for many years that her fair-skinned mother had actually been her father's slave. Interestingly, Harper begins the issue of education with the tale of Iola's mother Marie's early life. Eugene Leroy, Iola's father, takes great pains to give Marie a good education, sending her North to a boarding school before bringing her home to the South as his wife. Harper carefully describes Marie's commencement day, when Marie reflects on all she has learned not only from her formal studies but from the teachings of the abolitionists in the North. Harper tells us that Marie lectures on "American Civilization, its Lights and Shadows" [7] before the audience, speaking of slavery and freedom so eloquently that "[s]trong men wiped the moisture from their eyes, and women's hearts throbbed in unison with the strong, brave words that were uttered in behalf of freedom for all and chains for none," [8]although "[a]t times, a shadow of annoyance would overspread [Eugene Leroy's] face..." [9]

The fact that Harper places such emphasis on Marie's education and on her commitment to racial issues becomes critical as the story of the novel progresses. As the Civil War ensues, life changes drastically for the Leroy family. Iola and brother Harry are away at separate boarding schools in the North when Eugene, in the midst of visiting the children with Marie and their youngest child, Gracie, falls ill and dies, leaving his wife and children to the treacheries of his brother Alfred Leroy, who finds legal fault with both Marie and Eugene's marriage and Marie's manumission. This remands Marie and her children to slavery. Harry manages to stay North and joins the army, but Iola is tricked into returning home and is sold, along with Marie, by her uncle. Little Gracie dies before she tastes the evil of slavery. Iola mercifully finds herself soon rescued by the Union army and serves as an army nurse for the troops. Like Minnie in *Minnie's Sacrifice*, Iola embraces her African heritage and refuses to pass as white, even when urged by some to do so. Instead, she uses her intelligence and her education to work for the betterment of the race, focusing her efforts on the education of all African Americans, the independence of women, and the upholding of nineteenth century Christian ideals.

Throughout *Iola Leroy* the reader is made aware of the importance of these themes. Iola's Uncle Robert, in the midst of a discussion on the future of the race and ways to ensure the success of that future, declares, "The colored man has escaped from one slavery, and I don't want him to fall into another."[10] When Iola's family is back together again under one roof, after the war, Harry introduces his love interest, Miss Delaney, who is university educated and determined to open a school for freed blacks. Iola herself presents a paper on "The Education of Mothers"[11] at one of many intellectual gatherings at her home. Her paper leads to a lively discussion of the need for educated woman in both public and private settings. There is an underlying understanding that this is most critical for the black mothers, for it will be left to the devices of educated black mothers to steer their families in positive directions and to urge their children to an adulthood worthy of their talents. Harper leads the reader to believe that this is even more important for black women than for white women, as the future of an entire race is at stake. When Iola marries at the end of the novel, she carries on with her beliefs in education by working as a Sunday school teacher, just as Miss Delaney continues teaching even after her marriage to Harry.

Iola makes it a point to always carry her own weight economically. When she leaves her service to the army at the end of the war, she continues to work. She tells her uncle, "I have a theory that every woman ought to know how to earn her own living. I believe that a great amount of sin and misery springs from the weakness and inefficiency of women."[12] Part of her adventures in the world of work consists of Iola's facing continued racism when employers or coworkers discover her race. A more important part consists of the obvious development of self-esteem and self-sufficiency that comes from Iola's work. It is clear that Iola becomes a stronger and more confident woman because of her knowledge that she will always be able to care for herself and will never need to be financially dependent on another. This is illustrated particularly well as Iola works to spread this message to members of the race who did not grow up with the same advantages as did she. It is important to note that this message of Iola's/Harper's does not preclude a tendency for women, including Iola, to fall in love, marry, and hope for children. Rather, Harper seems to urge the reader to consider her options, realizing that without education and independence, one's options are already made for her. The fact that Iola is educated, possesses an independent spirit, and enjoys the freedom presented by the world of work does not keep her from falling in love and marrying. To the contrary, when Iola does fall in love and marry, it is with the understanding that her husband respects and embraces her intelligence and independence. In this sense, Iola embarks on a marriage with Dr. Latimer that was surely the exception to the rule.

Not all literary critics find the character Iola Leroy a plausible black leader. Cassandra Jackson, for instance, contends that Harper's positing of Iola Leroy as a teacher of blacks is problematic, as Iola Leroy had lived most of her life as a white woman; Jackson suggests that because of this Iola may not quite fit the ideal role model of a black teacher or a black leader of the race. Jackson does go on to admit the importance of Harper's focus on education, though, as she writes, "...teaching becomes the primary outlet for women to contribute to the self-help movement, and a way of positioning a public role for women not merely as a possible role, but as a duty of educated black women...Harper's emphasis on communal duty...reflects a desire for black women's political advancement." [13] When Harper uses biracial characters such as Iola Leroy to act in race-saving roles, she seems to be particularly cognizant of both the realities and the tragedies of slave-era miscegenation. She also was surely aware of the feminist political statement she was making by blending the two races into one female leader set on making things right for women.

In all of her fiction, most particularly in *Iola Leroy,* as well as through her own life, Frances Ellen Watkins Harper illustrates the necessity for black women in particular and all women in general to exercise their intellectual capacities and become more than a part of the Cult of True Womanhood. Critics such as Elizabeth Petrino assert that

> [o]ne way that Harper and her peers negotiated their identities for the public was to solidify their place in the emerging middle class and to manifest the conservative values of piety, domesticity, modesty, and sexual purity that were considered part of …'the Cult of True Womanhood.' Although these virtues were almost impossible for black women to achieve under slavery, they still set the terms by which freedwomen imagined they were guaranteed entry into the middle class during the Reconstruction era, and they used them to confirm their political alliance with white women to press for legal and social advancement."[14]

Despite Petrino's argument, Harper seemed to know better than to count on any white, middle-class driven social motive to serve the particular need of the black woman. Harper illustrates that, while True Womanhood may be useful—she did believe strongly in the Christian tenets at the base of the concept—the more a woman expects of herself personally, professionally, intellectually, and spiritually, the more freedom and true security she will experience.

Harper's inherent belief in the importance of education as a means of true freedom was based in the bitter reality of a lack of education opportunities available to African Americans, even after the promise of Reconstruction. As historian Eric Foner, writing in *Reconstruction: America's Unfinished Revolution, 1863-1877,* reports, "Over 90 percent of the South's adult black population was illiterate in 1860"[15] When the Freedmen's Bureau enlisted the help of largely Northern sympathizers to help educate the race, then, they faced a daunting task. Foner concedes that "[f]ew Northerners involved in black education could rise above the conviction that slavery had produced a 'degraded' people, in dire need of instruction in frugality, temperance, honesty, and the dignity of labor."[16] Nancy Hoffman reports that "[b]y 1870, five years after the end of the war, there were about 7,000 teachers in the South, instructing some 250,000 black students"[17]; many of these teachers were Northern white women who saw their Reconstruction efforts as a natural outgrowth of their Christian beliefs in doing charitable work while still abiding by the societal rules of what constituted acceptable work for women in the nineteenth century. Hoffman also reports that the efforts of these Northern teachers lasted no more than a decade, with the Northern teachers not expecting to make a lifelong career of educating the freedmen and with the hope that some of the newly educated black citizens would be ready to take on educational leadership roles. This change in leadership, while weak at first, did slowly take place—as much as the continued arena of racial strife and hatred in the South allowed.

While the Reconstruction education efforts were still heavily underway, social activist and writer Lydia Maria Child published *The*

Freedmen's Book, a volume meant to help educate the black population. The text includes many pieces by Child herself, including biographies of prominent black Americans and inspirational essays meant to steer the reader to proper, wholesome living. The volume also includes several selections by Frances Harper, works by black authors such as Phillis Wheatley and Harriet Jacobs, and works by white writers such as William Lloyd Garrison and Harriet Beecher Stowe, writers sympathetic to the plight of the African American. All selections are clearly chosen for what Child considered to be most useful to the delicate condition of the intended readers. Missing, though, are the challenging classical texts to which Harper had been subjected at William Watkins' school.

William Watkins had been trained as a shoemaker, yet he found his way to intellectual pursuits and a higher calling to education. His brand of education, as discussed above, was far more stringent than what Lydia Maria Child apparently thought African Americans capable of digesting. Along with his role as an educator, Watkins engaged in political writing and speaking, something he viewed as critical to impart upon his students as well.[18] When Frances Smith Foster refers to Frances Ellen Watkins Harper as "a member of the African American intelligentsia and one of its most successful writers,"[19] she is paying tribute to Harper's training under her uncle's tutelage, and she is correctly assessing the importance of Harper's work.

Harper's work, most especially her writing and lecturing, fit into the historical picture with a decided twist. Harper continually advocated the work of Reconstruction through education, but unlike the statistics that Foner presents, Harper seemed always to know that someone outside of the race could never quite be counted on to heartily fulfill the educational needs of the newly freed slaves and newly designated citizens. Her themes consistently point to the idea of the few blacks of privilege giving back to the many in need, never to an "outsider" attempting to assist in the efforts. In many ways her work follows what Hildegard Hoeller deems as an answer to Ralph Waldo Emerson's call to self-reliance:

> As if directly answering Emerson's essay, Harper's work addresses precisely those questions that Emerson's essay rhetorically excludes: What does self-reliance mean for women and others who are dependent and oppressed? How exactly can we envision the lives of self-reliant African Americans, working class people, and most importantly, women?"[20]

Hoeller goes on to state that Harper's work "...find[s] the greatest potential for self-reliance in women and blacks,"[21] an astute observation indeed, as Harper did in fact view a woman's independence and self-reliance as key to achieving her potential in life.

To be certain, other American women writers during the nineteenth century were concerned with the issues of women's education and independence, and some were concerned with the Reconstruction education efforts, but most did not bother in either instance to look at the implications for black women. Constance Fenimore Woolson, for instance, in her short story "King David," tells of the idealistic white Northerner David King who comes South during the Reconstruction to help the newly freed blacks to become educated so that they can best use their freedom, but who gives up on this notion in a relatively short time. King goes so far as to buy his own cotton field as a way to put idle hands—that is, the hands of the freed blacks--to work but soon begins to concur with the other (white) planters that "the negroes would work only when they pleased, and that was generally not at all."[22] One can hardly imagine Frances Harper finding this an amusing scenario. The fact that all freed blacks are lumped together, with no real understanding of the particular needs of the black woman, further illustrates that white Northern women writers like Woolson had a long way to go before being able to begin to understand Harper's motives and intentions.

Other nineteenth century American women writers such as the white writers Louisa May Alcott and Rebecca Harding Davis also dealt with issues of women and work, as did many others. Alcott's famous *Little Women* places female independence and education at a premium, as did her own life. Harding Davis's *Margret Howth* addresses women's place in society as well. And a fair number of women writers tackled race issues, although many, especially white writers, did so with a cautious gentleness. Those black women who wrote of race often wrote slave narratives, highlighting issues of especial importance to women. Harriet Ann Jacobs, for example, highlights the issue of sexual abuse in her narrative. But among the scores of women writers of all races and backgrounds in the nineteenth century United States, Frances Ellen Watkins Harper truly stands on her own as a woman who saw the importance of the black woman's perspective, role and needs in regards to both race issues and gender equality issues.

Frances Harper understood that equality and education issues differed for black women and black men. She also understood that the same issues differed drastically for black women and white women. While she shows an understanding of both black men's and white women's needs in her writings and in her lectures, she also consistently adheres to a belief that black women's education and economic independence must be put at the forefront of social thought in order for *any* issues of equality to become truly meaningful. In working for such, Harper left a legacy for her time that transcends to our own.

Notes

[1] Frances Ellen Watkins Harper. *A Brighter Coming Day*. (New York: The Feminist Press, 1990). 107.
[2] Harper, Brighter, 114.
[3] Frances E. W. Harper. *Minnie's Sacrifice, Sowing and Reaping, Trial and Triumph: Three Rediscovered Novels by Frances E. W. Harper*. (Boston: Beacon Press, 1994). 78.
[4] Harper, Minnie's, 91.
[5] Harper, Minnie's, 161.
[6] Harper, Minnie's. 239.
[7] Frances E. W. Harper. *Iola Leroy, or Shadows Uplifted*. (New York: Oxford UP, 1988). 75.
[8] Harper, Iola, 75.
[9] Harper, Iola, 75.
[10] Harper, Iola, 170.
[11] Harper, Iola, 253.
[12] Harper, Iola, 205.
[13] Cassandra Jackson, "'I Will Gladly Share with Them my Rich Heritage': Schoolteachers in
Frances E. W. Harper's *Iola Leroy* and Charles Chestnutt's *Mandy Oxendine*," *African American
Review* 37 (2003): 565.
[14] Elizabeth Petrino, "'We Are Rising as a People': Frances Haprer's Radical Views on Class and Racial Equality in *Sketches of Southern Life*," *American Transcendental Quarterly* 19 (2005): 138.
[15] Eric Foner. *Reconstruction: America's Unfinished Revolution, 1863-1877*. (New York: HarperCollins, 2005). 96.
[16] Foner, 146.
[17] Nancy Hoffman. *Woman's "True" Profession: Voices from the History of Teaching*. (New York: Feminist Press, 1981). 92.
[18] Melba Joyce Boyd. *Discarded Legacy: Politics and Poetics in the Life of Frances E. W. Harper, 1825-1911*. (Detroit: Wayne State UP, 1994). 36-37.
[19] Harper, Brighter, 3.
[20] Hildegard Hoeller, "Self-Reliant Women in Frances Harper's Writings," *American Transcendental Quarterly* 19 (2005): 207.
[21] Hoeller, 218.
[22] Constance Fenimore Woolson. *Rodman the Keeper: Southern Sketches*. (New York: D. Appleton & Co., 1880). 257.

Works Cited

Primary Sources

Harper, Frances Ellen Watkins. *A Brighter Day Coming: A Frances Ellen Watkins Harper Reader.* Ed. Harper, Frances Smith Foster. New York: The Feminist Press, 1989.

Harper, Frances E. W. *Iola Leroy, or Shadows Uplifted.* New York: Oxford UP, 1988.

Harper, Frances E.W. *Minnie's Sacrifice, Sowing and Reaping, Trial and Triumph: Three Rediscovered Novels by Frances E. W. Harper.* Ed. Frances Smith Foster. Boston: Beacon Press, 1994.

Secondary Sources

Boyd, Melba Joyce. *Discarded Legacy: Politics and Poetics in the Life of Frances E.W. Harper, 1825-1911.* Detroit: Wayne State University Press, 1994.

Foner, Eric. *Reconstruction: America's Unfinished Revolution: 1863-1877.* New York: HarperCollins, 2005.

Hoeller, Hildegard. "Self-Reliant Women in Frances Harper's Writings." *American Transcendental Quarterly* 19 (2005): 205-20.

Hoffman, Nancy. *Woman's "True" Profession: Voices from the History of Teaching.* New York: The Feminist Press, 1981.

Jackson, Cassandra. "'I Will Gladly Share with them my Rich Heritage': Schoolteachers in Frances E. W. Harper's *Iola Leroy* and Charles Chestnutt's *Mandy Oxendine.*" *African American Review* 37 (2003): 553-568.

Petrino, Elizabeth. "'We Are Rising as a People': Frances Harper's Radical Views on Class and Racial Equality in *Sketches of Southern Life.*" *American Transcendental Quarterly* 19 (2005): 133-53.

Woolson, Constance Fenimore. *Rodman the Keeper: Southern Sketches.* New York: D. Appleton & Co., 1880.

Chapter Sixteen

Work Among the People: How Susan La Flesche Picotte and Zitkala Sa Used Boarding School Education for the Benefit of Their Tribes

Sarah Jayne Hitt

The movement to educate Native American children, which reached the height of its fervor in the mid to late eighteen hundreds, is largely responsible for the success that Susan La Flesche Picotte (Omaha) and Zitkala Sa (Yankton) found in their personal and professional lives. Their education at white-run boarding schools gave them the opportunity to pursue careers in non-traditional and male-dominated fields: La Flesche was the first woman American Indian M.D. and Zitkala Sa was a nationally-renowned journalist and editor. However, becoming two of the most influential Native American women of their time came at the price of being torn from their homelands and communities, giving up their traditional cultures, and feeling isolated in a world where they were neither fully Indian nor fully white. Nevertheless, had it not been for the education they received at the hands of the dominant culture, they would not have been able to develop the skills that allowed them to become mediators who brought their disparate worlds closer together. In advocating for the rights of Indians while simultaneously gaining the respect and admiration of whites, Susan La Flesche and Zitkala Sa used their unique social positioning to help their people in ways they could not have done had they remained on the Midwestern reservations where they were born and raised.

On the Omaha reservation in Eastern Nebraska and the Yankton reservation in South Dakota in the mid-1800s, Susan La Flesche and Zitkala Sa (known as a child as Gertrude Simmons) were in some senses quite isolated geographically, economically, and socially from the industrial revolution sweeping across the East Coast and from Anglo-American societal constructs. But by no means were they living in a world completely removed from the dominant culture; the Sioux and Omaha had had encounters with white people for over two hundred years (both women were of mixed ancestry). At this period in history, there were missionaries on the reservations, white settlers at close proximity, and the army's constant presence at nearby forts. Yet while the two girls knew from their experiences early on that being Indian would almost completely alienate them from white culture unless they were willing to adopt it, their families reacted differently to the pressures of assimilation. The Simmons household was very traditional; Gertrude's mother Ellen, a full-blood Sioux, was vehemently opposed to white influence of any kind and was committed to educating her daughter at home in all of the Sioux ways and beliefs. In "Impressions of an Indian Childhood," Zitkala Sa writes of learning traditional crafts and cooking, and of hearing the legends of the tribe as well as stories about the continued white oppression of the Sioux. But in 1864, not long after her older brother Dawée returned from school in the east, Quaker missionaries came to recruit 8-year-old Gertrude as well. Her mother despaired at this additional intrusion into their world, saying, "Don't believe a word they say! Their words are sweet, but, my child, their deeds are bitter. You will cry for me, but they will not even soothe you. Stay with me, my little one! Your brother Dawée says that going East, away from your mother, is too hard an experience for his baby sister."[1] The lure of school was appealing to Gertrude, however, and she had other girl friends that would be going, so she persuaded her mother to let her go.

In 1868, Susan La Flesche also followed older brothers away to white-run schools, but her parents deemed this act a necessity. Her father, Chief Iron Eye (Joseph) La Flesche, was passionately dedicated to his people and a very strong leader, and because of his position and interactions with white people, he recognized the inevitability of modern progress. He felt that if Native people did not go along with the process of "civilization" and all its accoutrements, they would literally become extinct; if they hoped to gain rights, responsibility, and a decent living, they had to be able to move in the white sphere. Thus, he always stressed the importance of education to his children, telling his son Francis, Susan's stepbrother:

> That you might profit by the teachings of your own people and that of the white race, and that you might avoid the misery which accompanies ignorance, I placed you in the House of Teaching of the White-chests, who are said to be wise and to have in their books the utterances of great and

learned men. I had treasured the hope that you would wish to know the good deeds done by men of your own race, and by men of the white race, that you would follow their example and take pleasure in doing the things that are noble and helpful to those around you.[2]

This is a clear articulation of a plan for survival—not only of the people but of the culture, and it suggests that the important thing was not just to become educated and "civilized," but it was to use the skills bestowed by all educators, white or Indian, to ultimately help the community. Gertrude's mother and Susan's father represent the two extremes of reactions that parents had to the pressure of white boarding schools. But whether they were accepting of or rejecting of this pressure, these families became participants in the long tradition of Indian education in America.[3]

This movement officially began no later than 1606, when King James I urged the English settlers to educate, Christianize, and civilize the Indians in the First Charter of Virginia.[4] The Spanish and French had also established missions in the south and along the Great Lakes by this time, and various combinations of mission schools, private schools, and reservation schools worked at Indian education in fits and starts for two centuries. By 1819, though, Congress deemed it necessary to make education an official part of the government's Indian policy. Michael C. Coleman notes that following this provision, "each year the President could expend $10,000 to employ 'capable persons of good moral character, to instruct [the Indians] in the mode of agriculture suited to their situation; and for teaching their children in reading, writing, and arithmetic.'"[5] Now that there was a financial incentive rather than simply a moral one, education programs for Native children rapidly expanded, ultimately culminating in the boarding school program that would remove thousands of children from reservations and give them a crash course in becoming white. Richard Henry Pratt, famously (or infamously) founded the first of these government boarding schools, the Carlisle Indian Industrial School in 1879. In an 1892 speech about his goals for Indian education, he articulated his philosophy about the students in his care: to "kill the Indian and save the man."[6] American Indian children, after enduring the separation from family and community and tolerating the long journey east, bowed to the sometimes brutal methods of inculcating civilization, progress, modernity, and Christian morality, and adopted white styles of hair, dress, speech, and education. The boarding school experience has been extensively researched and commented on in fiction and in criticism, and these works have demonstrated the extremely negative consequences of this misguided government policy, including loss of language and culture, alienation, and in worst cases abuse and neglect. At the same time, however, these schools did allow some Native children to get a toehold in white society, and they were where Susan and Gertrude were headed.

It goes without saying that just making that long trip east was, in itself, another way that the dominant culture challenged these young children. Zitkala Sa says of the initial separation from her mother: "I was in the hands of strangers whom my mother did not fully trust. I no longer felt free to be myself, or to voice my own feelings."[7] Later, she writes of white people gawking at her on the train, making her ashamed of her clothes and moccasins. Upon first arriving at White's Manual Institute in Wabash, Indiana, she experiences pure culture shock, and writes about the trauma of being forced to have her hair cut short: "Our mothers had taught us that only unskilled warriors who were captured had their hair shingled by the enemy. Among our people, short hair was worn by mourners, and shingled hair by cowards!" After the deed is done, she says, "Then I lost my spirit."[8] Zitkala Sa also describes the difficulty of learning English while being strictly forbidden to use her native language among her peers. This language policy was touted in 1886 by J.D.C. Atkins, commissioner of Indian affairs, who said, "There is not an Indian pupil whose tuition and maintenance is paid for by the United States Government . . . who is permitted to study any other language than our own vernacular—the language of the greatest, most powerful, and enterprising nationalities beneath the sun."[9] The arrogance inherent in this statement demonstrates not only the vehemence with which the government's educational policies were promulgated, but also the extreme cultural pressures to which the students had to bow.

But not all Native students experienced such trauma during their education. Susan La Flesche was one of these fortunate ones. She had been going to the Omaha reservation's Presbyterian mission school since she was three. There, she learned about Christianity and women's vocations as well as English and other academic subjects.[10] This school was located on the eastern part of the reservation, at some distance from the tribal homes, and was a boarding school. After 1869, when the Presbyterians were pushed off the reservation by a new government policy, Susan would have attended the day school run by Quakers, who had taken over the mission. This school was only three miles from home, and Susan seems to have thoroughly enjoyed the education she received here; Benson Tong suggests this may be partly due to the Quakers' tolerance for Native ideas.[11] She soon followed her sister Susette to the Elizabeth Institute for Young Ladies in New Jersey, which provided Native girls with an extremely well-rounded and thorough academic training. Finally, in 1884, Susan went to finish her education at the Hampton Institute in Virginia, a school originally founded to educate African-American students (Booker T. Washington was a graduate). We don't know as much about Susan La Flesche's journeys to New Jersey or Virginia, or her first reactions to life at school, mostly because, unlike Zitkala Sa, these events were not the subjects of her later writings. But from what we can see in her letters, she seems to have accommodated to her surroundings, and wrote to her sisters that she was "doing pretty well."[12] Susan's years of experience at the reservation mission school and supportive family members like her brother Francis, who traveled with her on the train, and her sister Marguerite, who also enrolled at Hampton, probably helped her adapt to life far from home. Hampton was also a private school, founded by citizen philanthropists, and was therefore not so tied to strict federal regulations about courses and policies. For instance, it had a much more liberal stance on the use of native languages among students, and seems to have promoted its curriculum much less forcibly than schools like Carlisle.

Regardless of how the girls found their arrival at school, they both discovered, once they began their coursework, that they had extraordinary scholastic aptitudes. Curriculum at the time was divided along the "half and half" concept: half the instruction was devoted to academic subjects, and half to physical work that was "appropriate to 'proper' gender roles. The boys learned such skills as blacksmithing, woodwork, and . . . American methods of farming. The girls learned 'civilized' cooking, dressmaking, and other 'domestic arts.'"[13] Under this program, the emphasis was less upon knowledge and more upon vocation. In the last vestiges of the Victorian age, the appropriate vocation for girls like Susan and Gertrude was home-keeping. Nevertheless, within these confining expectations, they found ways to shine academically, and gradually gained the confidence to shake off such limiting roles for women. Gertrude won two oratory contests, one statewide in 1896, at which white contestants taunted her as a "squaw," and Susan ultimately became salutatorian of her class.[14] But though both women enjoyed learning and exhibited great capacity and intelligence, they graduated with uncertain futures. After her graduation in 1898, Gertrude was offered a position in the Carlisle school (a teacher being one of the acceptable professions for women), but couldn't decide if she wanted it, and upon leaving Hampton in 1886 Susan went back home because even though she knew she wanted to become a doctor, she didn't have the funds or the support to continue her medical education.

They had both made trips back to their respective reservations throughout the course of their education, and these were pivotal moments in each case. Gertrude had returned home after completing her first three years at Wabash, and even stayed on the reservation for four years, uncertain of what to do next. Apparently she was beginning to feel that her old way of life was irreconcilable with the new, which left her depressed and confused much of the time. She wrote, "My mother had never gone inside of a schoolhouse, and so she was not capable of comforting her daughter who could read and write. Even nature seemed to have no place for me. I was neither a wee girl nor a tall one; neither a wild Indian nor a tame one."[15] Obviously the cultural conflict that began when she left for school had only increased. She eventually decided to go to school again because she felt she couldn't get on where she was; she no longer fit in: "A few more moons of such a turmoil drove me away to the Eastern school."[16] Dexter Fisher explains that "to her mother and the traditional Sioux on the reservation where she had grown up, she was highly suspect because, in their minds, she had abandoned, even betrayed, the Indian way of life by getting an education in the white man's world."[17] She had become an outsider among her own family and friends, and resolved to attend Earlham College in Richmond, Indiana. Susan, meanwhile, was feeling more like an outsider in the white world. After graduating from Hampton, she had applied to the Women's Medical College in Pennsylvania, but all scholarship money had already been allocated, and she was dependent upon the generosity of the Women's National Indian Association and the Connecticut Indian Association for donations and support. Forced to go back to Nebraska and wait on the benevolence of others, she was left in limbo until the fall. While she was helping her father harvest crops in September, she finally heard that she had been given the means to attend medical school.

Here we see these women struggling to find a path that fit their new statuses as educated people. It had become clear to returning students that a boarding school education, as promising as it might be, really didn't prepare Indians for life back home; it was actually wasted because there were no economic or professional opportunities on the reservations. According to Coleman, "Many returnees soon discovered that the knowledge, skills, and trades they had struggled to acquire at school were often irrelevant on the reservation."[18] Gertrude's brother Dawée had initially been fortunate enough to get a position as a reservation government clerk when he left his Eastern school. But on one of Gertrude's visits home, her mother mentioned that "the Great Father at Washington sent a white son to take your brother's place . . . since then

Dawée has not been able to make use of the education the Eastern school has given him."[19] Susan La Flesche was also aware of this problem; there was nothing for her to do on the reservation after her graduation and no opportunities for business. She later wrote in the *Walthill Times*, a local white newspaper, "If [Native people] lack competency today it is because we are kept from developing as we ought to have by the experience gained through being brought into contact with the white man in a commercial way."[20] Boarding schools had gone to great lengths to assimilate the students to the values of white culture, but on the reservations, that culture didn't necessarily exist. Another problem was the disconnection and animosity they encountered in the community: "Many 'educated' Indians arrived home with a sense of cultural and indeed personal superiority, and this . . . produced strong resentment among the people."[21] In other words, the end of school left many students feeling a loss of identity, community, and vocation.

Susan La Flesche and Zitkala Sa were feeling this loss intensely as they attempted to make some decision about their futures. Susan was wholly dependent on white people far away who may at any time forget her, and Zitkala Sa felt like she was betraying her community in feeling more comfortable at school than at home. In this situation these students represent the very worst that colonization does to a people. They have had to use another language, attain another culture, develop a new set of values, and participate in a whole different way of seeing the world. To go so far as to participate in the system (even enjoy it), and advocate it for the rest of their people, smacks of the cultural betrayal personified by Frantz Fanon's colonized intellectual. He writes that "stumbling over the need to assume two nationalities, two determinations, the intellectual, . . . if he wants to be sincere with himself, chooses the negation of one of these two determinations. Usually, [he is] unwilling or unable to choose."[22] It would seem that at this crisis point, Susan La Flesche and Zitkala Sa chose to negate their Native American identities. But even as they went back East and continued to participate in white society, they were carving out unique positions for themselves which ultimately benefited Native people.

After spending an unsatisfactory year as a teacher at Carlisle Institute, Zitkala Sa finally decided to choose her own career. She moved to Boston to become a writer, saying: "Thus I resigned my position as a teacher; and now I am in an Eastern city, following the long course of study I have set for myself."[23] Now she would take ownership of her education, her status as an Indian woman, and her future. It is at this point that she adopts the name Zitkala Sa (Red Bird), perhaps to connect herself to home at the same time that she permanently divides herself from it. Amelia V.

Katanski notes that "[choosing] . . . a Lakota name for herself actually because of an accusation of her distance from that culture underscores the complex relationship between representative codes and identities in Zitkala Sa's life."[24] She is working with not one identity versus the other, but with two in concert. While she placed articles in the *Atlantic Monthly* and *Harper's*, bastions of Anglo-American culture, she used her chosen Sioux name. While she was apparently an embodiment of the success of the Indian education system, she wrote articles such as "Why I am a Pagan" which were surely calculated to undermine that very system. Though she was writing to a white audience, she was telling Indian stories and legends, giving her tribe's culture and concerns a prominent place among Eastern intellectual preoccupations. She eventually became the editor of *American Indian Magazine*, a position which she held for years until she resigned because she felt it had begun to pander to white interests. Charles Hannon believes her writing allowed her to find a place to exist between cultures: "In her [journalism] . . . she articulated a number of correspondences between the traditions of Native American tribes and those of 'Anglo-Saxon America.' In doing so, she contradicted the racial and cultural essentialism of the time."[25] Zitkala Sa's choice of career and her political advocacy for her tribe in issues such as Indian citizenship (Native Americans didn't become citizens of the United States until 1924), demonstrate how she could take her white education and put it to work for Indian causes. Without her cultural literacy, she could not have told her stories or made her appeals to both Indian and non-Indian audiences.

Susan La Flesche also found herself perfectly suited to her profession. In medical school, she cheerfully dissected cadavers while her white counterparts fainted; she describes the autopsies in detail in a letter to her family, calling them "splendid."[26] After graduation in 1889, she entertained no other plan than to go home and, in her words, "work as physician among [her] people."[27] Upon arriving on the reservation, she moved swiftly to improve the tribe's medical care. In her position as an Omaha citizen and as a doctor, she was able to persuade members of the tribe that were skeptical of Western medicine to accept treatment for illnesses. Her English fluency and ability to negotiate through political bureaucracy resulted in the tremendous success of a tribal hospital built at Walthill, Nebraska. La Flesche worked not only for health issues, such as for vaccinations and against alcohol and peyote abuse, but also for national issues—against allotment legislation that robbed Native people of the very land the government gave them, and for U.S. citizenship for Indians. She wrote about all of these issues in local and national newspapers, from Nebraska's *Walthill Times* to the *Southern Workman* and the *New York Times*, bringing the situation of the Omaha to the attention of whites.

Wilbert Ahern contends that La Flesche's medical work, like Zitkala Sa's career as a journalist, gave her the perfect opportunity to be a mediator on behalf of her people. Both women "neither cut ties with their community nor became apologists for either the Office of Indian Affairs or White neighbors at the expense of the tribe. They brought to their community a strong sense of mission, one that emphasized a selective retention of the old ways along with accommodation as a group to the surrounding population."[28] Granted, this position as cultural mediator and advocate came with the loss of some elements of Native culture. Zitkala Sa, especially, had mourned for the Sioux aspects of herself that she had to sacrifice for achievement in the modern world. But these choices were not made at a whim or at the exclusive behest of the dominant culture. Rather, she "meticulously constructed her identity as Zitkala Sa, emphasizing or excluding elements of her heritage, biography, languages, politics, and available literary forms to suit the needs of this situational self."[29] To recognize, and even promote a situational self, as Susan La Flesche and Zitkala Sa did with great success, is not an act of cultural sabotage, nor is it, as Fanon might suggest, a victory for the colonizer. Rather than having to choose one culture or the other, they took the best aspects of each and used their knowledge to benefit both—they could use the benefits of citizenship (literally and figuratively) in both nations for positive ends. In Sean Teuton's essay promoting American Indian national identity and sovereignty, he writes, "From this view of the tribal national citizen, we are able to . . . [avoid] simplistic or reified notions of how people participate in indigenous or human communities, modifying in fact as a consequence of complex allegiances. Knowledge of the self changes and even grows through this kind of engagement, reconstituting in response to one's surroundings in the midst of social change."[30] Zitkala Sa and Susan La Flesche were not just the losers of culture at the hand of trauma. They were also the gainers of culture at the hand of opportunity, and must be seen in both lights. Since their goal was to move freely within both Indian and white society, and above all to act on behalf of their communities, their status as educated women gave them the position of a mediator who could articulate needs and advocate for rights and policies that benefited Native Americans. By negotiating the expectations of the tribes who raised them and the white Americans who taught them, Zitkala Sa and Susan La Flesche used education as the essential tool that allowed them to write and act on behalf of their people.

Notes

[1] Zitkala Sa, "Impressions," 46.
[2] La Flesche, *The Middle Five*, 127-28.
[3] Coleman provides an interesting analysis of the reasons why American Indian children went away to school: out of 69 autobiographical narrators, he concludes that 17 were "compelled by authorities," 33 were sent by tribal members, often their families, 9 reported overlapping influences, and 10 went as a personal choice. *American Indian Children*, 60.
[4] Thorpe, *Federal and State Constitutions*, 58.
[5] Coleman, *American Indian Children*, 39.
[6] Pratt, "The Advantages of Mingling Indians with Whites," 260.
[7] Zitkala Sa, "Impressions," 47.
[8] Zitkala Sa, "School Days," 187.
[9] Coleman, *American Indian Children*, 105.
[10] Tong, *Susan La Flesche Picotte, M.D.*, 31-34.
[11] Ibid., 39.
[12] Ibid., 47.
[13] Coleman, *American Indian Children*, 40.
[14] Zitkala Sa, "School Days," 194; and Tong, 63.
[15] Zitkala Sa, "School Days," 191.
[16] Ibid., 192.
[17] Fisher, "Zitkala Sa," 230.
[18] Coleman, *American Indian Children*, 182.
[19] Zitkala Sa, "An Indian Teacher," 384.
[20] Picotte, "Dr. Picotte's Appeal."
[21] Coleman, *American Indian Children*, 180.
[22] Fanon, *The Wretched of the Earth*, 155-56.
[23] Zitkala Sa, "An Indian Teacher," 386.
[24] Katanski, *Learning to Write*, 114.
[25] Ibid., 192-93.
[26] Tong, *Susan La Flesche Picotte*, 73.
[27] Ibid., 87.
[28] Ahern, "The Returned Indians," 101-24.
[29] Katanski, *Learning to Write*, 114.
[30] Teuton, "Transnationalism and the American Indian Scholar," 277.

Works Cited

Primary Sources

La Flesche, Francis. *The Middle Five: Indian Schoolboys of the Omaha Tribe*. Madison: U of Wisconsin P, 1963.
Picotte, Susan La Flesche. "Dr. Picotte's Appeal." *Walthill Times*, March 4, 1910.
Pratt, Richard H. "The Advantages of Mingling Indians with Whites." In *Americanizing the American Indians: Writings by the Friends of the Indian 1880–1900*, edited by Francis Paul Prucha, 260-217 (Cambridge, MA: Harvard University Press, 1973).
Zitkala Sa. "Impressions of an Indian Childhood." *Atlantic Monthly*, January 1900.
—. "An Indian Teacher Among Indians." *Atlantic Monthly*, March 1900.
—. "School Days of an Indian Girl." *Atlantic Monthly*, February 1900.

Secondary Sources

Ahern, Wilbert H. "'The Returned Indians': Hampton Institute and Its Indian Alumni, 1879-1893." *Journal of Ethnic Studies* 10.4 (December 1983): 101-24.
Coleman, Michael C. *American Indian Children at School, 1850-1930*. Jackson, MI: University of Mississippi Press, 1993.
Fanon, Frantz. *The Wretched of the Earth*. Trans. Richard Philcox. New York: Grove, 2004.
Fisher, Dexter. "Zitkala Sa: The Evolution of a Writer." *American Indian Quarterly* 5.3 (August 1979): 229-238.
Hannon, Charles. "Zitkala Sa & The Commercial Magazine Apparatus." In *The Only Efficient Instrument": American Women Writers & The Periodical, 1837-1916*, edited by Aleta Feinsod Cane and Susan Alves, 179-201 (Iowa City, IA: University of Iowa Press, 2001).
Katanski, Amelia V. *Learning to Write "Indian": The Boarding-School Experience and American Indian Literature*. Norman, OK: University of Oklahoma Press, 2005.
Teuton, Sean. "Transnationalism and the American Indian Scholar: Native Studies and the Challenge of Pan-Indianism." In *Identity Politics Reconsidered*, edited by Linda Martín Alcoff, Michael Hames-García,

Satya P. Mohanty, and Paula M.L. Moya, 265-284 (New York: Palgrave Macmillan, 2006).
Thorpe, Francis Newton, ed. *Federal and State Constitutions, Colonial Charters, and Other Organic Laws of the States, Territories, and Colonies Now or Heretofore Forming the United States of America.* Washington, DC: Government Printing Office, 1909.
Tong, Benson. *Susan La Flesche Picotte, M.D.: Omaha Indian Leader and Reformer.* Norman, OK: University of Oklahoma Press, 1999.

CHAPTER SEVENTEEN

EDUCATION FOR MARRIAGE OR EDUCATION FOR LIFE? THE CHALLENGE OF POST-WAR SPANISH WOMEN NOVELISTS TO THE FRANCOIST APPROACH TO THE EDUCATION OF WOMEN

PATRICIA O'BYRNE

The regime of Francisco Franco (1939-75) marks one of the most repressive periods for women in Western Europe in the twentieth century. In sharp contrast to Spain's Second Republic (1931-36), when liberal left-wing governments had introduced full female enfranchisement, co-education, and even abortion on demand in Catalonia in 1936 before the outbreak of the Civil War (1936-39), under Franco's dictatorship women experience close to full female disempowerment. Gender becomes a "powerful signifier of social order": women are treated as minors before the law with fathers or husbands having the ultimate say in rights as fundamental as traveling alone, holding a passport or opening a bank account.[1] Legislation was introduced in the forties with view to ensuring that married women were virtually excluded from the workforce (*Fuero del trabajo* and the *Ley de Bases,* 1938) and bonuses and financial incentives were given to families with stay-at-home mothers. As a result, much of married women's labor was relegated to menial jobs, often on the black market, and they were now more vulnerable to exploitation. This legislation served not only to camouflage the true unemployment figures but was also instrumental in boosting the Spanish population to the dictator's desired target of forty million.[2] Employment figures for 1950 demonstrate the success of Franco's policies: 93.9% of males between the ages of 15 and 64 are engaged in remunerative employment in comparison to the figure of 14% for women, the lowest recorded rate in Europe.[3] Because young women were encouraged to enter marriage as early as possible, the working female population consisted almost exclusively of women belonging to the much derided category of *solteras* or spinsters.

The compliance of women with the Francoist agenda of domesticity and reproduction did not hinge solely on legislative enforcement. The Regime had a staunch ally in the Catholic Church, which also extolled Catholic motherhood as woman's true destiny. The Catholic lay organization *Acción Católica* ran educational programs for women targeting domestic skills and aimed at preparing young women for their future role as mothers. The Catholic Church in Spain, through its control of schools and because of the huge numbers attending masses and spiritual activities, was a powerful instrument in ensuring the subservience of women and promoting the virtues of abnegation and chastity. However, above all, Franco was indebted to the *Sección Femenina* of the Spanish fascist movement, the *Falange Española*, for mobilizing women to the service of the *Patria* and the Regime. Pilar Primo de Rivera, sister of the founder of the Spanish Falange, set up its female section in 1933 because the movement's fascist ideology, with its violent overtones, was considered unsuitable for female membership by its leader José Antonio Primo de Rivera.

While the Spanish Falange was one the least enduring of national fascist organizations in mid-century Europe, the *Sección Femenina* went on to become the most powerful women's fascist movement of the last century until its final dissolution in 1977. Pilar Primo recalls that there was a time when *all* Spanish women passed through the hands of the *Sección Femenina*, "millions of women".[4] While this may be a slight exaggeration, it does reflect the magnitude and scope of the organization and its activities. Franco was well rewarded for his promotion of the *Sección Femenina*. "A great prize from Franco's point of view", is how Paul Preston describes the organization that for more than forty years, through their compulsory Social Service initiative, "donated" millions of unpaid working hours of Spanish women to the nation's welfare.[5] Most of the energy of the *Sección Femenina* was devoted to their educational programs imparted in girls' high schools and as part of Social Service training. A Ministerial decree of 1941 included the compulsory subject Domestic Education (*Enseñanzas de Hogar*) in the high school curriculum for girls. The arrival of the *Sección Femenina* to the schools was referred to as "the invasion of Pilar's girls" and was generally viewed as an unnecessary intrusion. As Alcalde points out, neither the defeated nor the victorious sectors were happy about the appointment of the Falange instructresses to the schools.[6] Although there was some passive resistance from educators who considered this development a waste of valuable school time that should have been spent on academic learning, there was no collective protest. Girls were thus disadvantaged when competing with male students in State examinations or if they wished to attend university. In 1944, a further Ministerial directive instructed all high schools to set up Domestic Schools (*Escuelas de Hogar*) with responsibility for physical education, political education and a range of domestic courses from dressmaking, cookery and hygiene to childrearing: "Our Domestic Schools teach women to be truly good housewives, good mothers to their children and perfect companions to their husbands".[7] The *Sección Femenina* looked after the organization and delivery of all the Domestic School courses, which afforded them considerable time to mould and indoctrinate young women.[8]

Combating illiteracy and the education of women was central to the strategy of the *Sección Femenina*. However, the reason for educating women was to better equip them to serve. The following extracts, taken from the speeches and writings of Pilar Primo de Rivera are typical of the discourse of the first two post-war decades.

> We will build on the work we have already begun in our educational courses in order to make men's life in the family so pleasant that they will find what they did not have before in the home and then there will be no need for them to go to the bar or the casino to relax. (1939)

> Moreover, (*in addition to helping her husband with his work*) if women are educated they will be able to intervene directly in the education of their children by helping them learn what they need to know. (1948)

> I know that by educating mothers we will avoid the death of children, but this takes time and Spain is in a rush to double her population. (1946) [9]

The above were considered valid reasons for educating women: so as they could better serve their husbands, their children and the *Patria*. No references are made to the personal development or educational needs of women or to possible career or professional opportunity.

Women's magazines of the period, a number of which were publications of the *Sección Femenina* and of *Acción Católica*, reinforced the overwhelming importance of domestic efficiency, of marriage at the earliest possible opportunity, of mothering large numbers of children and of maintaining a happy husband at any cost. Intellectual activity was frequently discouraged. In a quiz entitled "Are you still young…?", one of the defining criteria of youth was that if a young woman went on a journey and could not remember a single place name of where she had been and could not remember the scenery well enough to describe it, but could describe all eligible men under thirty that she had met, she could then consider herself as still young![10] The respected author José María Pemán, considered an authority on the female psyche, was a regular contributor to women's magazines and encapsulates the contemporary views on women's intellectual capacity when he wrote: "It is always more difficult to understand beings who are close to instinct and are at a remove from the intellect…Women are more instinctive and primitive beings than men".[11]

The acceptance and reiteration of women's perceived intellectual deficiencies was a reason given for not overburdening them with too much intellectual content and it could also be used to justify the substitution of domestic skills courses in place of academic subjects. However detrimental this ludicrous assumption was to the education of middle-class girls, it should be borne in mind that in 1950, 28% of girls still received no formal education whatsoever because they were needed to work in the home.[12]

In the authoritarian society of the forties and fifties, in which they were dually repressed, both as citizens and as women, there were few fora available to women to effect change or even to express their grievances other than through artistic or literary means. However, all printed material had to be submitted to a rigid censorship process which imposed heavy fines on publishers, editors and authors who breached accepted political and moral codes. In the field of literary fiction, there is not a recorded tradition of women writers in the decades preceding the war, although a number of female authors published romantic novels in the 1930s. The romantic *novela rosa*, provided it stayed within safe moral boundaries, was not a cause for concern for the Regime's censors as it tended to be simplistic and conservative, rewarding the conforming woman with marriage to a dominant, authoritative male while punishing her morally inferior counterpart for her misguided or frivolous decisions. The 1940s witness the emergence of a new generation of women novelists, including better-known authors such as Carmen Laforet, Ana María Matute and Carmen Martín Gaite, who produced neorealist fiction depicting social issues affecting women, issues that fell beyond the safety net of the romantic *novela rosa* of the best-selling women authors. Brooksbank Jones has observed that these novelists used the *novela rosa* frame "to highlight the restrictions imposed on women under Franco".[13] It is quite probable that their recourse to a narrative structure similar to that of the *novela rosa*, provides the explanation why they were not unduly troubled by censorship.[14] This body of literature does not openly condemn the repression of women in post-war Spain; it is an oblique criticism that exposes injustices through the narration of the experiences of a young heroine in search of meaning and identity. The heroines of these novels are alienated figures who, motivated by curiosity or intellectual disquiet, present a challenge to the marriage and motherhood route that is meant to bring them fulfillment. Chris Perriam *et al* points to how these novels offer "an alternative life-narrative".[15] Among the recurring themes in this literature we find single women reduced to total dependency, unfaithful husbands, disillusioned housewives and mothers trapped in unhappy marriages and women who drift into prostitution; in short the unspoken aspects of Francoist society. The issues raised by the novelists stem from their unjust subordination in a patriarchal regime and also from their total lack of preparedness for life.

Carmen Martín Gaite (1925-2000), one of Spain's most accomplished twentieth century women novelists, published her second novel *Entre visillos* [*Behind the Curtains*] in 1958. This neorealist novel is highly critical of life in a provincial town where women lead vacuous lives and idle away the hours nurturing the hope that a half-acceptable suitor might come to the rescue. Although all the male characters have university studies and are preparing for state exams for senior positions, most are exposed as immature and unfaithful specimens. In sharp contrast, Martín Gaite's female characters are strikingly deprived of educational opportunities and discouraged from pursuing their studies by parents and fiancés and, inevitably, by one another. The non-conforming protagonist in this novel is Natalia who is determined to attend university in Madrid, despite opposition from her father and aunt, who has looked after her since her mother's death in childbirth. Natalia says of her aunt: "… Aunt Concha wants us all (*Natalia and her sisters*) to turn into dimwits and the only reason we are being educated is in order to find a wealthy fiancé. She wants us to be as inward looking and as ignorant as possible…"[16] The character of Aunt Concha epitomizes the attitudes of mothers in the forties and fifties, attitudes censured by women novelists. Natalia receives no encouragement to further her education from her authoritarian father who will not allow her to leave the family home to study. (He will not even allow her twenty-seven year old sister move to the capital.) Meanwhile, Natalia's sixteen-year-old friend Gertru is prevented from returning to school by her fiancé, who fears that her innocence might be at stake.

> She (*Gertru*) explained that she would not be registering this semester because Ángel does not consider the Institute a suitable place for her. When I asked why, it appeared that she had told him about the girl in fifth year that had had a baby last year.[17]

Having spoken to Natalia, Gertru then considers she should return for the semester and take her final exam but Ángel is adamant that his future wife has no need for academic education.

> You are marrying me and for that you don't need to know Latin or geometry; so long as you know how to be a good housewife, that's more than enough.[18]

The first time Ángel meets Natalia he refers to her as a "clever little monkey"[19] whose fame had reached him through Gertru. Gertru's subsequent interjection indicates the extent to which she has assimilated the discourse aimed at convincing women that it is more feminine and appealing to men if the woman is dim. She even changes her voice to tell Natalia and Ángel of her limited aptitude for study.

> "I told him how you've always helped me pass my exams and all that sort of thing. And about how smart you are".[20]

The majority of the girls in Natalia's class show similarly immature attitudes towards learning, referring to the three students out of a group of fifteen who regularly attend as "licks".[21] The naïve voice of the first person narrator, an Austrian teacher who arrives to the provincial town, is used by Martín Gaite to highlight the limitations and unbelievable attitudes towards girls' education. Pablo, the young teacher of German, is bewildered by the total lack of interest in learning shown by most of his female pupils. They spend their time giggling when they are asked a question and do not bother attending class. However, it is not just the girls for whom their education is a low priority. The accommodation available to the Institute is being eroded on an annual basis, ironically by the Jesuits–famed for their role as educators–, who claim space from the school and have priority of use of the stairs. The Jesuit quarters of the enormous building are well heated whereas the school area, due to budget restrictions, has no heating.[22] Pablo is also struck by the segregation of the sexes for educational purposes: the boys have their classes in the morning with a different complement of teachers.

By placing her bourgeois protagonist in an *Instituto* or state school, as opposed to the more elitist and expensive convent schools run by the nuns, Martín Gaite also manages to describe the experience of the working-class girl attending high school. Alcalde describes the two-tier educational system:

The daughters of these families (*those who had supported Franco and the Catholic Church in the Civil War*) would be educated by the nuns in convent schools, the "fee-paying schools" as they were known. The others, poor girls, daughters of the defeated Republicans or those who were unable or did not wish to mount the triumphalist bandwagon, would attend state schools.[23]

Natalia visits her friend Alicia Sampelayo in one of the poorer quarters of the town. She uses the cries of a baby to guide her up the stairs where she is met by Alicia's stepmother who is trying to remove the baby from the floor by threatening him. Natalia finds Alicia studying with her books spread over her bed, behind a curtain in a small alcove in the room her stepmother uses as a hairdressing salon. The former wonders how her friend could possibly study with all the noise from the dryers. (It is clear to the reader that there are more pressing issues in this household.) Alicia has a career dream, which could not be considered an ambition, as she is realistic enough to realize that: "Studying is very costly and it takes a long time". [24] She dismisses the possibility of ever becoming a primary school teacher and returning to her village to teach and live with her grandmother. Instead, she will present for state exams in the hope of securing a junior position in the public service. It is interesting to note that for women of the lower social classes it was acceptable that they take up employment before they married whereas for middle-class young women, in normal circumstances, it was not socially acceptable. The controlled protection of the family home was considered more propitious for the preservation of innocence and purity.

Carmen Kurtz (1911-1999) published fourteen full-length novels during the Franco years and to date has received surprisingly little literary coverage. In her novels written in the 1950s, she is extremely critical of the unnecessary limitations placed on women's lives. Moreover, her criticism is not limited to her fictional works. In an interview with the literary review, *Estafeta Literaria*, the author is extremely frank in her condemnation of the repression of women, calling for a complete revision of the existing Civil Code. She criticizes the practice of ending girls' education at a young age before they have acquired any academic or professional qualification.

> The number of girls who leave school at thirteen, fourteen, fifteen and sixteen to stay at home and help their mothers (which, in effect, means idling about, doing nothing, waiting for a boyfriend to turn up who will rescue them) is truly alarming. These young girls should be taught that studying, professional courses or training are essential in today's world and that work brings a sense of satisfaction that is not to be found in the tedium

of watching the days go by hoping for the dream solution. And of course earning one's own money provides women with an enormous sense of personal security.[25]

Even though the interview was given in 1959, Kurtz's outspokenness is quite uncommon; after all she is referring to the education of middle-class women for the workforce. While education is not the only target for her criticism of women's position in Spanish society,–she is also critical of early marriages and duplicity in relation to moral standards–the novelist prioritizes the theme of education, highlighting the need for the formal and general, including sexual, education of women. She vehemently rejects the cocooning of women from reality and in *Al lado del hombre* [*Beside the man*] (1961) she proposes that in all spheres, even in sexual relations, women should be free to take advantage of the same experiences and opportunities as their male counterparts.[26] Not surprisingly, the authorities heavily censored this novel and though the storyline loses some of its coherence and logic, Kurtz successfully communicates her message.

In her first novel, *Duermen bajo las aguas* [*They sleep under the sea*] (1954), the protagonist, Pilar, who finds herself alone with her child in France during the second world war, bemoans how her education has not prepared her to take up meaningful work.[27]

> The truth is that I was afraid. If they offered me a job, what would I do? [They] (*French working-class women*) could type, draft letters with minimum directions, file and could keep on top of things. I had never in my life written a business letter. Enrique used to say that my letters were beautiful, that they radiated love ... But what use was that to me now?[28]

The French working-class women are depicted as educated whereas coming from Spain, the assumption of the French is that Pilar is illiterate and she is frequently asked if she can sign her name.

The middle-class protagonist of Kurtz's third novel, *La vieja ley* [*The old Law*] (1956) has also acquired limited literacy tools. An intelligent young woman, she is incapable of writing basic Spanish: "According to him (*Ignacio*), my spelling was very suspect and my punctuation appalling".[29] When Victoria needs to find employment, she realizes how ill equipped she is:

> .... I was not qualified to do anything. My studies as a nice middle-class girl had not prepared me for any type of employment and the only means I had of earning was doing what I was actually doing.[30]

This is the conclusion of Victoria whose income supports her mother and grandmother and comes from a middle-aged wealthy lover with whom she has a sexual relationship. Prostitution and modeling–a profession considered morally degrading for middle-class girls–are her only means of earning a living. (In the post-war years thousands of Spanish women, out of dire necessity, drifted into prostitution in order to survive.) Her grandmother or mother had given no consideration to the possibility of Victoria ever working because for them the situation is quite clear: "Young ladies do not work".[31]

The most controversial of Kurtz's novels, *Beside the man*, challenges the myth that marriage is the destiny of all women. Carla's mother decided that she should not go to university because "the best profession for any woman is marriage".[32] The book exposes the fallacy of this myth and also the unwillingness of the protagonist's mother to confront this reality: two of Carla's mother's sisters had unsuccessful marriages. Unquestionably, the most convincing case underscoring the need to prepare women for destinies other than matrimony is exemplified in the tragic case of the Martínez sisters.

> When the Martínez girls opened their wardrobes to show their treasures to their new friends–the bed linen and the table cloths–, there was such a sense of despair. They had been deceived. They had been told that if they kept busy with their embroidery as soon as the trousseau was finished, husbands would come.[33]

The disillusionment of the Martínez sisters is shared by characters in the fictional narrative of Susana March.

> Leonor and Enriqueta were also female prisoners in the Castilian home, tireless embroiderers of trousseaus that would never see completion; pieces that would be added to the already bulging bottom drawers. They were women who had been prepared only for matrimony, and when this did not work out, as in this case, they watched their lives drift by with a bitter, harsh and melancholy feeling, deprived of any sense of hope or freedom.[34]

Susana March (1918-1991) is best known for her poetry collections and for historical narrative that she wrote jointly with husband Ricardo Fernández de Reguera, but her novels, although not well documented, are particularly relevant to the present discussion.[35] March's neorealist novel, *Algo muere cada día* [*Something dies with each day*] (1955) is a pessimistic work depicting the protagonist's trajectory from adolescence to entrapment in an unhappy marriage to an egotistical husband.[36] María's attempts to educate herself as an adolescent and later to attend university are frustrated through lack of support and understanding and finally through her own personal disillusionment. When, as a young girl with a hunger for books and study, she informs the family doctor that she intends to graduate from high school, he unjustifiably opposes her decision on health grounds and believes he is reassuring her when he adds: "[Besides], a pretty girl like you, why would you need a *bachillerato*?".[37] Because she is from a lower middle-class family with financial difficulties, and indeed because of the extraordinary circumstances of the ongoing war, María is allowed work outside the home. While employed as a secretary, she tries desperately to prepare for university exams, notwithstanding the scorn of her lecherous boss, whom she informs: "I was not born merely to be secretary for another".[38] Interesting to note in the case of March's protagonists is that they demand more than education as a means to employment; they want to attend university and to scale the professional ladder. In one of March's earliest published works, *Nido de vencejos* [*Nest of Swallows*] (1944) quoted above–a novel which contains more features of the romantic *novela rosa* than it does of the neorealist novel–, untypically the heroine is a university professor who has spent years furthering her career. In keeping with the *novela rosa* tradition, she realizes that what is missing from her life is the love of a man. However, when she finds a suitable life partner, based on criteria informed by compatibility, not desperation, he does not oppose when she tells him that she intends to continue with her career after they marry.

The reluctance not just of society but also of the parents of young women, especially mothers, to accept that not all women were destined to marry and that they needed education to survive in life, is difficult to comprehend and perhaps is a reflection of the extent of the brainwashing of women by the dominant discourses. March, like Kurtz and Martín Gaite also censures parents for their compliance.

> Of Aunt Javiera's three children, only Aurora, the eldest, had married. And now she was the mother of four little girls, whom, like all the women in the family, would not receive from their parents the education necessary to defend them against the challenges of life ahead.[39]

Many novelists depict the plight of the middle-aged single woman, who moves from financial dependence on her parents to dependence on the married brother who remains on in the family home. One of March's most memorable characters is the maiden Aunt Celia in *Something dies with each day*, who was resigned to her role as "a defenseless creature who had been brought into this world for the sole purpose of darning the clothes of her nieces and nephews and obeying those around her".[40]

The documenting of repressive gender educational practices in order to serve the interests of patriarchal Spain, as illustrated above, was a recurring feature of the neorealist fiction written by women in the first two post-war decades. The three authors discussed are representative of a number of novelists who sought to address educational discrimination and other injustices and contradictions affecting women of mid-century authoritarian Spain. Regrettably, most of these women novelists have received inadequate literary coverage and remain outside the literary canon but in recent years there is some evidence that the significance of their contribution is finally being recognized.[41] Akiko Tsuchiya describes the neorealist narrative written by women in the forties and fifties as "a muted discourse, often in camouflaged form, that represents possibilities of resistance to the repressive ideology of Francoism".[42] The criticism by novelists of women's situation, of necessity, had to be oblique because of the repressive political and social climate in which they lived, but nonetheless their courage in daring to tell the unofficial version deserves unreserved recognition.

Notes

[1] Vincent, "Spain", 212.

[2] The first birth prizes, the *Premios de Natalidad*, were awarded in 1941. The male recipients of the birth prize–it was always presented to the father–often headed families which had up to twenty children.

[3] Miguel, *Manual de estructura social de España*, 280.

[4] "millones de mujeres". Moya, *Últimas conversaciones con Pilar Primo*, 19. All translations from Spanish in this article are my own.

[5] Preston, *Franco*, 270.

Servicio Social consisted of a six-month period of service, three of which were devoted to domestic, physical and political education and three months were spent working in a hospital, orphanage or other community service. All women over the age of sixteen were obliged to undertake social service although exemptions did exist in a number of circumstances e.g. nuns, married women or the mentally incapacitated.

[6] "[L]a invasión de las chicas de Pilar en los colegios, [...] Ni a los derrotados ni a los vencedores les agradaban las «mandonas»." Alcalde, *Mujeres en el Franquismo,* 75.

[7] "En las Escuelas de Hogar de la Sección Femenina se enseña a la mujer a ser verdadera ama de su casa, buena madre de sus hijos y perfecta compañera de su marido." Taken from the *Sección Femenina Anuario* of 1954. Reproduced in Otero's *La Sección Femenina,* 153.

[8] Suárez Fernández, 136. The *Sección Femenina* instructors were paid significantly less by the Ministry of Education than regular school teachers.

[9] Published in *Discursos, circulares, escritos* (year of publication not given) "Ampliaremos la labor iniciada en nuestras escuelas de formación, para hacerles a los hombres tan agradable la vida de familia, que dentro de la casa encuentran todo aquello que antes les faltaba y así no tendrán que ir a buscar en la taberna o en el casino los ratos de expansión." (52-53)
"Además, si la mujer es culta, puede también intervenir directamente en la formación de los hijos, ayudándoles en los estudios que deban realizar." (259)
"Ya sé que, educando a las madres, evitaremos la muerte de los hijos; pero esta tarea es lenta y España tiene prisa en doblar el número de habitantes." (33)
Spain's Second Republic–in sharp contrast to the Franco years–had stressed the need to educate women so that they could participate more fully in life and in the workforce. The concept of educating women for the sole purpose of serving others underscores the retrograde patriarchal forces informing the Francoist ideology in relation to women.

[10] Published in the magazine *Y*, January 1943. Reproduced in Martín Gaite's *Usos amorosos de la posguerra española*, 158.

[11] "Son siempre más difíciles de explicar los seres cuanto más cerca están de lo instintivo y más lejos de lo intelectual. [....] La mujer es un ser más instintivo y elemental que el hombre." Pemán, *De doce cualidades de la mujer,* xiii. Pemán, who was closely linked to the Spanish Falange in the 1940's, echoes Hegelian views on the primitive nature of the female intellect. Hegel was an inspirational force for young Falangist intellectuals.

[12] Capel Martínez, *Mujer y sociedad en España (1700-1975),* 370.

[13] Brooksbank Jones, *Women in Contemporary Spain,* 160.

[14] There is evidence from a large number of the censors' reports I have examined, that the censors often did not bother to read novels written by women authors. While there are a number of novels that experienced problems with censorship (e.g. Mercedes Salisach's *Una mujer llega al pueblo* (1956) or Dolores Medio's *Diario de una maestra* (1961), it is surprising that many other novels, critical of women's role in society, had no difficulties whatsoever with censorship.

[15] Perriam *et al*, *A New History of Spanish Writing:1939 to the 1990s*, 86.

[16] "[T]ía concha nos quiere convertir en unas estúpidas, qué sólo nos educa para tener un novio rico, y que seamos lo más retrasadas posible en todo [...]." Martín Gaite, *Entre visillos*, 232.

[17] "Dice que ella este curso por fin no se matricula, porque a Ángel no le gusta el ambiente del Instituto. Yo le pregunté que por qué, y es que ella por lo visto le ha contado lo de Fonsi, aquella chica de quinto que tuvo un hijo el año pasado." Ibid., 11.

[18] "–Para casarte conmigo, no necesitas saber latín ni geometría; con que sepas ser una mujer de tu casa, basta y sobra." Ibid., 174.

[19] "un rato lista" Ibid., 65.

[20] "–Es que yo le he contado ¿sabes?, que siempre me has ayudado a aprobar y todas las cosas. Lo salada que eres." Ibid., 65.

[21] "pelotilleras" Ibid., 213.

[22] Ibid., 210-11.

[23] "Las niñas de estas familias serán educadas en los colegios de monjas, los colegios de «pago», como seguía diciendo la expresión popular. Y las otras, las pobres, las hijas de los vencidos, o de los que no quisieron o no pudieron subirse al carro de la exaltación nacional, aprenderían en las escuelas nacionales." Alcalde, 67.

[24] "–Es muy caro hacer carrera y se tarda mucho." Martín Gaite, 192.

[25] "La cantidad de chiquillas de trece, catorce, quince y dieciséis años que dejan el colegio y se quedan en casa para ayudar a la madre (lo que equivale a no hacer nada más que esperar el novio que les saque del apuro), en España es aterradora. A esas chiquillas se les debiera enseñar que unos estudios, una especialización y un oficio son esenciales en el mundo de hoy, y que en el trabajo cumplido se encuentra una satisfacción mucho mayor que en el tedio de ver pasar los días esperando hipotéticas soluciones. También ganar dinero gracias al propio esfuerzo da una enorme seguridad en sí misma." "Entrevista con Carmen Kurtz", *Estafeta Literaria*, 8.

[26] Although *Al lado del hombre* was not published until 1961, the novel was first submitted to the censor in 1959 and it took two years of correspondence and subsequent changes to the original text before permission was granted for publication. Quotations are from the first edition.

[27] Kurtz, *Duermen bajo las aguas*. Quotations are from the 1961 Círculo de Lectores edition.

[28] "La verdad es que tenía miedo. Si me ofrecían un empleo ¿qué haría? ... [Ellas] escribían a máquina, redactaban cartas con las cuatro palabras que les había dicho el director, sabían encontrar fichas en el fichero y se acordaban de todo. Yo no había escrito nunca una carta comercial. Enrique me decía que mis cartas eran muy hermosas, [...] que estaban impregnadas de amor [...] Pero ¿de qué iba s servirme todo eso?" Ibid., 180-81.

[29] "Según él, mi ortografía era dudosa y la puntuación francamente mala." Kurtz, *La vieja ley*, 167. Quotations are from the 1956 edition.

[30] "[Y]o no estaba capacitada para nada. Mis estudios de pequeña burguesa no estaban a la altura de ninguna colocación y para lo único que yo servía era para lo que estaba haciendo." Ibid., 233.

[31] "–Una señorita no trabaja." Ibid., 197.

[32] "[L]a mejor carrera para la mujer [...] –Es el matrimonio." Kurtz, *Al lado del hombre*, 29. Quotations are from the 1961 edition.

[33] "Cuando las Martínez abrían el armario de los tesoros y enseñaban, a las nuevas amistades, los juegos de cama y las mantelerías, había en ella mucha desesperanza. Las había engañado. Les habían dicho que la mujer debía ser hacendosa y que en cuanto tuvieran el ajuar, tendrían marido." Ibid., 148.

[34] "Así eran también Leonor y Enriqueta, mujercitas presas en el hogar castellano, bordadoras incansables de labores que jamás llegaban a concluirse y que, aunque así sucediese, no servirían más que para engrosar la serie que en lo profundo de los cajones dormía. Mujeres sólo educadas para el matrimonio y cuando el matrimonio fallaba – como en este caso –, veían pasar la vida con una melancolía rencorosa y dura en los corazones, huérfanas de toda esperanza y de toda

liberación." March, *Nido de vencejos* [*Nest of Swallows*] (1944), 144. Quotations are from this first edition.

[35] In the 1940s and '50s, March was recognized as a successful novelist. Her novel, *Something dies with each day* [*Algo muere cada día*] (1955) was translated into several European language.

[36] March, *Algo muere cada día*, 88. Quotations are from the first edition.

[37] "–[U]na chica tan bonita como tú, ¿para qué necesita estudiar el Bachillerato?" Ibid., 75.

[38] "–[N]o he nacido para ser secretaria de nadie." Ibid., 128.

[39] "De las tres hijas que había tenido tía Javiera únicamente Aurora, la mayor, se había casado. Ahora era madre de cuatro chiquillas que, como todas las hembras de la familia, no recibirían de sus padres la menor arma con que luchar contra la vida." *Nido de vencejos*, 14.

[40] "[U]na indefensa criatura, que había venido al mundo sólo a poner remiendos en la ropa de los sobrinos y a obedecer las órdenes de los demás." *Algo muere cada día*, 88.

[41] Raquel Conde Peñalosa has sought to address the neglect of this group of writers in her recent publications: *La novela femenina de posguerra (1940-1960)* and the bio-biographical guide *Mujeres novelistas y novelas de mujeres en la posguerra española (1940–1965)*, both of which were published in 2004.

[42] Tsuchiya, Akiko. "Women and fiction in post-Franco Spain", 214.

Works Cited

Primary Sources

Kurtz, Carmen. *Al lado del hombre.* Barcelona: Planeta, 1961.
—. *Duermen bajo las aguas.* Barcelona: Planeta, 1954.
—. *La vieja ley.* Barcelona: Planeta, 1956.
March, Susana. *Algo muere cada día.* Barcelona: Planeta, 1955.
—. *Nido de vencejos.* Barcelona: Selecciones Literarias y Científicas, Colección VESTA, 1944.
Martín Gaite, Carmen. *Entre visillos.* Barcelona: Destino, 1983.

Secondary Sources

Alcalde, Carmen. *Mujeres en el Franquismo.* Barcelona: Flor del Viento Ediciones, 1996.
Brooksbank Jones, Anny. *Women in Contemporary Spain.* England: Manchester University Press, 1997.
Capel Martínez, Rosa María, *Mujer y sociedad en España (1700-1975).* Madrid: Instituto de la Mujer, 1986.

Conde Peñalosa, Raquel. *La novela femenina de posguerra (1940-1960)*. Madrid: Pliegos, 2004.
—. *Mujeres novelistas y novelas de mujeres en la posguerra española (1940-1965)*. Madrid: Fundación Universitaria Española, 2004.
Kurtz, Carmen. "Entrevista con Carmen Kurtz", *Estafeta Literaria* No. 178, 1959.
Martín Gaite, Carmen. *Usos amorosos de la posguerra española*. Barcelona: Anagrama, 1987.
Miguel, Amando de. *Manual de estructura social de España*. Madrid: Tecnos, 1974.
Moya, Antonio-Prometeo. *Últimas conversaciones con Pilar Primo*. Madrid: Caballo de Troya, 2006.
Otero, Luis. *La Sección Femenina*. Madrid: EDAF, 1999.
Pemán, José María. *De doce cualidades de la mujer*. Madrid: Alcor, 1957.
Perriam et al. *A New History of Spanish Writing: 1939 to the 1990s*. England: Oxford University Press, 2000.
Preston, Paul. *Franco*. London: Harper Collins, 1993.
Primo de Rivera, Pilar. *Discursos, circulares, escritos*. Madrid: Afrodisio Aguado, no year given.
Suárez Fernández, Luis. *Crónica de la Sección Femenina y su tiempo*. Madrid: Asociación Nueva Andadura, 1993.
Tsuchiya, Akiko. "Women and fiction in post-Franco Spain." In *The Cambridge Companion to the Spanish Novel*, edited by Harriet Turner and Adelaida López Martínez, 212-31. England: Cambridge University Press, 2003.
Vincent, Mary. "Spain." In *Women, Gender and Fascism in Europe 1919-45*, edited by Kevin Passmore, 189-213. New Brunswick, New Jersey: Rutgers University Press, 2003.

Chapter Eighteen

Cultural Preservation Through Education and Literacy: Isabel Juárez Espinosa

Abbey Poffenberger

Five hundred years after the Conquest, the indigenous peoples of the Americas are joining in unprecedented solidarity against hegemony to ensure their cultural survival. While some native languages are on the verge of extinction (or already extinct), others are flourishing due to movements that emphasize literacy in the native languages.[1] In Mexico, sixty-two native languages exist,[2] spoken by an estimated 6.7 million indigenous peoples according to the 2000 census.[3] The current renaissance of Mexican indigenous literature reflects the evolving social reality of the indigenous peoples of Mexico. According to a 1995 study by Michael Kearney and Stefano Varese,

> After five centuries of colonization and oppression and the best efforts of modern nation-states and their international agencies to develop the indigenous out of existence, it was clear that they were still very much present and in a number of cases growing in numbers and in political significance. . . . [T]hey have assumed new social forms, new relationships with nation-states that seek to contain them, and indeed in many cases are assuming new identities that no one had previously imagined.[4]

This essay focuses specifically on the Tzeltal Mayan artist, Isabel Juárez Espinosa, who is from Chiapas, and analyzes how she utilizes theatre and performance to promote literacy in the native languages and to educate and empower, particularly targeting Mayan children and women. The first section provides an overview of her participation in the current renaissance of Mexican indigenous literature and the second half provides an analysis of one of her representative works, "Te tatil/El padre," or "The Father."[5]

The written word has gained particular prominence in Mexico, catalyzing an unprecedented revitalization in literary production which has become a didactic tool for both social change and resistance to hegemony, such as one sees in the works of the Juárez Espinosa. According to the Mazateco poet and critic Juan Gregorio Regino:[6]

> The process of educating contemporary indigenous writers is not introduced in the universities, nor is it part of an *indigenista* project, but rather results from the movements of resistance, self-development and consciousness raising by the Indians, about their subaltern ethnic condition. It is one more defense mechanism to preserve and develop indigenous culture as seen from the perspective of the Indians themselves.[7]

As Gregorio Regino has indicated, contemporary indigenous literature coincides with and fortifies current social movements: "The renaissance of indigenous literature is not an isolated phenomenon isolated from the rest of popular movements, it is closely related to the sectors that demand democracy, autonomy, self-determination and a worthy and representative space within the national context.[8] Juárez Espinosa and other contemporary Mexican indigenous authors join Rigoberta Menchú, the Zapatistas, and other indigenous peoples throughout the Americas in the dialogue regarding the future for native peoples. Her works underscore the role of literature as a tool for empowering women through education, literacy and performance.

The computer has proven instrumental in the creation of standardized alphabets, which in turn combats the centuries-old notion that indigenous languages are inferior dialects without a written code. Instead, the texts now provide for the diffusion of anthropological studies, literature, and dictionaries created by the indigenous peoples in their own language as a means to preserve their communities' identity and culture.[9] According to Jesús Salinas Pedraza[10], contemporary technology permits the publication of "more texts in less time," creating a viable option to the official government policy of "teaching Spanish and denying the maternal language."[11]

Similarly, the adaptation of Latin script to indigenous languages provides a cultural tool that actively resists assimilation of the indigenous population into the majority mestizo culture, and promotes the continued reaffirmation and revision of the indigenous cultures. One of the founding members of the (Writers in Indigenous Langauges) *Escritores en Lenguas Indígenas, A.C.* (ELIAC), Feliciano Sánchez Chan (Maya Yucateco), describes how the adoption of Latin script has initiated an innovative phase in indigenous literary production, and in some cases has brought indigenous thought outside of the "zones of refuge" where "knowledge has historically been guarded, exercised, and sustained:"

> I don't know if we can talk of a 'resurgence' because there is continuity, it's just that sometimes it's guarded in the caves, it seeks refuge in the pueblos. I've heard when I go into the countryside, people, who while they're working, suddenly singing a song in Maya, then I say that's where you can find the zones of refuge and now we're only proposing a new way to present it before the eyes of the world, and that's through written literature, which existed before just in different forms among the Maya, but now we're using a tool that practically all of humanity masters which is the alphabet . . . to write in our language starting from our own cultural concepts and our own cosmogony and goes into a parallel manner with the life of the nation and the universe.[12]

Correspondingly, the publication of literature written in indigenous languages marks a rupture with the assimilationist policies of the Mexican government which have previously focused on the Mexicanization of the nation according to Western notions of modernization. Marking the shift towards the acceptance of diversity, the 1992 amendment to Article Four of the Mexican Constitution affirms the multi-cultural and pluri-lingual status of Mexico, thus theoretically ending the discriminatory processes, as well as allocating government funds specifically for the preservation of the nation's indigenous communities and cultures.[13]

Born in Aguacatenango, Chiapas in 1958, Juárez Espinosa is one of the most prominent female authors of contemporary Mexican indigenous literature. Her work *A 'yejetik sol Ta' jimal/ Cuentos y Teatro Tzeltales*, or *Tzeltal Short Stories and Theater* (1994) is the only one written by a woman writer among the more than twenty authors represented in the ground-breaking *Letras Indígenas Contemporáneas (Contemporary Indigenous Writers)* series.[14] While this fact does not necessarily suggest that women are not actively engaged as writers across literary genres at the local level, it does demonstrate that they did not initially benefit from the same access to publication as their male counterparts in the early 1990s.[15]

Her literary production includes short story, essays, and theater; she is also renowned as the first female Mayan actress from the region.[16] In this arena, she was later joined by her colleague Petrona de la Cruz Cruz,[17] and together the artist-activists also established themselves as the first Mayan women playwrights.[18] Like most contemporary Mexican indigenous writers, Isabel Juárez Espinosa publishes her works in bilingual Tzeltal[19]/Spanish editions and includes her own translation of each work into Spanish.[20]

Along with her male counterparts, Juárez Espinosa advocates the preservation of native customs and language as a tool to resist assimilation and the exploitation of the indigenous peoples. However, her works are also imbued with messages of female empowerment through the deconstruction of gender roles. Similarly, many of her plays and short stories are directed towards a primarily female audience with whom she seeks to explore didactic themes including issues concerning health, the (bilingual) education of the younger generations[21], and combating violence. In the following quote, Juárez Espinosa celebrates revolutionary potential and agency granted by her role as a female actress-activist:

> For example, we as indigenous women are pioneers in entering into work as actresses, so supporting and encouraging other women so that they also initiate projects and make theater. Theater is the means by which we can send the positive message of what we want to do, of our goal. Our goal of, for example, what we've already mentioned with regards to domestic violence, violence in the community, education, health ... Because we have various plays. We stage plays with children, with women... And that's what we want to do: to pass it on, above all else, to the younger generations.[22]

Juárez Espinosa shares the prestigious position of being among the first recipients of the *Beca para Escritores en Lenguas Indígenas (Sponsorship for Writers in Indigenous Languages)* in 1992-1993, and was the only woman recipient of this honor. In 1988, Juárez Espinosa and Petrona de la Cruz Cruz were the only women among the founding members of the Tzeltal- and Tzotzil-speaking theater collective *Sna Jtz'ibajom/Asociación de Actores y Escritores Tzotziles y Tzeltales, Cultura de los Indios Mayas*[23] based in San Cristóbal de las Casas and established in 1983.[24] Juárez Espinosa and de la Cruz Cruz then co-founded the *Asociación Fortaleza para la Mujer Maya (FOMMA*[25]*)*, as they became dissatisfied with *Sna Jtz'ibajom's* failure to "adequately address issues of concern to women."[26] La FOMMA is renowned both locally and internationally as an all-female troupe that performs throughout Mexico, the United States, Canada and Europe. In the introduction to *Cuentos y Teatro Tzeltales (Tzeltal Short Stories and Theater)*, Juárez Espinosa describes La FOMMA[27] as a group whose goal is to "apoyar el trabajo literario y creativo de mujeres tzeltales y tzotziles en los Altos de Chiapas y empezar a formar a sus niños."[28] In a 2003 interview with Diana Taylor, she further emphasizes the empowering potential of theater, which provides women with the opportunity to "auto-estimarse un[a] mism[a] . . . [y] darle la confianza."[29]

The bilingual editions of her works promote the further dissemination of her Tzeltal language and its literary and oral traditions. The fact that each work is written in both Spanish and the indigenous language acts symbolically as a political and educational tool to advocate literacy in the native languages and to propagate indigenous works among a national and even international audience, as well as among indigenous members of non-Tzeltal communities. According to the Otomí writer Margarita de la Vega, the development of this work serves to "guarantee its survival."[30] Writing in the native language is crucial to the preservation of both the language and culture for future generations as well as to challenge the stereotypes that have labeled the indigenous as inferior based on the perceived lack of a written language. Instead, according to Gregorio Regino, "the old myths and prejudices that considered indigenous languages as dialects without the possibility of being written are erased."[31] Similarly, by writing in their own language about their own communities, indigenous authors combat centuries of "othering" where non-indigenous peoples continuously portray the communities according to their own stereotyped perspectives, often as means to justify domination by portraying them as inferior.

In essence, Isabel Juárez Espinosa utilizes literature as a vehicle to reaffirm and rewrite her Tzeltal cultural traditions, customs and languages, according to her communities' own experience, putting them into print so they will be available for posterity. This is not to suggest that the written word is in any way superior to oral tradition, a belief that the indigenous writers adamantly challenge, but rather it provides another platform for the dissemination of indigenous thought. This is particularly relevant through Juárez Espinosa's role as an actress, as her partner Petrona de la Cruz Cruz notes in an interview:

> In the case of Chiapas, where there are many, many people who write, there are also many people who are illiterate. And through writing or a book.... Those people didn't have the opportunity to go to school ... and it will take them a long time now to learn how to read. So through theater they can receive messages . . . [o]n the one hand they're enjoying themselves, but at the same time they're educating themselves by way of theater. So it's a way we've chosen to bring them education and the lesson of a written text.[32]

In spite of her increasing visibility in the world of theater[33], Juárez Espinosa's own published works have received little critical attention, with the notable exception of the play "La migración" ("The Migration") which has been analyzed by critic Tamara Underiner.[34] Many of her short stories remain without critique, or even dismissed as revealed in the following quote of Carlos Montemayor, one of the leading non-indigenous critics and promoters of Pre-Colombian and contemporary Mexican indigenous literature:

> Her dramas are largely didactic and thus often her characters lack their own individual development. Her works argue against the exodus to the cities . . . and when she writes about the family, she exaggerates the evil traits in her characters, especially when the victims are women, like in "The Father".[35]

This blatant disregard for her work is indicative of the sexism that has hindered the publication of the works of other female indigenous writers. I contend that this same play about combating domestic violence in fact underscores women's agency; her female characters refuse to be victims.

The Mayan people, as represented by the *Popul Vuh*,[36] have a history of theatrical performance that predates the conquest. During the colonial period, Spanish priests employed indigenous actors for the missionary theater, using this already familiar genre as a tool for conversion to Christianity.[37] Theater regained popularity in the early twentieth century as a tool to reach the Mayan communities through "cultural missions"[38] that were "designed to convert the countryside to the aims of the Revolution."[39] The genre continues to function as a successful didactic cultural communicative tool, as evidenced by the achievements of *Sna Jtz'ibajom*,[40] joined in 1994 by the all female La FOMMA, given its accessibility for multi-lingual, literate and illiterate audiences.

The play "Te Tatil/El padre," addresses the issue of domestic violence and sends a message of female empowerment to resist abuse. This play underscores the revolutionary potential of literature, and theater in particular, as a means to resist dominance and promote social change, while promoting a reevaluation and revision of the status of indigenous women. Furthermore, it encourages the spectators to analyze the actions of the characters and apply the proposed solutions to themselves, as explained by Petrona de la Cruz Cruz in an interview with Cynthia Steele:

> In our case, the theater . . . makes us feel useful, because we realize how influential it is in improving our communities' way of life. Through drama we can explore family and social problems that couldn't be expressed any other way. People learn to value their mother tongues and the virtues of their culture, and they are made aware of the vices and defects of our society, all the while being entertained, not feeling attacked or scolded.[41]

It embodies the blending of the public and private spheres earlier advocated by Juárez Espinosa in other works from this collection. The play "El padre/The Father" reaffirms female agency and corroborates Underiner's assertion that "indigenous women are becoming key actors in defining an alternative world order, envisioned theatrically, to be enacted beyond the boundaries of the stage."[42]

The father in this play is an alcoholic who both verbally and physically abuses his wife and children on a regular basis. Pedro is condemned by his family (including his own parents) for his violent behavior, while Pascuala, "la madre/the mother," is venerated for her role in the preservation of family values and culture. In this portrayal of domestic abuse, Pascuala makes the transition from a victim to a woman with agency. By the end of the play, she separates from her abuser with the support and blessings of both her in-laws and her own parents.

The first scene begins with stage directions that introduce Pascuala in her home as a "mother of a provincial family who is busy doing her accustomed housework."[43] This description highlights her role both as a mother and the preserver of tradition through the maintenance of the domestic sphere. In contrast, Pedro, "el padre," is introduced as a violent and uncaring father who shuns his daughter when she attempts to greet him as he returns home early from work: "Move aside! You do not want me to let loose on you. Where is your mother?"[44] He immediately ruptures the sanctity of the domestic sphere through his verbally abusive entrance: "Shut up! You are the one that I have a problem with, stupid. Instead of making allegations and asking questions, you should be serving me my food, since that's the only thing you are good for."[45] Despite the verbal abuse, Pascuala remains calm, suggesting that his misdirected anger stems from his unnamed and distant workplace. Although neither his occupation nor his work place is specified, the fact that he lives away from home implies that he is abandoning his native culture.

Pedro's behavior threatens Tzeltal cultural values on multiple levels. The verbal and physical abuses, combined with alcohol consumption, are destructive to the family structure. Furthermore, Pedro does not fulfill his obligation to educate his children, which Juárez Espinosa describes in the essay "Te nojptes wanej ta jlumaltik/La educación de nuestros pueblos"[46] as one of the primary responsibilities of the parents in order to ensure cultural survival. She explains that Tzeltal parents share the responsibility of educating their children to preserve their indigenous customs and practices:

> Through family education the parents are responsible for educating their children; from a young age they teach the children to respect their elders,

particularly the most elderly, to speak their maternal language correctly, how to take care of the land, to pray before planting and after the harvest . . . everything has a ritual, even the daily food . . ."[47]

Pedro's lack of respect for his elders is consistently mentioned throughout the play by Pascuala and her parents, and finally by his own mother who states: "It deeply saddens me to see my son behave like this, he no longer respects us either."[48] Furthermore, he is absent from the home on a regular basis due to his employment, and therefore does not represent a viable option for cultural survival.

The over-consumption of alcohol is blamed as a contributing factor to the father's vicious behavior. Although he spends a considerable amount of his time working out of town, Pedro prefers to spend his visits socializing with his "drunken friends," rather than at home with his children. Both family and community members repeatedly condemn his presence in the bar, and his consistent drunkenness is one of the reasons his own mother eventually supports Pascuala's decision to separate from him.

Pascuala does not begin the play with the intent to leave her husband, but only builds confidence to do so after witnessing Pedro's physical abuse of their children. Initially, Pascuala makes excuses for Pedro to their children, suggesting that the solution to the abuse is to simply avoid him:

> **Miguel:** But mom, why is it that every time Dad comes home he yells at us or beats us?
> **Pasquala**: That's just how he is, everything bothers him. The best thing for us to do is stay out of his way.[49]

As the play progresses, the violence increases, and Pascuala acquires the confidence to exert her agency and leave him. Maintaining the status quo by attempting to hide from Pedro is not seen as a viable solution for the future of the family or their culture. The pattern of alcohol-induced abuse is highlighted in the following dialogue that takes place between the children after their mother exits in search of her mother-in-law, Petrona. They discuss the hiding places they will use to avoid their father when he arrives inebriated:

> **Juanita**: If I see that he is going to begin to hit us, I am going to hide under the bed.
> **Tomasa**: Do you really think that he is going to give you time to hide? You really think that he isn't going to find you if that's where he always looks for us. I am going to climb Anona's tree, all the way to the very top and I'll stay hidden up there, that way he'll never find me!![50]

Miguel: Look who's talking! And what if he finds you distracted or if he comes when we are asleep?

This compelling dialogue emphasizes their terror, highlighting the history and frequent occurrences of violence. The youth of the children and the innocence of their comments provide a poignant criticism of the horrors of domestic abuse on the family.

The close relationship between Pascuala and her mother-in-law, Petrona, transmits a message of solidarity to the audience/reader. Pascuala seeks the advice of her mother-in-law, before approaching her own parents. Petrona, like Pascuala, initially advocates that her daughter-in-law and grandchildren remain obedient to patriarchal power, and merely hide from Pedro when he returns from the cantina: "Please hide, and don't let him hit you."[51] She changes by the end of the play, however, as she witnesses the detrimental effects of Pedro's violent behavior on the family. She exerts her status as the matriarch when her grandchildren seek her assistance and protection, after their father returns from the cantina in a drunken rage, striking the children and their mother. Even as a mother, she demands his exile when his behavior threatens the family structure. In her book *Mayan Visions: The Quest for Autonomy in an Age of Globalization* (2001), anthropologist June Nash emphasizes that women hold a significant role in cultural preservation: "Women as caretakers for the young and old, are central actors in the emergent social movements of indigenous peoples in the hemisphere, precisely because of their connectedness to the issues of the survival of past traditions and future generations in their own lives."[52] In this play, Pedro's behavior represents a threat to future generations, and thus the adults agree to his exile to ensure both the physical and cultural survival of Petrona's family.

The honored status of motherhood is further reinforced in the play, as Pedro at first acquiesces to his own mother's wishes. In the following interchange, Petrona exercises her power to protect her grandchildren, insisting that her son leave town rather than corrupt the children with his violent behavior and lack of respect for the family structure:

> **Pedro:** It's better for me to leave! And I am never returning, let's see how you make it without me, this way you won't have to blame me, if I make you sick, if I mistreat you . . bah.
> **Petrona:** Well, that would be the best thing. Since we have already called this to your attention several times and you just don't understand. Your children are big and they can work to support their mother and we are going to help them, because you are only setting bad examples for them . . . .[53]

She emphasizes his role as a father in preserving culture and tradition, and condemns him for not fulfilling his responsibilities. Nevertheless, to Pascuala's dismay, Petrona defends her son when he begrudgingly agrees to Juanita's requests to accompany him out of town. She argues that the presence of his daughter may serve as inspiration for her son to change his ways. Petrona is proven incorrect, at the end of the play, when Juanita returns to her family without her father.

Pascuala undergoes a transition after this episode, refusing to be further victimized by Pedro. Although Petrona cautions her, warning of the financial difficulties of raising children without paternal assistance, she eventually pledges her support after realizing the dangers of exposing the children to Pedro's destructive behavior and acknowledging the strong bond between the two women. Pascuala asserts her position as caretaker of the upcoming generation: "I don't want to see any more abuses in this house, just look at what they are learning, and later, they may turn out the same as their father. No, Mrs. Petra, I am not going to allow your son to kill me, and if only it were just me, the bad thing is that he even hits the kids."[54] The play sends a strong message to the audience/reader that the family must unite against the abuser in order to protect the children. It further demonstrates that women do not have to remain victims of domestic violence, and instead can form alternatives through their solidarity.

The children and their mother maintain a close relationship throughout the play. The three children assist with the domestic chores and attempt to protect their mother from their father's abuse, even at the risk of becoming targets themselves. It is interesting to note that this bond between mother and children translates into her children's self-sufficiency by the end of the play, when Pascuala defends her decision to separate from Pedro: "Well, that is what I want, besides I alone can take care of our business. Miguel and Tomasa are older and they can help by working and raising the other children."[55]

Pascuala also benefits from a social network of women that assists her in achieving financial stability, notably through the exercising of traditional commerce and artisanry. She embroiders blouses that a friend later sells for her in the city. She also sells corn to her comadre, Felipa, who offers her words of support: "It's not good that my friend is behaving like this, what more does the dummy want if he has you? You aren't ugly and the two of you already have your kids. He should think about them."[56] Solidarity between the two families is reinforced when Petrona offers to accompany Pascuala to inform her parents of her decision to leave Pedro: "Now we have to go and inform my friends [Pascuala's parents] of your decision."[57] This gesture is a reflection of relationships that serve to preserve cultural traditions. It is interesting to note that it is Petrona who informs her *compadres*, Pascuala's parents, of the decision to separate, thus lending generational authority and approval to the younger woman's decision.

Pascuala's parents both appear relieved to learn of the decision, yet voice the concern that the separation be permanent so as to not cause them further embarrassment. In the following quote, her mother, Margarita, expresses her relief: "I was thinking that you were going to let him beat you to death. I am happy for you, if it is your decision and you have thought it out. The only thing I am going to ask of you is that you do not embarrass us by going back with him later, because we will not like that."[58] Both parents pledge their support to their daughter and to her children, noting that they will attempt to fulfill the paternal void by educating the children themselves. Similarly, the grandparents provide for reaffirmation of culture, as Pascuala's father offers to teach the children how to work the land and Pedro's father requests Miguel's assistance with selling corn in the city.

The play ends on a happy note with the return of Pascuala's daughter, Juanita. She is delivered to her family by a male character symbolically named Santos. Santos provides a stark contrast to Pedro, as he insists upon returning to his own family after working away from home. The characters are overjoyed to see the return of *la niña* (the little girl), and together they cry "out of happiness." Pedro's absence will not be mourned, as he does not represent a viable option for the future given his role as a rupturer of tradition rather than a cultural preserver. Instead, Pascuala's role as the preserver of culture and the family is solidified, and she will raise her children with indigenous values with the assistance of the elder generations and the other women. She escapes her abusive relationship and stands as an inspiration to women as a survivor of domestic abuse. This play encapsulates the author's views as articulated in a recent interview, where she explains that her works advocate "telling women how valuable they are how they have their rights. . . [and] showing them they can solve their problems. And men must understand that we have to support each other" (qtd. in Erdman 164).

As mentioned in the introduction to this chapter, Juárez Espinosa's role as an actress and playwright for La FOMMA in Chiapas with Petrona de la Cruz Cruz is well documented by several North American academics, including Donald Frischmann, Natividad Guitérrez, Robert Laughlin, Miriam Laughlin, Cynthia Steele, Diana Taylor, and Tamara Underiner. This play was published in 1994, the same year as the formation of La

FOMMA. It reflects the author's social consciousness for cultural survival and a strong message of empowerment which continues to be celebrated by the actresses of La FOMMA twelve years later, particularly for the marginalized audience.

The public performance of "El padre" demonstrates the author's commitment to challenging the gendered division of the public and private spheres. Although Juárez Espinosa celebrates the home as a sacred space for cultural preservation and resistance, she demands that men recognize their role in the domestic sphere as well. Furthermore, her public role as an actress and writer embodies the notion that women must engage in the public sphere on equal terms as men. For Juárez Espinosa, is only through unity that Tzeltal men and women will effectively resist cultural assimilation by the dominant mestizo culture, through the revision and reaffirmation of the traditional values they share.

Notes

[1] See the 1992 study by the Catalán linguist Franesc Ligorred, "Lenguas indígenas de México y Centro América" for a detailed overview of the status of indigenous languages in Central America and Mexico.

[2] In her article, "The Power of Native Languages and the Performance of Indigenous Autonomy: The Case of Mexico," the Nez Perce/Chicana activist and scholar Inés Hernández Ávila, notes that 24 of the 62 languages are in danger of extinction.

[3] Hernández Ávila further notes that the "official" count of indigenous speakers from the 2000 census is low, and that, according to Stefano Varese, the indigenous organizations include between 12 and 17 million indigenous peoples in Mexico (50, 69). There is also a debate regarding the number of Mexican indigenous languages; the number ranges from 56-62, as some are dismissed as "dialecta" or dialect.

[4] Kearney and Varese, "Latin America's Indigenous Peoples. . .", 215

[5] This article contains excerpts from my dissertation titled "The Renaissance of Mexican Indigenous Literature: Resistance, Reaffirmation and Revision" (2006).

[6] Juan Gregorio Regino is a Mazateco poet and critic from the State of Oaxaca and the author of "Escritores en lengua indígena" (Writer's in Indigenous Languages) published in 1993 in *Situación actual y perspectivas de la literatura en lenguas indígenas* (The Current Situation and Perspectives on Literature Written in Indigenous Languages). He is distinguished as a founding member of ELIAC and once served as president of the organization.

[7] Gregorio Regino, "Escritores en lengua indígena", 119. "El proceso de formación de los escritores indígenas contemporáneos no se presenta en las universidades ni es parte de un proyecto indigenista, pues resulta de los movimientos de resistencia, autodesarrollo y toma de conciencia de los indios, de su condición étnica

subalterna. Es un mecanismo más de defensa para preservar la cultura indígena vista desde la perspectiva de los indios mismos y para desarrollarla." (119)

[8] Gregorio Regino, "Literatura indígena", 3 "El renacimiento de la literatura indígena no es un fenómeno aislado del resto de los movimientos populares, está vinculado estrechamente, con los sectores que demandan democracia, autonomía, autodeterminación y un espacio digno y representativo dentro del contexto nacional" (*Literatura indígena"* 3). All translations are mine unless otherwise indicated.

[9] Contemporary indigenous literature reflects innovative modifications in the Latin alphabet to represent phonetic variants from Spanish. For example, the Huichol language overcomes linguistic differences with character adaptations: "i̱", while the Mazateco language employs "a̱", "e̱" and "i̱" to identify sounds that are not represented by the Spanish phonetical system.

[10] Jesús Salinas Pedraza is the author of "La computadora y sus aplicaciones en la escritura de las lenguas indígenas" (The Computer and its Applications to Literature Written in Indigenous Languages), published in 1992 in *Los escritores indígenas actuales II: Ensayo*. His native language is Ñhañu, previously known as Otomí.

[11] Jesús Salinas Pedraza, "La computadora y sus aplicaciones. . .", 103.

"Más textos en menos tiempo"/"enseñar el español y negar la lengua materna"

[12] Hernández Ávila, *The Power of Native Languages*, 38

[13] The amendment states: "La nación Mexicana tiene una composición pluricultural sustentada originalmente en sus pueblos indígenas. La ley protegerá y promoverá el desarrollo de sus lenguas, culturas, usos, costumbres, recursos y formas específicas de organización social, y garantizará a sus integrantes el efectivo acceso a la jurisdicción del Estado." (The Mexican nation has a pluricultural composition sustained originally by its indigenous peoples. The law will protect and promote the development of their languages, cultures, traditions, customs, resources and specific forms of social organization, and it will guarantee that constituents have effective access to the jurisdiction of the State. (qtd. in Hernández, *in tlahtoli* 138)

[14] Some volumes of the series *Letras Indígenas Contemporáneas* include not original texts but rather compilations of oral folktales. Among these texts there is one, *Cuentos y leyendas en lengua Tének* (Tenek Stories and Legends), co-edited by a woman, Clementina Esteban Martínez. However, apart from Juárez Espinosa there are no women producers of original literature in this series.

[15] The Nez Percé/Chicana scholar Inés Hernández Ávila writes that "perhaps one of the greatest challenges facing ELIAC [Escritores en Lenguas Indígenas] is the involvement of more women at the national level. Women are very active at the local and regional levels, and some organizations, such as FOMMA (Fortaleza de la Mujer Maya) . . . have gained international recognition as well" (*Power of Indian Languages* 57).

[16] The taboo against public performance is attributed to what Underiner describers as a "strong cultural pressure on Mayan women not only to stay put but also to keep quiet" (*Contemporary Theater* 48). She further notes that the "womanly

virtues of immobility, invisibility, and silence hardly lend themselves to work in the theatre; indeed opportunities for indigenous women in Chiapas even to see theatre are practically nonexistent" (48). In her article "'A Woman Fell into the River': Negotiating Female Subjects in Contemporary Mayan Theatre", Steele notes that Juarez Espinosa and de la Cruz Cruz's previous work with Sna "has entailed great risk . . . they have aroused suspicion among their townspeople regarding their sexual virtue" (251).

[17] De la Cruz Cruz is a Tzotzil actress from Zinacantán, Chiapas and co-founder of Fortaleza de la Mujer Maya (FOMMA).

[18] In her 2003 article "Eso sí pasa aquí: Indigenous Women performing Revolutions in Mayan Chiapas," Teresa Marrero notes that Juárez Espinosa was the first, and for a time, the only, female indigenous actress in los Altos de Chiapas (316).

[19] The Catalán linguist Francesc Ligorred estimated the number of Tzeltal speakers to be approximately 200,000 in 1992; Frishmann and Montemayor put the estimate as high as 547,000 at the end of the 20th century (Ligorred *Lenguas indígenas* 223; Montemayor and Frischmann 133). Ligorred further notes that Tzeltal is amongst the twelve Mayan languages "vivas o en resistencia" (alive or in resistance) (*Cuestiones de habla* 469).

[20] This is particularly significant for this author, given the lack of formal education in her native language. She states: "yo no me imaginaba que pudiera escribir en mi lengua, porque la habl[o], pero no la había visto escrita, porque en la escuela nunca nos enseñaron" (I never imagined that I would be able to write in my native language, because I speak it, but I had never seen it written, because in school they never taught us) (Gutiérrez, "Escritoras mayas" 15). Both de la Cruz Cruz and Juarez Espinosa graduated from *secundaria* (junior high). According to Teresa Marrero, this is "considered higher education since most indias are not allowed by their families to finish primary school" ("Eso sí pasa aquí" 317).

[21] It is still unusual for indigenous children to receive a bilingual education in the public (and private) school system. The emphasis continues to be on assimilating the youth into the dominant culture by promoting literacy in Spanish, according to a recent conversation with the Zapotec novelist Javier Castellanos Martínez.

[22] Hazas interview, 2003

[23] Association of Tzotzil and Tzeltal Actors and Writers, Culture of the Mayan Indians

[24] In his article, "Viviencias de nuestra palabra: El resurgimiento de la cultura maya en Chiapas" (1992) Manuel Pérez Hernández describes the function of *Sna jtz' ibalom* as follows: "Consideramos prioritario recopilar cuentos, leyendas, conocimientos e historias de los personajes más ancianos y reconocidos por su sabiduría de nuestras comunidades. Una de las grandes preocupaciones de los ancianos y principales de las comunidades es gran parte de sus costumbres, tradiciones y conocimientos ancestrales se están perdiendo demasiado rápidamente, ya que los jóvenes salen a trabajar a las ciudades y están transformando su idioma, costumbres y conocimientos." (We consider it a priority to compile the short stories, legends, knowledge and histories of the oldest living

amongst us who are recognized for their knowledge and wisdom of our communities. One of the great preoccupations of the elders and leaders of the communities is that a great part of their customs, traditions and ancestral knowledge is being lost too quickly, since the young people are leaving to work in the cities and are transforming their language, customs and knowledge) (84).

[25] Erdman explains the "distancing strategy" from the EZLN of the two artists, explaining that "while La FOMMA (Strength of the Mayan Woman) was created the same year as the Zapatista uprising, both women are careful to distance themselves from the guerilla movement. Both La FOMMA and the Zapatistas are responding to the same material conditions of struggle and exploitation . . . but the women assert their neutrality in the ongoing conflict. While such a public stance of 'neutrality' may be a necessary survival strategy, particularly given the company's need to avoid harassment from the Mexican government, it is probably more useful to see La FOMMA's work as providing a different perspective on injustices endemic to the region rather than one that is merely 'neutral'"(Erdman 160).

[26] Erdman, "Gendering Chiapas", 160 For more information about this rupture see Cynthia Steele's article "'A Woman Fell into the River': Negotiating Female Subjects in Contemporary Mayan Theatre."

[27] See Diana Taylor's 2003 interview with the co-founders Juárez Espinosa and de la Cruz Cruz at http://www.hemi.nyu.edu/eng/seminar/usa/text/fomma_bio.html.

[28] Juarez Espinosa, *Cuentos y teatro Tzeltal*, 9.
"Support the literary and creative works of Tzeltal and Tzotzil women from Altos de Chiapas and to initiate the education of their children."

[29] "Build her self esteem and give her confidence"

[30] De la Vega , *Crónica Otomí*, 9 "garantizar su permanencia"

[31] Gregorio Regino, "Escritores" 124. "Se desechan los viejos mitos y prejuicios que consideraban a las lenguas indígenas como dialectos sin la posibilidad de escribirse."

[32] Hazas interview, 2003

[33] Juárez Espinosa's role as an actress and playwright for La FOMMA in Chiapas with Petrona de la Cruz Cruz is well documented by several North American academics, including Donald Frischmann, Natividad Guitérrez, Harley Erdman, Robert Laughlin, Miriam Laughlin, Cynthia Steele, Diana Taylor, and Tamara Underiner.

[34] See Underiner's *Contemporary Theater in Mayan Mexico* (2004) as well as "Incidents of Theatre in Chiapas, Tabasco, and Yucatán: Cultural Enactments in Mayan Mexico" (1998).

[35] Montemayor, *La literatura actual* 101. "Sus dramas son sumamente didácticos y por ello a menudo sus personajes carecen de relieve propio. Sus obras provienen contra el éxodo a las ciudades . . . [y] [c]uando trata temas familiares, extrema los rasgos de maldad en sus personajes, particularmente cuando las víctimas son mujeres, como en *Te Tatil* (El Padre)."

[36] According to Underiner, the twin-gods perform an "act of theatrical allusion" when one beheads the other, cuts out his heart, and then resuscitates him in front of the gods of death. This "command performance" was so exciting to the spectators,

that they requested that the twins perform the same act on them. The twins knowingly obliged, defeating the death gods since the act was no longer an illusion, and they remained beheaded (*Contemporary Theatre* 19).

[37] Underiner, "Contemporary Mayan Theatre" 525

[38] Underiner, *Contemporary Theatre, 31*. She further notes that one of the main endeavors of the "Cultural Missions" was to "reduce monolingualism" in the indigenous languages while "improving literacy" in Spanish (30).

[39] Rosario Castellanos wrote plays for the *Teatro Petul* in Chiapas and served as Director from 1956-57. She and six Tzotzil and Tzeltal Mayans presented plays throughout Chiapas, presenting "current problems in health, education, or agriculture, and each proposed a concrete and practical solution" (Underiner, *Contemporary Theatre* 30).

[40] For more information on *Sna Jtz'ibajom*, Cultura de los Indios Mayas A.C. see Frischmann's "New Mayan Theatre in Chiapas: Anthropology, Literacy, and Social Drama" (1994), "Active Ethnicity: Nativism, Otherness, and Indian Theatre in Mexico" (1991). Also see Robert Laughlin's works, including "The Mayan Resistance: Sna Jtz'ibajom" (1994) and "En la vanguardia: Sna Jtz'ibajom"(1993).

[41] Steele, "A Woman Fell Into the River", 255.

[42] Underiner, *Contemporary Theatre, 48*.
Domestic violence is addressed in the 1993 *Ley Zapatista Revolucionaria de la Mujer* which states: "Ninguna mujer podrá ser golpeada o maltratado físicamente ni por familiares ni por desconocidos. . . ." (No woman shall be beaten or physically mistreated by either family members or strangers . . .)

[43] Juarez Espinosa, *Cuentos y teatro tzeltales*, 189. Madre de una familia de provincia [que] se encuentra haciendo sus acostumbrados labores domésticos.

[44] Ibid. ¡Hazte a un lado! No vaya a ser que contigo me desquite. ¿En dónde está tu madre? Move aside! You do not want me to let loose on you. Where is your mother?

[45] Ibid, 190. ¡Cállate!, que es contigo con quien tengo que arreglar cuentas, estúpida. En lugar de estar alegando y preguntando, deberías de servirme de comer, que es para lo único que sirves.

[46] This essay, "The Education of Our People," is found in the collection *A 'yejetik sok Ta 'jimal/Cuentos y Teatro Tzeltales* (1994).

[47] Ibid 54. En la educación familiar los padres se encargan de educar a sus hijos; desde pequeños les enseñan a respetar a la gente mayor, más a los ancianos, a hablar correctamente la lengua materna, cómo cuidar la tierra, rezarle antes de sembrar y después de la cosecha. . . todo tiene rito, hasta la alimentación de cada día . . .

[48] Ibid 203. "A mí me da mucha tristeza que mi hijo sea así, ya tampoco a nosotros nos respeta."

[49] Ibid 191. "Pero, mamá, ¿por qué cada vez que regresa papa de su trabajo, nos regaña o nos golpea?"

"Es que así es su carácter, todo le cae mal. Lo mejor será hacernos a un lado."

[50] Ibid 191. "Si veo que empieza a golpearnos, me voy a esconder debajo de la cama."

"Y a poco crees que te va a dar tiempo de esconderte, y crees que no te va [a] encontrar, si es ahí donde siempre nos busca. ¡Ah, pero yo sí me voy a subir al árbol de Anona, hasta la mera puntita y ahí me quedo escondida, así no me encontrará."
¡Mira quien habla! Y que tal si te encuentra distraída o llega cuando estemos bien dormidotes.
[51] Ibid 193 "Se esconden por favor, y no vayan a dejar que los golpee."
[52] Nash, Quest for Autonomy, 25
[53] Juárez Espinosa, *Cuentos y teatro*, 200. "¡Mejor me voy! Y ya no vuelvo nunca, a ver cómo se las ven sin mí, así no tendrían que echarme la culpa, si los enfermo, si los maltrato... ¡bah!."
"Pues sería mejor. Porque ya te llamamos varias veces la atención y tú nomás no entiendes. Tus hijos ya están grandecitos y pueden trabajar para sostener a su madre y nosotros les vamos a ayudar, porque tú sólo malos ejemplos les estás dando..."
[54] Ibid 202. "Lo que no quiero es que haya más maltratos en esta casa, mire nada más lo que están aprendiendo, y luego, si me salen igual que su padre. No, doña Petra, no voy a dejar que su hijo me mate, y bueno fuera que sólo a mí, lo malo es que hasta a los niños les toca."
[55] Ibid 202. "Pues eso quiero, además puedo arreglármelas yo sola, Miguel y Tomasa ya está[n] grandecitos y me pueden ayudar a trabajar y criar a los más chicos."
[56] Ibid 195. "No está bien que haga eso mi compadre, pues, ¿qué más quiere el tonto?, si te tiene a ti. No cres fea y ya tienen sus hijitos. Debería pensar en ellos."
[57] Ibid 202. "Ahora tenemos que ir a avisarles a mis compadres tu decisión."
[58] Ibid 203. "Yo había pensado que ibas a dejar que te matara a golpes. Me alegro por ti, y si es tu decisión y ya lo pensaste bien. Lo único que voy a pedir es que no nos pongas en vergüenza y te rejuntes otra vez luego luego, porque eso no nos gusta."

Works Cited

Primary Sources

Juárez Espinosa, Isabel. *Cuentos y Teatro Tzeltales: A 'yejetik sok Ta 'jimal*. México D.F.: Editorial Diana, 1994.

Secondary Sources

Castellanos Martinez, Javier. Interview with author. Oct., 2007
De la Vega, Margarita. *Crónica Otomí del Estado de México*. Mexico: Instituto Mexquense de Cultura, 1998.

Erdman, Harley. "Gendering Chiapas: Petrona de la Cruz and Isabel J.F. Juárez Espinosa of la FOMMA (Fortaleza de la Mujer Maya/Strength of the Mayan Woman)." *The Color of Theater: Race, Culture and Contemporary Performance.* Roberta Uno and Lucy Mae San Pablo Burns, eds. London: Continuum, 2002. 158-169

Frischmann, Donald. "New Mayan Theatre in Chiapas: Anthropology, Literacy, and Social Drama." *Negotiating Performance: Gender, Sexuality, and Theatricality in Latin/o America.* Diana Taylor and Juan Villegas eds. Durham: Duke UP, 1994.

—. "Active Ethnicity: Nativism, Otherness, and Indian Theatre in Mexico." *Gestos.* 11 (April 1991): 113-126.

Gregorio Regino, Juan. "Escritores en lenguas indígenas." *Situación actual y perspectivas de la literatura en lenguas indígenas.* Carlos Montemayor, coord. México: Seminario de Estudios de la Cultura, 1993. 119-138.

—. "Literatura indígena." *La palabra florida* 1 (Invierno, 1996): 3.

Gutiérrez, Natividad. *Nationalist Myths and Ethnic Identities: Indigenous Intellectuals and the Mexican State.* Lincoln: UP of Nebraska, 1999.

—."Escritoras mayas." *La Jornada Semanal* 1992 (Feb.1993): 14-15.

Hazas, Tracy. Interview with FOMMA and the Coatlicue Theater Company. 4[h] Annual Encuentro of the Hemispheric Institute of Performance and Politics, New York University, July 11-19, 2003. http://hemi.nyu.edu/eng/seminar/usa/studentwork/hazas/fomma_english.html.

Hernández Ávila, Inés. "The Power of Native Languages and the Performance of Indigenous Autonomy: The Case of Mexico." *Native Voices: American Indian Identity and Resistance.* Richard Grounds and George Tinker, et al, eds. Lawrence: UP of Kansas, 2003. 35-76.

Hernández Hernández, Natalio. *in tlahtoli, in ohtli: la palabra, el camino: Memoria y destino de los pueblos indígenas.* México: Plaza y Valdés Editores, 1998.

Hernández Pérez, Fernando. "Through the Mists of Transformation: Excerpts from a Conversation with Petrona de la Cruz Cruz and Isabel Juárez Espinosa." *Canadian Theatre Review* 68 (Fall 1991): 32-36.

Kearney, Michael and Stefano Varese. "Latin America's Indigenous Peoples: Changing Identities and Forms of Resistance." *Capital, Power, and Inequality in Latin America.* Sandor Halebsky and Richard Harris, eds. Bolder: Westview Press, 1995.

Laughlin, Robert. "The Mayan Renaissance: Sna Jtz'ibajom, the House of the Writer." *Cultural Survival Quarterly* 17 (Winter 1994): 13-15.
—. "En la vanguardia: Sna Jtz'ibajom." *Situación actual y perspectivas de la literatura en lenguas indígenas.* Carlos Montemayor, coord. México: Seminario de Estudios de la Cultura, 1993.
Ligorred, Franesc. *Lenguas indígenas de México y Centroamérica (De los jeroglíficos al siglo XXI).* Madrid: Editorial MAPFRE, 1992.
Ligorred, Franesc. and María Josefa Iglesias Ponce de León. "Cuestiones de habla, de lengua y de literatura mayas (estudios y propuestas)." *Perspectivas antropológicas en el mundo maya.* Madrid: Sociedad Española de Estudios Mayas, 1993.
Marrero, Teresa. "Eso sí pasa aquí: Indigenous Women Performing Revolutions in Mayan Chiapas." *Holy Terrors: Latin American Women Perform.* Diana Taylor and Rosalyn Constantino, eds. Durham: Duke UP, 2003. 311-30
Montemayor, Carlos. *La literatura actual en las lenguas indígenas de México.* México D.F.: Universidad Iberoamericana, 2001.
— and Donald Frischmann, eds. *Words of the True Peoples/Palabras de los Seres Verdaderos: Anthology of Contemporary Mexican Indigenous-Language Writers.* Vol. I Prose. Austin: U of Texas P, 2004.
Nash, June. *Mayan Visions: The Quest for Autonomy in an Age of Globalization.* New York: Routledge, 2001.
Pérez Hernández, Manuel. "Viviencias de nuestra palabra: El resurgimiento de la cultura maya en Chiapas." *Los escritores indígenas actuales II: Ensayo.* Carlos Montemayor, ed. México: Fondo Editorial Tierra Adentro, 1992.
Poffenberger, Abbey. "The Renaissance of Mexican Indigenous Literature: Resistance, Reaffirmation and Revision." Diss. U of Kentucky, 2006.
Salinas Pedraza, Jesús. "La computadora y sus aplicaciones en la escritura de las lenguas indigenas." *Los escritores indígenas actuales II: Ensayo.* Carlos Montemayor, ed. México, D.F.: Editorial Tierra Adentro, 1992. 103-112.
Steele, Cynthia. "A Woman Fell into the River." *Negotiating Performance: Gender, Sexuality, and Theatricality in Latin/o America.* Diana Taylor and Juan Villegas, eds. Durham: Duke UP, 1994. 239-256.
Taylor, Diana. "FOMMA Interview with Isabel Juárez Espinosa and Petrona de la Cruz Cruz." New York. July 2003.
<http://www.hemi.nyu.edu/eng/seminar/usa/text/fomma_bio.html>

—. "Contemporary Mayan Theatre." *Literary Cultures of Latin America: A Comparative History*. Mario Valdés and Djelal Kadir, eds. New York: Oxford UP, 2004.

—. "Incidents of Theatre in Chiapas, Tabasco, and Yucatán: Cultural Enactments in Mayan Mexico." *Theatre Journal* 50 (October 1998): 349-69.

Underiner, Tamara. *Contemporary Theater in Mayan Mexico: Death-Defying Acts*. Austin: U of Texas P, 2004.

Contributors

Karin Baumgartner is Assistant Professor for German literature at the University of Utah, Salt Lake City. She has published numerous articles on the early 19th century, in particular, on the political writings of nineteenth-century German women. Other articles address issues of masculinity and nationhood in early nineteenth-century Germany and France. Her article "Staging the German Nation: Caroline Pichler's Dramatic Writing" (*Modern Austrian Literature*) won the Max Kade Award for best article in 2004. Her book, *Public Voices: Political Discourse in the Writings of Caroline de la Motte Fouqué,* is forthcoming in 2008.

Sandy Feinstein is Honors Coordinator and Associate Professor of English at Penn State Berks. She has published on alchemy in Chaucer's *The Canon's Yeoman's Tale* (in *Alchemization of the Mind*, eds. Bialas, et al), on the alchemical images in the *Splendor Solis* (*Sixteenth Century Journal*), as well as on both alchemy and chemistry in Milton's *Paradise Lost* (*Ben Jonson Review*). She has also published articles and chapters on innovative teaching, including the teaching of alchemy and chemistry (*Learning Literature in an Era of Change*, eds. Hickey, et al).

Sarah Jayne Hitt is a 3rd year Ph.D. student in Literary Studies at the University of Denver. Her primary interest is literature of the American West, and she is beginning work on a dissertation which will examine late 19th and early 20th century immigration narratives from the Great Plains.

Beatrice Jacobson is Professor of English and Director of Women's Studies at St. Ambrose University. She earned her doctorate at University of Iowa, writing a dissertation on Emily Dickinson. Current interests include Latin American women's issues and she serves on the board of Centro de Estudios Internacionales in Cuenca, Ecuador.

Jane E. Jeffrey is a Professor of English at West Chester University. Her recent publications include "Radegund" in *Women and Gender in Medieval Europe: An Encyclopedia*, Routledge, 2006, and *Women Writing in Latin*, 3 vols., eds. Laurie Churchill, Phyllis Brown, and Jane E. Jeffrey, Routledge, 2002.

Julia Kiernan is a doctoral student in Composition and Rhetoric at the University of Louisville. Her three primary areas of scholarly interest include early modern women's rhetorics and writing practices, Canadian multilingual student writing practices, and writing center pedagogy and theory.

Charlotte Liddell completed her doctoral studies in the Department of Spanish and Portuguese, University of Manchester, in 2006. Her thesis analyzes the work of Nísia Floresta. Her article, "Nature, Nurture and Nation: Nísia Floresta's Engagement in the Breast-Feeding Debate in Brazil and France," was published in *Feminist Review*.

Dorothée Mertz-Weigel received her PhD in French Literature from The Ohio State University in 2005, and is now an Assistant Professor of French at Armstrong Atlantic State University in Savannah, GA. Her interests are the representation of melancholy in medieval French literature, as well as the integration of technology in the classroom. Dr. Mertz-Weigel has published numerous book reviews for *The French Review* and is currently working on a manuscript centered on three medieval authors (Jean de Meun, Christine de Pizan, and François Villon) and the way that they portray melancholy and similar illnesses in addition to the suggestions that they propose to cure the all-consuming black bile.

Claire Emilie Martin received her B.A. and M.A degrees from the University of Massachusetts, Amherst, and her Ph.D. from Yale University. She is Professor of Spanish and Chair of the Romance, German, Russian Languages and Literatures Department at California State University, Long Beach. She published *Alejo Carpentier y las crónicas de Indias: orígenes de una escritura americana*, Hanover, N.H.: Ediciones del Norte, 1995, and with Cristina Arambel Guiñazú, *Las mujeres toman la palabra: escritura femenina hispanoamericana del siglo XIX*, Volumen I, and *Antología de escritoras hispanoamericanas del siglo XIX*, Vol II, Frankfurt-Madrid: Iberoamericana, 2001. She has published numerous articles and book chapters on nineteenth-century women writers and Argentinean novelists of the last two decades.

Terry Novak is Professor of English at Johnson & Wales University in Providence, Rhode Island, where she teaches literature and composition courses. She has published several articles on 19th century African American women writers, most recently "Frances Harper's Poverty Relief Mission in the African American Community," which was published in *Our Sisters' Keepers.*

Patricia O'Byrne is a lecturer at Dublin City University, Ireland, in the School of Applied Language and Intercultural Studies, where she lectures on the comparative literature program and contributes to a range of undergraduate literature and intercultural modules. She was awarded a PhD by the National University of Ireland for her thesis entitled *La novela neorrealista femenina.* Her recent publications on women writers include the following articles "Representaciones de la maternidad en la novela española 1940-1960" (2006) and "Testimonial Literature and Spanish Women Novelists" (2008).

Julia C. Paulk is an Assistant Professor of Spanish at Marquette University in Milwaukee, Wisconsin, where she teaches Spanish American literature and culture classes. In 2003, she earned her doctorate at Indiana University, Bloomington, with a dual specialization in Spanish American and Comparative Literature. Dr. Paulk's areas of research interest are nineteenth-century antislavery literature, Inter-American literary studies, and women's studies. Her work has been published in *Revista Hispánica Moderna* and *The Luso-Brazilian Review.*

Abbey Poffenberger is an Assistant Professor of Spanish and Women's Studies at Eastern Kentucky University. In 2007 she earned her doctorate in Latin American Literature from the University of Kentucky. Her research interests include contemporary Mexican Indigenous literature and her publications include "Iretemai Gabriel Pacheco Salvador: literatura huichol actual" in *Graffylia: Revista de la Facultad de Filosofía y Letras* (2007) and "Desmontando la casa: la desmitificación de la interpretación de los papeles públicos y privados tradicionales asignados a la mujer" in *Confluencias en Mexico: Palabra y Genero* (2007). She is currently working on an annotated critical translation of *Cantares de los vientos primerizos* by the Zapotec author Javier Castellanos Martínez.

Mar Soria López is a PhD student at the University of Illinois at Urbana-Champaign. She specializes in 19th and 20th century Spanish cultural studies with a focus on gender and working-class representations. She is currently coeditor for the summer 2008 special issue of *Letras Femeninas*, "Families Under Construction: Migratory Female Identities in the Remaking of Iberian, Hispanic Caribbean and Latina Cultures."

Ulrike Tancke pursues research interests in early modern English literature and contemporary British fiction. She received her Ph.D. in English Literature from Universität Trier (Germany) in 2006. Her doctoral thesis investigated early modern women's strategies of identity formation in their autobiographical writings. Having previously taught at Universität Trier (Germany) and Lancaster University (UK), she is currently an Associate Lecturer at Johannes-Gutenberg-Universität Mainz (Germany).

Magdalena Tarnawska received her Ph.D. degree in the Department of German at the University of California, Irvine. She has researched and taught many aspects of nineteenth- and twentieth-century German culture, literature, and social history at the University of California at Irvine, University of Colorado at Boulder, and DePauw University in Indiana. Currently she is an Assistant Professor at the University of Wyoming in Laramie. Her research is interdisciplinary, including the fields of literature, gender and women's studies, and history of medicine and education. She recently published her book, '*...und Medea war eine Ärztin': Constructions of Femininity in Public Debates about Medical Education for Women in Germany and Austria between 1870 and 1910*.

Hülya Yıldız is a doctoral candidate in the Program in Comparative Literature, University of Texas at Austin. She is currently writing a dissertation on the print culture in the Ottoman Empire during the long nineteenth century. This work is tentatively titled, "Literature as Public Sphere: Gender and Sexuality in Ottoman Turkish Novels and Journals."

INDEX

Abelard p. 14-16, 18-19
African American p. 7, 197-207, 213
Alchemy p. 4, 53, 55-58, 60-62
Americas, The p. 1, 2, 5, 6, 7, 8, 184, 185, 236, 237
Angel of the Home p. 138, 189
Aristocracy (see "Class, Upper")
Author, Female p. 23, 37-38, 54, 59-61, 71-73, 75-78, 98, 107, 111, 130-136, 138, 149, 185, 188-190, 201, 205, 224, 227, 231, 237-238, 246-247 (see also "Writer" and "Journalist")
Autobiography p. 5, 14, 38-40, 59, 98-107, 110-120, 206

Beecher, Catharine p. 3, 6, 157, 159-161, 192-188, 191-192
Boarding School p. 7, 85, 156, 201-202, 209, 211-212, 214-215
Book of the City of Ladies p. 23, 25, 26-30
Bourgeoisie (see "Class, Middle")
Brazil p. 6, 170-179

Catholic Church p. 57, 222, 227
Catholic Government p. 138
Catholicism p. 10, 136, 173, 177-78
Chemistry p. 3, 4-5, 53-62, 88, 119, 164
Christian p. 10-12, 14, 76, 134-135, 145, 160, 162, 185-187, 197, 199, 202, 204, 211
Christianity p. 19, 212, 241
Christianize p. 211
Class
    Lower p. 5, 6, 69-75, 78, 145, 176, 197, 205

Middle p. 41, 69, 73, 78, 83, 84, 90, 91, 92, 156, 161, 204
Upper p. 3-4, 5, 12, 68, 72, 74-75, 77-78, 86, 88, 91, 90, 134, 135, 145, 184
Coeducation p. 70, 103
Colony p. 5, 98, 101, 133
Colonial p. 130-131, 241
Colonization p. 215, 217, 236
Christine de Pizan p. 3, 4, 23-35, 54
Creole p. 5, 98-107
Cuba p. 5, 98, 101-104, 106, 133
Cult of True Womanhood p. 6, 158, 160, 185, 186, 197-199, 204

Dickinson, Emily p. 156-157, 163-166
Dominant Culture p. 1-9, 10, 15, 19, 37, 46, 209, 210, 212, 217, 247, 249
Domestic Sphere p. 2-4, 77, 82-84, 87-88, 99, 130, 152, 157, 159, 161, 171, 186, 188, 242, 247
Domesticity p. 5, 45, 82, 100, 104, 166, 186, 204, 222

England p. 4, 5, 37, 38, 70,
Europe p. 1, 4, 5, 6, 8, 23, 27, 101, 102, 110, 121, 144, 145, 149, 171, 173, 175, 176, 177, 188, 221, 222, 234, 239,
Eustochium p. 10-12

Fatma Aliye p. 6, 143, 146, 148, 150-152
Feminism p. 23, 30, 42, 129, 133-135, 137-138, 148
Floresta, Nísia p. 6, 169-179

Fouqué, Caroline de la Motte p. 5, 82-92
France p. 4, 17, 24, 26-27, 55, 58, 61, 173, 177, 228
Franco, Francisco p. 7, 138, 221-222, 224-225, 227, 231

German Women's Movement p. 83-84, 91
Germany p. 5, 17, 83, 86-87, 111-112, 173
Great Britain p. 129, 173
Gleim, Betty p. 84-90

Harper, Frances p. 7, 197-207
Heloise p. 4, 15-19
Hildegard of Bingen p. 4, 15, 17-19,
Hrotsvit of Gandersheim p. 13-14

Illiteracy p. 223
Indian p. 130,
    North American p. 209-217 (see also "Native American")
    Mexican p. 236-247
    Indigenous Peoples
    Mexico p. 7, 236-247
    Peru p. 188
    United States p. 209-217
Islam p. 128, 146, 147 (see also "Muslim")

Juárez Espinosa, Isabel p. 7, 236-247
Jerome p. 2, 4, 10-13, 15, 17, 19
Jewish p. 111-112
Journalist, Female p. 209, 217 (see also "Author" and "Writer")
Journals for Women (see "Periodicals for Women")
Judaism p. 128

Kurtz, Carmen p. 7, 227-229, 230

Lady Grace Mildmay p. 38-40

Latin p. 1, 2, 4, 8, 10-22, 41, 43, 116, 164-65, 171, 226
Lejárraga, María p. 128-138 (see also "María Martínez Sierra")
Literacy p. 2-4, 6-7, 10, 12, 14, 42, 69, 146, 170, 216, 228, 236-237, 240
Lyon, Mary p. 3, 7, 156-166

Magazines for Women (see "Periodicals for Women")
Makin, Bathsua p. 5, 68-79
March, Susana p. 7, 229-231
Marie de France p. 14
Marriage p. 3, 7, 13, 24, 43, 44, 59, 68, 71, 77-79, 84, 87, 98-101, 131, 136, 162, 171, 173, 184, 188, 192, 198, 199, 202, 203, 221-225, 228-229
Martín Gaite, Carmen p. 7, 224-226, 230
Martínez Sierra, Gregorio p. 133-134, 137-138
Martínez Sierra, María p. 6, 128-138 (see also "María Lejárraga")
Matto de Turner, Clorinda p. 6, 184-192
Medicine p. 40, 55, 60, 88, 186, 187, 216
Medical Students p. 110-120
Medieval Education p. 2, 4, 11, 14, 18, 19, 23, 61
Medieval Women p. 13, 17, 23, 24 26, 30
Memoire (see "Autobiography")
Menchú, Rigoberta p. 237
Merlin, Mercedes p. 5, 98-107
Meurdrac, Marie p. 4, 53-62
Mexico p. 7, 236-247
Millet, Kate p. 184-185, 187, 192
Misogyny p. 19, 27-30
Mother p. 2, 5, 23, 24, 41, 44, 69, 72, 78, 82-85, 87, 89, 99, 101, 103-106, 113, 132, 136, 143, 150-152, 158, 163, 166, 169, 173, 174, 177, 189-192, 201-202, 210-212, 214,

221-223, 225, 227, 229-230, 242
246
Motherhood p. 68, 71, 77-79, 100, 105, 106, 131-132, 136-137, 158, 169, 172-173, 222, 225, 244
Moulsworth, Martha p. 40-43
Mount Holyoke Female Seminary p. 6, 156-166
Muslim p. 143-145, 148-150 (see also "Islam")

Nation-building p. 132-133, 169, 172-173, 177-178
Native American p. 7, 130, 209-220 (see also "Indian")

Ottoman Empire p. 6, 144-152

Pardo Bazán, Emilia p. 6, 128-138
Periodicals for Women p. 6, 146, 144-150, 223-224
Personal narrative (see "Autobiography")
Peru p. 184, 188-192
Picotte, Susan La Flesche p. 7, 209-217
Pliny p. 54, 56
Prussia p. 83, 85, 87-89, 91
Public Education p. 144-145, 151, 174, 185,
Public Sphere p. 3-4, 25, 39-40, 77, 83, 88-92, 120, 128, 133, 135, 143-144, 150, 152, 161, 171-172, 185-186, 202-203, 242, 247

Radegund p. 4, 12-13, 15,
Religion p. 1, 24, 75-76, 146, 158, 160, 186
Rousseau, Jean Jacques p. 5, 87, 98-107, 130

Salonnière p. 4, 5, 83, 90, 104, 106
Science p. 5, 25, 57, 59-62, 82, 85, 103, 128, 131,
Schubert-Feder, Cläre p.110-120

Slavery p. 7, 149, 188, 198, 201, 202, 204
Spain p. 6, 7, 98-99, 101-103, 128-138, 221-231
Stowe, Harriet Beecher p. 205
Straus, Rahel p. 110-120

Teachers p. 129, 130, 174, 204
 Education of p. 143, 145, 149-152, 158-166, 174, 186
 Female p. 4, 6, 16, 54, 62, 129, 143, 145, 149-152, 157-165, 174, 186, 190, 202-204, 213, 215, 227
 Male p. 14-15, 19, 37, 117, 129, 226
Tiburtius, Franziska p. 110-120
True Womanhood (see "Cult of True Womanhood")

United States of America p. 3, 7, 8, 157, 173, 184, 186, 187, 206, 212, 216, 239

Vives, Juan Luis p. 37, 128

Whitney, Isabella p. 36-37
Willard, Emma p. 157-160
Wilson, Lucy p. 5, 68-79
Wollstonecraft, Mary p. 5, 68-70, 72-79
Womanhood p. 6, 14, 44, 99, 100, 128, 135, 136, 150, 178, 186 (see also "Cult of True Womanhood")
Working Class (see "Class, Lower")
Writer, Female p. 3, 4, 6, 14, 17-19, 23-31, 36-37, 42, 46, 54, 56, 61, 71, 84, 99, 100, 120, 128-130, 134, 137-138, 146-147, 169, 178-179, 185-188, 190-192, 204, 206, 215, 224, 238-241, 247 (see also "Author" and "Journalist")

Zitkala Sa p. 7, 209-218